Badkhen, Anna,
Walking with Abel :
2015

8|15

WALKING
WITH
ABEL

ALSO BY ANNA BADKHEN

The World Is a Carpet: Four Seasons in an Afghan Village

Afghanistan by Donkey: One Year in a War Zone

Peace Meals: Candy-Wrapped Kalashnikovs and Other War Stories

Waiting for the Taliban: A Journey Through Northern Afghanistan

RIVERHEAD BOOKS

New York

2015

WALKING
WITH
ABEL

Journeys with the Nomads
of the African Savannah

ANNA BADKHEN

RIVERHEAD BOOKS
An imprint of Penguin Random House LLC
375 Hudson Street
New York, New York 10014

The author gratefully acknowledges permission to quote from the following:
"Cuckoo your footprints," by Yosa Buson, translated by W. S. Merwin and Takako Lento,
from *Collected Haiku of Yosa Buson*. Translation copyright © 2013 by W. S. Merwin and
Takako U. Lento. Reprinted with the permission of The Permissions Company, Inc., on behalf of
Copper Canyon Press, www.coppercanyonpress.org. "Cymatics (Frequencies)" by Hassen Saker,
from the film-poem triptych *terra lingua: three aspects*. Used by permission of the author.
Kaïdara by Amadou Hampâté Bâ, translated by Daniel Whitman. Copyright © 1988 by
Lynne Rienner Publishers, Inc. Used with permission of the publisher. "Reality Demands,"
from *Miracle Fair: Selected Poems of Wisława Szymborska* by Wisława Szymborska, translated by
Joanna Trzeciak. Copyright © 2001 by Joanna Trzeciak. Used by permission of W. W. Norton &
Company, Inc. "Sometimes Pleasing, Sometimes Not" by Jenn McCreary, from *& now my feet are maps*.
Used by permission of the author. "We Travel Like Other People," by Mahmoud Darwish,
from *Victims of a Map: A Bilingual Anthology of Arabic Poetry*, edited by Abdullah al-Udhari
(London, Saqi Books, 1984). Reprinted with permission of Saqi Books.

Library of Congress Cataloging-in-Publication Data

Badkhen, Anna, date.
Walking with Abel : journeys with the nomads of the African savannah / Anna Badkhen.
p.   cm.
ISBN 978-1-59463-248-8
1. Fula (African people)—Sahel.   2. Fula (African people)—Mali.   3. Fula (African people)—
Migrations.   4. Badkhen, Anna—Travel—Sahel.   5. Badkhen, Anna—Travel—Mali.   I. Title.
DT530.5.F84B34   2015   2015004476
305.896'322—dc23

Printed in the United States of America
1   3   5   7   9   10   8   6   4   2

Book design by Gretchen Achilles
Maps by Jeffrey L. Ward
Illustrations by Anna Badkhen

No matter how far the town, there is another behind it.

—FULANI PROVERB

I walked on knives
to get here & now
my feet are maps.

—JENN MCCREARY

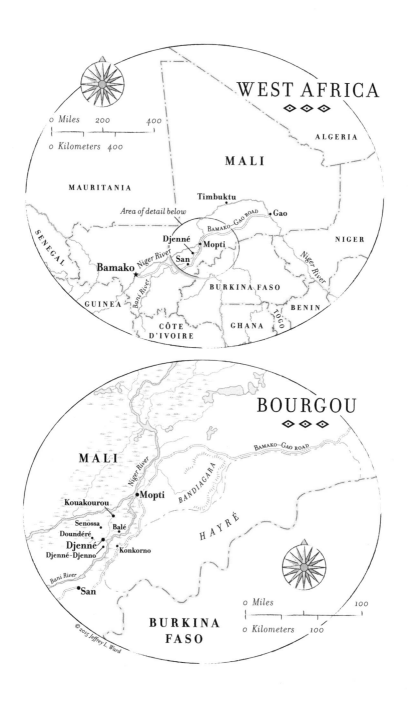

WEST AFRICA
◇ ◇ ◇

o Miles   200   400

o Kilometers   400

ALGERIA

MALI

MAURITANIA

Area of detail below

Timbuktu

●**Gao**

Bamako–Gao road

SENEGAL

Djenné

●**Mopti**

NIGER

Bamako
★

Niger River

●**San**

Bani River

BURKINA FASO

Niger River

GUINEA

BENIN

TOGO

CÔTE
D'IVOIRE

GHANA

BOURGOU
◇ ◇ ◇

MALI

Niger River

BANDIAGARA

Bamako–Gao road

Kouakourou

●**Mopti**

HAYRÉ

Senossa

●**Balé**

Doundéré

Djenné
Djenné-Djenno

●**Konkorno**

o Miles   100

Bani River

o Kilometers   100

●**San**

© 2015 Jeffrey L. Ward

**BURKINA
FASO**

THE
HOPING

◇ ◇ ◇

If you set out on a journey pray that the road is long

–Zbigniew Herbert

You could hear them from miles away. They went *tprrr! tprrr!* and they went *jet jet jet!* and they went *jot jot jot!* and they went *ay, shht, shht, oy, trrrrrr, 'uh, 'uh!* Repeating with proprietary virtuosity the calls their ancestors had used to talk to their own herds since the dawn of time. As if they journeyed not simply across distance but across eras and dragged with them through the land grooved with prehistoric cow paths all the cattle and all the herders who had laid tracks here before. You could almost make out all of them in the low scarf of shifting laterite dust, cowboys and ghosts of cowboys driving true and phantom herds on an ageless migration that stretched forever.

The Fulani and their cows tramped along the edge of the bone-white savannah, restless slatribbed wayfarers weaving among slow cattle just as slatribbed. Nomads chasing rain in the oceanic tracts of the Sahel. The cowboys wore soiled blue robes that luffed in the wind like sails, and their gait flowed smooth and footsure. Each step stitched the waking earth with a sound smoothed by millennia of repetition, a sound of sorrow and hope and loss and desire: the sound of walking.

They whistled and laughed and hurled their clubbed staffs underhand at the cows that were too hesitant or too distracted or out of step and they called "Girl! *Shht!*" and "Die! Die, bitch!" to such cows, but never in anger. They filled the soundscape with the chink of hooves and staffs upon filaments of shale, with yips and ululations, with incessant banter about cows and women and pontifications about God and swagger about migrations past. They moved in tinny bubbles of bootleg music that rasped from the cellphones they dangled on lanyards from their necks. Some had strapped to their chests boomboxes they had decorated with small mirrors, like disco balls. Their music said go on, go on, go on, go on, go on, in the same iambic beat as the songs of the Kel Tamashek camel riders of the Sahara, the Turkoman goat-herds of the Khorasan, the horsemen of the Kazakh steppes. Music made for walking and cowbells. Music made out of walking and cowbells.

Their herds fell together and drifted apart and even when the cattle drive swelled to many thousand head, the Fulani always knew which cows belonged to whom. They seared lines and dots and crosses into the hides of their cattle with sickle-shaped branding irons, but these hieroglyphics mostly were of no need to them because they recognized their livestock and the livestock of others from the serrated silhouette of the herd, from the way dust billowed in its wake, from the particular gait of the bulls. You learned such knowledge somehow.

"Those are Afo's cows, Papa."

"No they aren't."

"How can you tell?"

"That's just how it is."

"But how can you tell?"

"When I see cattle, I know."

Oumarou Diakayaté squinted at the procession of cattle and cattle drivers filing into the sunrise. He had risen in the cool blue pre-dawn from the wide reed pallet he shared with his wife, Fanta, their youngest son and daughter, and two small grandchildren, and washed from a small plastic kettle and prayed while most of the camp still slept. In the modest manner of his generation he had wrapped his indigo turban three times around his head and under the gray stubble on his narrow chin and across his thin mouth, in which a few teeth still remained, and dragged his millet-straw mat out of the cold shadows of the hut.

Then day crashed into the Sahel in a crescendo of birds. A rooster crowed once and right away clouds of tiny passerines in twilit shrub let loose a delirious trill. Starlings shrieked the world's oldest birth-song: alive, alive, alive, alive. A kingfisher warbled. The sun hurtled upward red and elliptic from beyond the sparse scrublands, grazed the low umbrella crowns of acacias, slowed down, and hung glaring in the fierce African sky.

Oumarou sat attentive and quite like a bird himself in the canted light of that July morning, with his knees drawn and a blue-checkered fleece blanket wrapped shoulder to toe around his tall and rawboned frame, and watched the herds pass. By the time the sun rose a palm above the treeline, his family would roll up their mats, pilfer the best thatch and rope from their shelters, pile calabashes and gunnysacks of blankets and clothes onto donkey carts, and join the other pilgrims ambling off from the

Sahel's most coveted pasturage to allow farmers a turn with the land.

Oumarou's dry-season grazing grounds lay in the fecund seasonal swamplands in the crook of the Niger's bend, in central Mali. The Fulani called the region the bourgou. Bourgou was hippo grass, *Echinochloa stagnina*, the sweet perennial semiaquatic species of barnyard grass that grew on the plains from late summer till winter's end, when the anastomosing stream of the Bani River flooded the Inner Niger Delta. Hippo grass shot its spongy blades up to nine feet out of the wetlands. Its rhizomes floated. It was a drifter, like the Fulani. Cows went wild for it.

The Diakayatés had arrived in the bourgou in January, after the rice harvest. Oumarou and his sons and nephews and grandnephews had raised their domed grass huts in a slightly swerving line of six beneath a few contorted thorn trees on a strip of dry land that bulged out of a fen so deep that the cows had to swim to return to camp from pasture. The thorn trees had fingered the soft wind of early winter with feathery peagreen leaves.

By July the island was a cowtrodden knuckle barely manifest on an enormous spent plateau. The fen was a foul sike, fragmented and not ankle-deep. All about, the oldest continental crust in the world lay bare, its brittle rusted skin ground to red talc by cattle and the dry harmattan winds of February and the cruel spring heat. The three thorn trees that flanked Oumarou's hut had no more leaves, and in the dusty naked branches agama lizards with orange heads rotated their eyes and pressed up and up in a laborious Triassic mating dance. To the northeast, the millet fields of slash-and-burn farmers smoked white against dark gray rainclouds that refused to break. The rain was late.

Oumarou had not heard the planetary-scale metastory of the most recent global warming. He had not heard much about the planet at all. He had not even heard about Africa. He could not read, did not listen to the radio. He took bearings by other coordinates calibrated in other ways, brought into existence billions of years before the Earth itself. He sought counsel from the stars.

For centuries the Fulani had aligned the annual movement of their livestock from rainy-season to dry-season pasture and back again with the orderly procession across the sky of twenty-six sequential constellations. Each signified the advent of a windy season, of weeks of drizzle or days of downpour, of merciless heat or relentless malarial mosquitoes that danced in humid nights. But for decades now the weather had been chaotic, out of whack with the stars. The rainy season had been starting early or late or not arriving at all. Oumarou was searching for the promise of rain conveyed across millions of light-years, and he could not reconcile the cycle.

In this part of the Sahel, the first week of June was the brief season the Fulani called the Hoping, when people looked at the sky expecting rain any day. This year the Hoping had stretched into two excruciating weeks, then three, then four. Oumarou's cows hung deflated humps to the side and let down little milk. Milk made up most of the old man's diet. He was nauseous with hunger.

"Three things make a man live a long and healthy life," he

would repeat over a succession of disappointing dinners of bland millet-flour porridge with sauce of pounded fish bones. "Milk, honey, and the meat of a cow that has never been sick." Honey was a rare treat in the bush. As for beef, that was a conjecture, a hypothesis. The Fulani very seldom ate meat, and when they did, it usually was goat or lamb. No Fulani would readily slaughter a healthy cow.

Oumarou freed an arm from his blanket and paced off the sky to the sun with a narrow hand. Half a palm's width. A flock of birds burst out of a low shrub, chirped, circled, settled again. The uninterrupted horizon quivered with birdsong, lizards' click-tongue, the whimper of goats, the hoof-falls and lowing of moving cows. Eternal sounds. Ephemeral sounds. Three more fingers and the cows would be gone. Time to pack.

Oumarou looked at Fanta, his wife, his fellow rambler, who now stood by his side listening to the faraway herds also.

"Ready?" he said.

Oumarou's restlessness dated back to the Neolithic, to the time when a man first took a cow out to graze.

It was an outsize brown cow that stood six feet front hoof to shoulder and bore a pair of forward-pointing, inward-curved horns such as the ones that eventually would gore tigers and bears in the coliseums of Rome. The last of her undomesticated tribe, a female wild aurochs, would die of disease or old age or hunger or loneliness in the Jaktorów forest in Poland in 1627. Around 10,000 BC, ancient humans began to encourage the *Bos primigenius* to stay close. How? Maybe they used salt to entice the massive ruminants, as people did in the twenty-first century with the wild mithans of the Assam hills, with northern reindeer. Or maybe, like the Diakayatés did on cattle drives, they simply sweet-talked the aurochs into sticking around. "*Ay, ay,* girl!" One way or another, sometime in the early Holocene a colossal proto-cow felt trusting enough around people that she allowed herself to be milked. Milking would become like walking: essential, innate. It was why God gave man opposable thumbs.

In Africa, herders preceded farmers by some three thousand years. In Asia, pastoralism evolved after agriculture. Anthropologists disagree whether people domesticated cattle on these two continents independently or whether itinerant Asian traders brought the cow to Africa, though DNA studies indicate that all taurine cattle came from eighty female wild aurochs. In any event, during the Agricultural Revolution, Cain and Abel parted ways, and from then on, "the nomadic alternative," as the writer-wanderer Bruce Chatwin called it, developed parallel to, and in symbiosis with, the settled culture.

Antecedent herders grazed their kine in the lush pastures of East Africa. Around 8000 BC, people at Nabta Playa, an interglacial oasis in the Nubian Desert, littered their primeval hearths with pottery and bones of ovicaprids and cattle. Ten thousand years from now, archaeologists of the future will scrape the same refuse from the midden of Oumarou's campsite—cow bone and goat crania and cracked bowls, plus some empty glass vials of commercially manufactured vermicide.

Around 6000 BC, some bands of nomads hit the road. Perhaps, as sedentary farmers carved pasturage into millet and sorghum fields, they had run out of country. They drove before them lyre-horned zebu cows: much smaller than the wild aurochs, requiring little water, able to withstand high temperatures, docile, and partially resistant to rinderpest. The herders were tolerant to lactose and lived mostly on milk. Their limbs were stretched by protein. Their bones were strong enough to chase clouds. Like Hollywood cowboys, they hooved it west.

Today the unlettered Fulani in the bourgou without effort can trace the beginning of their passage to the very birthplace of mankind. I don't know how they know. Western anthropologists, linguists, and ethnographers have puzzled over Fulani origins for more than a hundred years, measuring skulls, divining cadences of language. But ask a cowherd in Mali where his people came from, and he will reply: "Ethiopia."

The nomads marched their cattle through a Neolithic Sahara. The land was lush, sodden with the subpluvial that had followed the last glaciation. Herds of hippopotamus and giraffe and ostrich and zebra grazed along mighty rivers. The rivers were full of fish. You can still see their dry courses from space.

Around 4000 BC they stopped at the Paleozoic obelisk forest of Tassili n'Ajjer, the Plateau of the Rivers, a migrants' oasis in what today is Algeria. There, on sandstone, the nomads painted and engraved Bovidian odes to cattle. Herds on the run. At pasture. Humped. Unhumped. Longhorned. Piebald. One painting shows a person milking a cow as a calf stands by, probably to encourage the cow to let down her milk. Someone picked into a rock a cow weeping rock tears. What was the artist's dolor? The beautiful stones of Tassili are silent.

By 2000 BC a great drought had returned. The desert—in Arabic *sahra*, the Sahara—pushed the herders south. Perhaps for the first time these land-use innovators had to adapt to climate change. They hooked down toward the westernmost edge of the region that Arab traders and conquerors later would call *sahel*, the shore: the savannah belt that stretches from the Indian Ocean to the Atlantic, linking the Sahara and the tropics roughly along the thirteenth parallel.

Trapped between the lethal tsetse forests of the south and the northern desert, Fulani cattle herders ambulated the semiarid grass-lands of western Sahel. They plodded toward the Atlantic, into the coastal reaches of modern-day Senegal, Guinea, Côte d'Ivoire, Ghana. But just south of the town walls of modern Djenné, less than a day's walk from the Diakayatés' dry-season camp, one of the oldest known urban centers in sub-Saharan Africa, Djenné-Djenno, pokes its ruins out of the earth. Excavations at Djenné-Djenno have revealed bones of domesticated cattle and goats and sheep that date back to the beginning of the first millennium AD. Oumarou's fore-fathers may have passed through already then.

The Fulani thrust inland in the twelfth and thirteenth centu-ries. Many of them were Muslim. "Generally of a tolerant disposi-tion," the Nigerian scholar Akin L. Mabogunje wrote in his essay "The Land and Peoples of West Africa," the Fulani were embraced "for the manure their cattle provided on the fields and for the milk and butter which could be exchanged for agricultural products." That arrangement never has changed. When I met them, the Diakayatés lived on the millet and rice and fish Oumarou's wife, Fanta, swapped for butter and buttermilk, and villagers welcomed his cow dung on their fields as long as it was not at the time of planting, during the rainy season, or at the time of harvest, right after. As the Fulani had been doing for thousands of years, the fam-ily notched and notched the routes of ancient transhumance deeper into the continent's bone, driven by a neverending quest for pastur-age, a near worship of cattle, and the belief that God created the Earth, all of it, for the cows.

In the early nineteenth century, a Fulani scholar, cleric, and trilingual poet named Uthman dan Fodio launched one of West Africa's earliest jihads. Hurtling camelback and horseback, dan Fodio and his followers delivered Sufi Islam to the mostly animist rural savannah on the tips of their spears and broadswords. In the floodplains of the Inner Niger Delta, one of dan Fodio's disciples, a Fulani orphan named Ahmad bin Muhammad Boubou bin Abi Bakr bin Sa'id al Fulani Lobbo, led an Islamic uprising and created the theocratic empire of Massina. Twenty-first-century Fulani remember and revere him by his preacher sobriquet, Sekou Amadou: Sheikh Muhammad.

Sekou Amadou made his first capital at the village of Senossa, a sparse oasis of low adobes and doum palms above a swale that separates the village from Djenné. Then he set out to purify what he saw as his subjects' corrupt mores. He banned tobacco and alcohol, established purdah, set up social welfare for widows and orphans, and regularized land use, drawing up seasonal timetables that distributed pastures and rivers among Bozo fishermen, Songhai traders, Mandinka and Bambara farmers, and Fulani herders. He favored the cattlemen; the nomads thrived. Almost two hundred years later the amplitudes of Oumarou's migration still abided by the transhumance schedules Sekou Amadou had drawn in 1818.

By the beginning of the twenty-first century an estimated thirty to forty million nomads roved the world, herding cattle, deer, goats, sheep, yak, camel, horses. Some twenty million of them were Fulani.

Their ruinously swelling herds, confined by state borders, frontlines, and megalopolises that were recharting the Sahel, competed with expanding farmsteads for depleted and dwindling resources. Demographers in the West predicted that the next big extinction would be theirs. That in a hundred years, we all would be settled, and living in cities.

When I relayed this to Oumarou he was distressed. For more than seventy years, since the first year he could remember, he had spent the dry season on the narrow island right here, in the middle of the sweetgrass marsh an hour's walk northwest of Senossa.

"How will we keep cows in the city?" he asked.

Nomad, νομάς, *nomas*: a vagabond for pasture.

To enter such a culture. Not an imperiled life or a life enchanted but an altogether different method to life's meaning, a divergent sense of the world. To tap into a slower knowledge that could come only from taking a very, very long walk with a people who have been walking always. To join a walk that spans seasons, years, a history; to synchronize my own pace with a meter fine-tuned over millennia. For years I had wanted to learn from such immutable movement. In January of 2013—a number meaningless to the nomads, who ignored man-drawn borders and man-defined time—I came to the bourgou to follow a Fulani family on a yearlong cycle of transhumance, to learn from their journey lessons of adaptation and survival. *"Solvitur ambulando,"* Diogenes promised: "It is solved by walking."

Long walks in open spaces are like ujjayi breath for the mind. Human feet evolved to measure out steady steps on hot, dry, flat land, and the human brain evolved to absorb boundless geology at the speed of three miles an hour. The sheer volume of lucid air fills the mind, the distant skyline paces off a spirit level of peace. The expanse around you unburdens the space within.

To join the nomads I needed an introduction, a benediction, consent. I needed advisors. I went looking in the unpaved bezel of Djenné's market square.

The town's Sudanic skyline jabbed at the early-evening sky and in the faded air over the three soaring clay minarets of the Grande Mosquée swallows dashed among pale stars. Dust mixed with the potent scent of strong green gunpowder tea that was boiled and reboiled with sugar and sometimes mint and then poured, bubbling and syrupy, from great heights into small shot-glasses sticky from hours of tea ceremonies previous. Women floated past in single-file columns and quarreled and chaffed and balanced on their heads trays of fresh Nile perch, calabashes of buttermilk, plastic bags of peanuts, baskets of smoked catfish, lozenges of sugared sesame, baguettes, papayas, hot peppers, laundry, water, the world.

A small boy on a bicycle dragged a donkey on a rope at a gallop. Teenagers strolled importantly between shops carrying redhot birds' nests of wire braziers with lit coal for tea. Itinerants with goatskin bags and short broadswords in tooled leather scabbards

shuffled through hot dust. Two young Fulani men walked arm in arm, their fingers clasped in huge silver rings. The broad brims of their spiked burgundy cowhide-and-canvas hats touched as they gossiped. Rimaibe girls, descendants of the slaves who once grew their Fulani masters' millet and rice, who grew and spun and wove their cotton, unloaded from their heads tall stacks of firewood for the townswomen to cook the day's dinner, then stood fanning themselves. They wore cotton pagnes printed with giddy M. C. Escher designs of fish and pineapples and flowers, and nylon soccer jerseys: Mali, Manchester, Liverpool, Barcelona, Brazil. Elders passed in lace boubous of incredible neon hues. The color screamed like some heat-induced delirium in the antique clay monochrome of the town. A three-legged goat pulled on the rope that tethered it to a thorn tree, bleated miserably, pulled again.

It was Sunday. Africa Cup of Nations blared from television sets propped on crates outside shops. South Africa was playing Morocco. Halftime news delivered dispatches of death from Mali's north, where a latter-day jihad was converting traditional nomadic routes into the newest frontline of the global war on terror. Al Qaeda fanatics were chopping off hands in Gao, blowing up old Islamic shrines in Timbuktu. French troops had arrived in Mali a week earlier and now rumbled in armored personnel vehicles into the Sahara. Half a century after gaining independence from France, Malians gathered roadside to wave at her soldiers with blue-white-and-red tricolors.

Afo Bocoum sat under the thatched awning of a shabby mercantile on a long backless wooden bench varnished with years of sweat. Afo's father had forsaken transhumance to serve as a translator for French colonists, and Afo had grown up in Djenné. A settled Fulani, a homesick Fulani. To satisfy his nomadic yearnings he rode his motorcycle twice daily to the pastures where hired cowboys herded his many hundreds of cows. He would lean the bike against a tree and talk to his cattle and feed them cottonseed by hand.

"Cattle," he would say, in a mix of English and French, "c'est pas business, c'est l'amour."

When he was home and there was electricity in the house, he watched nature channels in French. Discovery Channel France, National Geographic, Nat Geo Wild, Planète+. He sought out shows about herders.

"Texas! I've seen it on television. They have a lot of cowherds there. They ride horses. And they have hats like the Fulani, only bigger."

Afo was a *diawando*, a member of a Fulani caste of mediators between the nomads, who despised and feared government in all its incomprehensible forms, and the officialdom, which considered the nomads arrogant, rich, and obsolete, and took advantage of their illiteracy by fleecing them recklessly: in the modern world, God seemed to favor Cain. A *diawando* advised his clients on all matters legal, formal, veterinary, and financial. The relationship was passed down from father to son and the loyalty between a *diawando* and the pastoralists was nonpareil. The Diakayatés were Afo's clients and they worshipped him.

Afo picked at bad teeth with a match and considered my request.

"In this life you have to feel love for what you do. If you don't feel love for what you're doing you won't do it well."

He fell silent. Late January heat made everything lazy, moved listlessly through legs, slowed circulation. A small boy slouched by, swallowing hard some insult or injury, tears running down his pouting face. A teenager with wandering eyes came under the awning and drooled and stood fingering his green stone prayer beads. The gloaming softened all color. An old muezzin in a dusty blue boubou limped up to his post at the southeastern corner of the mosque wall, stopped, spat a sizable ball of phlegm over the rampart, put his bony hands to his ears. The mosque loudspeaker crackled like bursts of distant gunfire and the muezzin began his first summons to evening prayer. The quarter tones ricocheted gently off banco walls, spilled into the immense famished horizons beyond.

The French adventurer René Caillié, the first European to return from Timbuktu, stopped in Djenné in 1828. The massive mosque built of daub and wattle in the twelfth or thirteenth century, during Islam's early and erratic years in the Niger Delta, stood mostly in ruins by then: Sekou Amadou had disapproved of its ostentatiousness and allowed it to fall into disrepair, while he built his own, smaller, simpler mosque a block away. The Grande Mosquée, Caillié wrote, was "rudely constructed, though very large. It is abandoned to thousands of swallows, which build their nests in it." The modern mosque, the largest mudbrick building in the world, was a replica, built at the order of French colonists in 1907. The swallows remained.

I waited. Swallows chirred. At last Afo pronounced:

"Bon! Your work is good. We'll go to the bush tomorrow."

On the other end of the square two elders stopped me. Babourou Koïta, a *diawando* like Afo, held court each day next to a pharmacy in a chair made of bamboo and goatskin, while in the secrecy of his compound, cowboys in his employ raised gigantic interbreeds of zebus and Holsteins. In an identical chair next to Babourou sat his best friend, Ali the Griot.

A griot: a bard, an entertainer. An ambulatory madman spewing blessings and augury. An oracle for the powers that shaped the universe, as feared as the blacksmith who transforms the Earth's elements. A hereditary oral chronicler of the land who alone knows all the secret iniquities and virtues of its gentry.

Griots dumbfounded the fourteenth-century traveler Ibn Battuta. "Each of them has got inside a costume made of feathers to look like a thrush with a wooden head made for it and a red beak as if it were the head of a bird. They stand before the sultan in that ridiculous attire and recite their poetry," he wrote in the chronicle of his journey through the Malian kingdom. "It was mentioned to me that their poetry is a kind of preaching." Ibn Battuta didn't understand: you submitted to the griot and feared his judgment because how he pronounced you to be was how you would be. His words tweaked destiny. He was the keeper and twister of history who castigated and flattered and who from his praise and reprimands molded prophecies and delivered such news and advice as he saw fit so he could stoke or resolve conflicts, forge or disband unions, bestow or retract fame.

"In Africa, when an old man dies, it's a library burning," said Amadou Hampâté Bâ, Mali's most renowned writer. When a griot died, histories of entire families and empires dissolved underfoot. The world lost gravity.

Modern griots no longer dressed in feathers. They were court jesters set loose in a new world, a world without kings. Some cut records and performed in front of African and European and American crowds. Most dispensed wisdoms at weddings, at political rallies, in public squares. They were ronin. Ali was one of those.

Ali had a two-packs-a-day habit and looked like my grandfather who had died when I was a girl. I told him that. He nodded and informed me he was broke. "That makes two of us," I said. He giggled and nodded again. I told him my grandfather had been an orchestra conductor, an entertainer, and that my grandfather's name—my name, *badkhen*—meant a fiddler, an irreverent jester-rhymer who ad-libbed at Jewish weddings. I came from a long line of Yiddish griots, I said. That wasn't good enough. Ali stubbed out a Dunhill in the dust and motioned to Babourou for another and said that to walk in the Sahel I needed a different name, a Fulani name.

He looked at Babourou. Babourou looked at the sky, presumably for instruction.

"Bâ!" he said. "Your name will be Anna Bâ."

Ali nodded once more. "Good name. Noble name. One of the oldest Fulani names." And he grabbed my hand and yanked it up in the air and sang me my new ancient family history. It began in no remembered time with the arrival from a faraway desert of four Fulani progenitor families—the spiritual leaders the Diallos, the logisticians the Sows, the largest cattle owners the Bâs, their helpers the Barris—and it ended like this:

"Anna Bâ, Bâ the owner of cattle, Bâ the owner of white cattle, white is the color of milk, Bâ the owner of the color white. First came the Diallos the Sows the Bâs the Barris. Bâ is the owner of many animals, Bâ is the owner of butter, Bâ smells of butter, Bâ the sweetest-smelling Fulani. Bâ. Bâ. Bâ. Bâ."

He did not let go of my hand the whole time.

The naming ceremony would be held the next day. I was to buy a sacrificial goat. On television screens around the square, South Africa and Morocco tied, two–two.

A friend hosted the ceremony at his bar, an eyesore of poured concrete on the outskirts of town. Its courtyard had a bandstand under a leaky cabana. It served Malian beer and lukewarm soft drinks and inside it had low benches upholstered with artificial leather and mirrored disco balls and a small television set tuned to a channel that showed Ivorian and Senegalese dancers in bikinis and hot pants grinding to hiphop. The bar owner was a settled Fulani wheeler-dealer who wore copious perfume, spoke seven or eight languages, including French, Spanish, and English, was afraid of cows, and went by the nickname Pygmée. "Peul moderne," Afo called him: the modern Fulani. Out of respect for the Muslim sensibilities of my elder guests Pygmée turned off the television. His friend Allaye the Butcher had roasted a goat in town and delivered it to the bar in the evening and carved it in the yard.

My three godfathers, my three magi, arrived on three motorcycles in flowing robes. Afo wore a boubou white as an egret's wing and had two helpings of roast goat and pronounced it very good. Babourou, in a handwoven mantle of black and turquoise wool embroidered with gold thread, told me that to be one hundred percent Fulani I needed a Fulani man, and that—this was a segue—he and the other elders would assist me in any manner possible. Ali the Griot promised that my new name would protect me from evil.

"Anna Bâ! Fulani Bâ! General de Gaulle! Bienvenue, bienvenue." We toasted with orange Fanta.

I walked up to the flat roof. Effervescent dusk. White guinea-fowl perched in a eucalyptus grove. The town's sole generator droned. In a thin web of orange streetlights Djenné's oblique adobes crowded narrow and asymmetrical and surreal. The floodplains around the town reflected the mauve and blue and crimson of the dying sky and the town seemed suspended in air. Beyond spread the thorny and flat Sahelian wilderness that belonged to the cows and their cowboys. I would be joining them in the morning.

Then the generator quieted and the lights went out, the town disappeared, and a full moon rang into the sky like a bell.

Early the next day, Afo, Pygmée, and I sat in the freckled shade of a windtwisted thorn tree with Oumarou Diakayaté and Fanta and their many kin and watched cattle egrets float down from the sky into hippo grass thickets that scissored in the wind. The white birds parted the grass and puckered the fen's glossy surface with their long legs. A low northbound warplane thundered overhead. A few days' walk away from the camp the French air force was bombing the Sahara. In the fen terrified cattle jolted and tripped and bawled. On the other side of the thorn tree a cow calved quietly and licked the calf to life. The Diakayatés had been in the bourgou a week.

"This is Anna Bâ," Afo said and the Diakayatés laughed. "Bâ? Anna Bâ? A Fulani? Good, good. Welcome, Anna Bâ."

Oumarou asked me if I had any cows, and whether it had rained where I came from. Was America in France? Afo said it was on the other side of Mecca, which meant very far. One of Oumarou's nephews said: "In your land don't you also have a city that loves cattle, named Kentucky?"

I had no cows. But I, too, went on pendular journeys in the world's margin lands. I grazed for stories, I explained. I herded words.

Oumarou laughed again and said I could tag along as far as I wished. The women laughed as well and said I would have to take turns pounding their millet. They showed with their arms—and *down!* and *down!* and *down!*—in case I didn't understand.

One of Oumarou's nieces said, "There are three ways to study, Anna Bâ: with your feet, with your eyes, and with your mind. Now I know you study with your feet because you have come here to live and walk with us."

I had come to study, it was true. I also was pursuing something, a measure of healing. I was not on a pilgrimage—that would have been fatuous, a folly. But secretly I hoped that all the old pathways of my hosts somehow could triangulate into an inarticulable and uncharted solace, because just four months earlier, as I was readying, in cold autumn, to travel to West Africa, my beloved had left me.

We passed around a calabash with foamy buttermilk that Fanta had churned that morning. A communion, a nomad's toast. From the northeast the harmattan blew minuscule particles of the Sahara. Sand granules. Tiny travelers. Each speck a capsule delivering to the Sahel echoes of drought, of war, of a space vast and arid and pitiless. The cow had licked her calf dry and clean and had eaten the afterbirth and the calf was trying to push away the ground with its new legs. Oumarou sent a grandnephew to take a look. It was a male calf, the boy reported. More likely to be sold in case of emergency: the females were valued for their milk. The old man said that he would name it Anna Bâ, in my honor, and everybody laughed some more.

Only Mama, his stepdaughter, was worried. She was thirty-two, and she lay on a mat feverish and curled up with a migraine and a bad sinus infection.

"You say you want to tell our story," she said. "But we don't know how the story ends."

Besides, she said, how would I walk? I didn't know how to carry water on my head.

Carrying water was woman's work. Water for laundry and washing and cooking came mostly from the triangular hippo grass swamp west of the camp that each morning exploded in spalls of reflected sunlight.

"Aren't you worried about drinking water from that marsh?"

"Oh no. Our cows drink from it, so we know it's good. But who knows who put water in your plastic bottle? Aren't you worried about drinking from it?"

But it was true, the women conceded, that well water was less cloudy. The closest well was about half a mile away. Two or three times a day the women would balance empty jerrycans and plastic pails on their heads and slowly flipflop to it.

The path to the well changed with the seasons from morass to mud to the hard corduroy of fossilized footsteps, as though each season the most recent itinerants recast out of oblivion the traces of the ancients. It linked Oumarou's campsite to the two mostly parallel ruts that bore tracks of horsedrawn carts and pack donkeys and of feet bare and sandaled and the serpentine imprints of motorscooters and wobbly Chinese bicycles, and that meandered north deeper into the bourgou and south toward the sewage-sluiced snarl of the narrow daub alleys of Djenné.

Settled people lived along that unnamed road. Nearest the camp, each less than half a mile away, sat two hamlets, Doundéré and Dakabalal.

Doundéré, to the southwest, was an old outpost of compact adobes that crowded uphill toward a tiny steepled clay mosque. Doundéré's elevation was a compression of cultural layers, of uncounted generations of mudbrick homes raised and crumbled and raised anew. Everyone knew it was very old but whether it was three hundred years old or a thousand no one could tell: years did not count, were not counted in these parts. Its residents were Bambara rice and millet farmers and rimaibe, former Fulani slaves who treated the nomads with a combination of respect and mistrust. Oumarou's sons and grandnephews who were old enough for such things sometimes went to Doundéré to drink tea and prattle with other cowboys and for a few pennies to charge their cellphones, using a motorcycle battery one rimaibe family owned, and to buy cigarettes and small paper cubes of gunpowder green tea from China and counterfeit medicine. Married Diakayaté women avoided Doundéré. On some nights, after their parents had fallen asleep, teenage girls would sneak out to the village to flirt with young visiting cowboys in smoky rooms.

Dakabalal, to the northwest, was a haphazard cluster of homes that an extended family of Bozo fishermen had tossed upon a slight rise, in Oumarou's lifetime. The Bozo traced their ancestry to capricious man-eating water spirits and amphibians and may have been seining and trapping the Niger and the Bani since the Stone Age; their name, bo so, was an epithet given them by the Bambara that, in Bambara, meant "bamboo hut," for the riparian dwellings they would set up when they moored. Many remained transient, floating down rivers in redwood pirogues. They were nominally Muslim but they worshipped the river, did not wash for burial the people who had died by drowning, and considered drowned animals halal to eat. Dakabalal had no mosque. I once saw Dakabalal children play with a white egret the way children elsewhere would with a cat. The women in the village kept small and silent yellow dogs and smoked fish on large gridirons day and night, and around these gridirons toddlers played with tackle. The women were heavy from lifetimes of childbirth and they often sat in front of their grills like river goddesses, naked from the waist up, knees spraddled inside colorful pagnes, a small child on the breast.

Two or three miles north of Dakabalal lay Somena, a carefully swept arrangement of fifty or so tidy clay huts. Settled Fulani cattlemen had built it half a century earlier on a mound left by some previous village of some previous people no longer remembered. To the south, past Doundéré, on the way to the Massina Empire's first capital at Senossa, tall mopped doum palms and mango trees in geometric bloom of dirty pink flanked the villages of Weraka and Wono. These villages were larger than Doundéré, and rimaibe and Bambara and settled Bozo lived and farmed behind their tall mudbrick walls, and during the dry season the Diakayaté women walked there to barter buttermilk for grain. Two fastpaced hours farther south lay Djenné, with its fabled mosque, its disorienting and overwhelming Monday market, its perfunctory district hospital, the only one around. Costly pharmacies, indifferent magistrates, extortionist gendarmerie.

This was the southern tip of the bourgou. In satellite images it looked like the big toe print of a southpointing green flat foot, the foot of a nomad.

Most winters each village was an island until the end of February. The swales filled with stagnant water in which small black herons slouched and cheery white-faced whistling ducks grazed on sodden leftovers of the grain harvest. By January scores of nomadic families set up camp on the low rises dry enough to sleep on, each campsite a neatly swept circle of mats, chicken, guinea hens, goats, sheep, cattle. To the black kites that wheeled over the fens in silent concentration they must have looked like salvages from a shipwrecked ark, their poultry like something to snatch up and eat. For centuries, slavers had shuttled the wetlands between the villages and camps in pirogues during the rainy season and kidnapped luckless children and young women to sell at the markets of Djenné, of Ségou, of Timbuktu. Some of their victims became rimaibe. Some were resold out and out toward the Atlantic coast and of those many ended up toiling on plantations in the West Indies, in the American South. For the most part the abductions ended when France colonized western Sahel, swapping one kind of bondage for another.

The well the Diakayaté women favored sat beside Dakabalal: a stack of concrete rings in a rectangular enclosure of poured concrete. Water laced with clay sloshed piss-yellow in the fourteen-foot drop. But on some days within the rings there quivered a blue disk of sky.

At the well the women would remove their sandals and leave them at the enclosure's threshold as if they were entering a hut or a house, the house of water. They would pull up hand over hand a pail

of rubber or goatskin on a yellow manila rope and drink from the pail and let the water run down their chins. Luxuriously, even decadently. They would fill their containers and sometimes they would strip out of their boubous and shirts and wash their shoulders and arms and breasts and laugh at water running down their spines to tickle under their calico pagnes and between their skinny legs. And sometimes, though the Fulani women considered themselves more worthy as a race because of their lighter skin tone and almost Semitic profiles, they would condescend to joke with the Bozo laundresses in Bozo or in Bambara and the laundresses would respond, and women's laughter and the slapping of laundry would bounce off the concrete in playful echoes.

Then they would set the buckets and canisters on their heads again and walk single file back to camp, the containers in static equilibrium. The weight would compress painfully the vertebrae in the women's necks. The women always walked back to camp quickly, almost on the double, the sooner to offload their freight, and to pour the water into the earthenware jugs each of them kept inside her hut by the door, and to stretch. They kept joking to distract themselves.

About halfway to the camp the path skirted a small grove of eucalyptus planted here during some bygone reforestation campaign. Even during the rainy season the grove always stood above the tideline. Its hard topsoil hid at least two unmarked graves.

One belonged to Oumarou's firstborn, Djamba, who already had been married when she died many years ago at the age of seventeen. The other belonged to Oumarou's eleven-year-old son Amadou. They were his children from his first wife, Hajja, who died on transhumance during the great famine thirty years earlier and was buried far away, north of the Niger River. The acacia branches Oumarou had felled upon the graves of Djamba and Amadou to keep away wild animals were long gone. Maybe the wind had dragged them away. Maybe women had collected them for kindling. Maybe the termites had eaten them into frass that simply had disintegrated with time.

"You only have one child?" Oumarou's niece Salimata clicked her tongue, turned toward me her head of long grayhaired cornrows, squinched her aquiline nose. The golden hoop she had threaded through her septum jiggled. She walked briskly; ten kilos of water on her head were crushing her sixty-year-old bones. "Oh, oh, oh. You must have a lot. At least five."

"How many do you have?"

"Seven are still alive."

"And the others?"

"There were three more. God took them. We move. They died on the move."

The Diakayatés did not discuss the graves much. The Fulani code of honor was strict and punitive: a woman who cried over her dead child weighed him down, barred his soul from entering the heavenly gates, and barred the child, too, from testifying in heaven on her behalf. The Fulani submitted to the awesome and unlearnable omnipotence of God. They celebrated impermanence the way the Japanese watched cherry blossoms in spring. The way the Tibetans poured the entire vibrant universe of a mandala into a river. Sufi teachers promised that freedom lay in the absence of choice, but the nomads' practice may have predated their conversion to Islam. Stoicism was the discipline of suffering, and transhumance demanded both. In the second century BC the Greek historian Agatharchides wrote of a pastoral sub-Saharan people he called the Troglodytes who lived on milk and blood of cattle and buried their dead to the accompaniment of laughter. The Roma, Europe's last remaining nomads, dance in mourning.

By the beginning of the second millennia, around the time Islam's early forays into the bourgou delivered spindle whorls, rectilinear houses, and brass, people had abandoned the settlement of Djenné-Djenno. A hundred acres of culture painstakingly carved out of the hardscrabble geography since the third century BC had simply withered, become effaced. Why? The oral epics are mum. From midsummer to late winter, when the wadis around the prehistoric grounds run with water, laundresses spread their bright pagnes over the relics to dry.

A different story survives. A thousand years ago, around the time of Djenné-Djenno's mysterious decline, nomadic Bozo fishers began to settle into permanent banco villages along the Bani, the

Niger's tributary. On a large island hammocked in the vascular tangle of the river's braided stream the Bozo sacrificed the young maiden Tapama Djennepó, alias Pama Kayantau, asking the genii of the floodplains to bless a new settlement they called Djenné. They immured the girl alive.

The city grew to eminence. It became a medieval stopping point on the trans-Saharan caravan route for traders of gold, salt, and slaves. A "blessed town," the seventeenth-century Timbuktu scholar Abd al Rahman al Sa'adi called Djenné in *Ta'r-īkh al Sudan*, the earliest surviving written history of the Songhai Empire, which in the fifteenth and sixteenth centuries stretched more than two thousand miles from the Atlantic Ocean to the heart of modern-day Niger. Camels and pack donkeys clacked by Tapama's tomb. Islamic scholars flocked past it to madrassas. Sekou Amadou's purist jihadis let it be. A thousand years after the sacrifice, in 1988, the United Nations designated Djenné a World Heritage Site—like the Mayan city of Chichén Itzá, like the Taj Mahal—and town fathers erected next to the tomb a signboard that read TOMBE DE LA JEUNNE FILLE TAPAMA GENEPO SACRIFEE POUR PROTEGER LA VILLE CONTRE LES MAUVILLES ESPRITS. In the twenty-first century the tomb's clay hexahedron still slanted toward the river on the southern edge of the town, next to a fetid black rivulet of refuse. Slanted toward the necropolis of the Sahel, where a child's grave always watched over the living.

Oumarou had three other dead children. They were buried at two different resting stops on his migration route. Each campsite was a gravesite. Each season the old cowboy measured with his footsteps the distance from one dead child to the next.

Two thousand footsteps per mile. Twenty to forty thousand footsteps a day. Seven to fifteen million footsteps a year on the raw hide of the Earth: the drawn-out journeys of biannual migration, and in between, the constant movement of twice-daily pasturage, of daily roundtrips to waterholes and distant markets. Every footfall contains the kernel of our becoming, the meganarrative of our time-less hejiras, our common travelogue writ large. Every footfall brings the walker closer to the next patch of shade, the next well, the next resting spot. Every footfall is a leap of faith that at the end of the trek lie pasture and water for the cows, redemption, forgiveness, self-compassion.

Every footfall begets a separation. Each time the Diakayatés moved camp they left behind huts sedulously wainscoted and torn down, loved ones, lovers, graves.

Salimata pitied me. She knew the heartbeat of the savannah with the soles of her feet and she knew that the land preserved all the memories past and future and replayed them again and again in cycles that lasted a season, a decade, an eternity. Cycles of plentitude and uncertainty, of holding on and letting go, of life and death and life again.

"Is there a land without death, Anna Bâ?" she said. "We are used to leaving everything."

To spend a lifetime walking away. To bid farewell over and over, all the time. To anchor your heart to the next campsite and then move on. To have your heart broken and reset like a bone.

For a while my beloved had lived in the desert. When the land stilled in the late-afternoon heat and ocotillos cast shadows blue and long like sundial gnomons we would watch stormcells collide sixty miles away. But he was not free to give me his love and did not give it freely. He was a landscape of desire, and I was always trespassing, and every goodbye was our last. Each time we met it was to walk away.

Don't you know, Mama? Carrying water has nothing on grief.

Above the graves in the eucalyptus trees there lived a murder of pied crows. Whenever the Diakayaté women passed by the grove the birds would fling themselves out of the fragrant grove at the women's repartee and caw their own carnivorous tattles.

A pied crow is the best medicine for epilepsy. You pluck it, cook it in a pot, and eat it whole. But it is hard to find a pied crow even in Djenné's fetish market on a Monday because a crow is very difficult to kill. The hunters who do sell it charge a lot of money for it.

If you catch a pied crow alive, which is all but impossible because it is such a cunning and evasive bird, and pull down its eyelids, you will find a sentence from the Koran written in Arabic on the sclera of its eyes. If you read that sentence, spit into your palm, and wish for anything—a lot of cows, or money—your wish will come true. But pied crows are even harder to catch alive than to kill.

A pied crow does not lay eggs, not ever. It steals the eggs of other birds, takes them to its nest, and whispers an incantation over them, turning the fetus birds inside into pied crows.

Perhaps sorcery is the kind of covenant one needs to level with this land, to live and walk in the bush of ghosts.

Sunup in the Sahel. Thousands of cattle egrets hung on the blue wind, laced the air with dawn-coppered wingbeat. A bright scarlet sun pushed away the night and in the west there appeared a gauze of dust. A hint of cattle. Hairatou, Oumarou's youngest daughter, quit poking the manure fire she had lit with the coals she'd borrowed from an uncle's camp and rose to see. The animals no larger than gilded peppercorns on the miraging horizon between Dakabalal and Doundéré, the cattle driver himself invisible.

"That's Ousman with the cattle, Papa."

"Where—oh yes. So it is."

"I knew it!"

The Bedouin who in the nineteen forties accompanied the British traveler Wilfred Thesiger through the Empty Quarter of Arabia knew camels that way. The dark oval beauty tattoo around Hairatou's lips grew broader with her proud smile.

Hairatou was fifteen. A day earlier, with a forefinger dipped in Ultra Blue No. 1 Tulip clothes dye, she had painted on the pale clay wainscot of her parents' hut images of cattle and cowherds, stick figures with crosses for the broadbrimmed hats of men and ovals for the cows' humps. She had painted larger standalone crosses for birds aflight and gargantuan spoons that looked like Venus symbols. Were the hut to remain standing, some future scientists would wonder about those, and about the large and hairy vulvae that were

Hairatou's renderings of the calabash lids she wove in her spare time out of grass and colored thread.

Hers was not the elegant artwork of Tassili n'Ajjer, painted with mineral pigment that silica had bound to rock. Nor had she ever heard of ancient pictographs, those or any others. Her own art would in fact disappear at the onset of the rainy season, when her parents dismantled the hut. The cuticle of her finger would remain bluestained for days.

"Ousman's coming, Mother!"

Ousman was Oumarou's second-eldest living son. The eldest was Boucary, a gaunt and withdrawn man who lived separately from his father and herded almost exclusively goats and sheep because he was a lousy cowboy and could not be trusted with cattle. Ousman was thirty years old and had a wife and two small sons and because of that raised his own hut, which, wherever the family camped, he built three dozen yards south of his father's. Like Oumarou he was reed-thin and tall. Under his various faded blue boubous he always wore a Los Angeles Lakers singlet of yellow rayon. On his feet, the narrow plastic lace-ups made in Côte d'Ivoire that all nomads wore irrespective of gender and that market vendors who sold them for two dollars a pair called Fulani shoes. They came in combinations of blue, white, and green, and their dense soles stopped thorns, mostly. Ousman's eyes were strange. Milky faraway eyes. Not cataractic but as though patinated with silver. They made me stare immodestly.

Ousman had been herding his father's cows since midnight and now was whooping them back to camp at a trot on a red clay path

that folded out of the end of the Earth, past indigo hollows that still cradled last night's cold against the long light of early morning.

The cows slowed to a walk as they approached, and at the western edge of Oumarou's campsite they jostled and stepped in place, lowing in earnest satiation just to the west of a shaggy yellow and frayed rope strung from a thorn tree to a short stake in the ground a few paces away. The first thing a Fulani family did whenever it arrived at a new campsite was to drive into the ground the stake to which the calf rope was tied, to claim an outpost and to divide the new landscape into the domestic and the animal, the female and the male. Only after Oumarou or Ousman or Oumarou's youngest son, Hassan, had tied the calf rope would the Diakayaté women hang their pagne bundles and calabashes from an acacia, steady their kneehigh mortars in its shade, drag three rocks together to build a new fire site, sweep the ground clean of thorns. The cows knew to stand to the animal side of the rope. Only rarely a wayward yearling, not yet educated in the way of the world, would venture hearthside to pick at leftovers in cooking pots or steal some roofing grass from a hut.

Ousman did not slow at the calf rope. He arrived the way Fulani cowboys usually arrived: a determined and rapid heel strike, then an abrupt full stop within handshaking distance. Now they were striding fast, their hips hinged, their staffs yokewise across their necks, wrists resting on either end—and now they were standing still, one knee bent, foot shucked out of a slipper and propped against the opposite knee, leaning on their staffs as they exchanged extensive and ornate salaams. Now they were striding off again. Fulani men did not slow down except for the cows.

Ousman raised both hands to his chest palms-forward in greeting and from the shrinking shade of the hut his father raised his own two hands in response. Long and narrow palms, cracked from dust, shingled and callused. Miniature maps of the Sahel.

"Peace upon your morning, Papa. Did you have a peaceful night?"

"And upon yours, Ousman. How was your road? Was your night peaceful?"

"Nothing but peaceful. How is your health?"

"Fine. How are the animals?"

"They are well. The bay's foot has healed. How is Mother?"

"She is well. Did the animals eat well?"

"Yes, plenty. There's a lot of sweetgrass out there. How are the children?"

"All healthy, *al ham du lillah*. How are the animals of your cousins?"

"All healthy. I saw Sita's animals west of Doundéré. They are on their way, too. Was your night peaceful, Anna Bâ?"

Mornings dissolved in patient and lengthy salutations, each question asked in order and methodically answered, palms raised in greeting and raised again in response, as if to rebate the kindness of the wellwisher. The newly arrived always greeted the already present, the solo walker always greeted the group, the younger always greeted the older. Each day, each encounter began by reestablishing the immemorial perimeters of tradition, the unspoken boundaries.

Borders give our world the structure we can define and defy, and the Fulani world is riven by them: brittle divides of water rights, marches of pasturage, manmade state partitions, shifting modern frontlines, borders between the primeval and the ultramodern, and, most profoundly, their own internal cadastres of the permissible. For those of us who are settled, the most common borders are the walls of our homes, the doors we shut against the rest of the world. When the physical home is ephemeral, structure begins with the uncompromising and reverential observation of rituals.

Paul Riesman, an American anthropologist who lived with the nomads of Upper Volta, wrote that being Fulani meant not so much belonging to a specific ethnic group as possessing certain traits of behavior considered essential. "The Fulani," he wrote, "should be: . . . refined, subtle, responsible, cultivated, endowed with a sense of shame, and master of his needs and his emotions." If you are a woman, never cry over your dead child. If you are a man, never eat where strangers can see you. Never, in public, express discomfort or pain. Never use the milking calabash to store or transport anything other than fresh milk. Never boil the milk. When you drink milk, drink it seated or squatting and hold the calabash with both hands. Shake right hands when you say farewell for a few days. Shake left hands when you say farewell for a long time so that God may grant you another reunion. Never count cattle.

Never count cattle. Yet even without counting everyone knew the devastating boundary that bisected Oumarou's life into the time before and after the cataclysmic famines of the nineteen seventies and eighties, when more than a million cadaverous people wasted away in the Sahel, folded into unmarked mass graves. Oumarou's first wife, Hajja, died then. Mummified livestock dropped dead unnumbered. The nomads, who disparaged any labor of the settled peoples, of slaves, learned to dig wells. They sold some cows to buy cattle feed for the others and to pay marabouts for potent leather-bound gris-gris they would hang for protection around the horns and necks of the cows that remained. Not even magic helped. Before the famine Oumarou had more than a thousand head of yellow roan cattle and other herders knew him as Oumarou the Yellow, one of the best and richest herders in the bourgou. Forty years later the nickname remained. But his herd was around fifty head, give or take. Among the four Diakayaté patriarchs who in the dry season pastured their cattle and camped together on a hummock near Doundéré, he was the eldest, and the poorest.

"It was just bad luck," Afo the *diawando* told me once, and pursed his lips in pity. "After the famine the cattle of all the other people reproduced, and Oumarou's did not."

When I asked Oumarou about the famine and about the cyclical droughts that for half a century had been punishing the Sahel, he simply said:

"The cattle suffered a lot and life changed forever. We have less grass now. The milk before and the milk now taste different, and the river doesn't get as full. The wind is hotter and dries out the water faster. But everything else is normal, *al ham du lillah*. We are here now, we are alive."

As if he remembered congenitally mankind's survival of all the droughts that ever had pushed migrants to their feet. The interglacial that may have forced early humans out of Africa a hundred and fifty thousand years ago on one of our earliest migrations, and the dry spell that shoved South American hunter-gatherers off the plateau that would become Chile's high-altitude Atacama Desert, and the famine that drove the Jews of Canaan into Egypt. The droughts that blew off the Colorado River's mudbanks the entire civilization of the Ancestral Puebloans in an exodus archaeologists later would call the Great Abandonment. They split carrying their infants and their tongue and the men who came after knew no better than to call them by their Navajo name, the Anasazi: "enemy ancestors." Droughts punished the Sahel in the fifth century, the fifteenth, the sixteenth, the seventeenth, the eighteenth, the nineteenth. There had been a drought two years before I met Oumarou. After each devastation came a recovery. Oumarou's chromosomes carried the impressions of both.

With a single impatient flap of a bony wrist the old man waved away into the thin morning air any remorse about his cattle's past, any concern about its future, and Mama's anguish that the end of the journey was unknown, unknowable, that it was possible altogether.

"It doesn't end," he said. "It only pauses here, at this camp, during the dry season."

Never show regret. Never display sorrow. Submit to the omnipotence of God. I had been told that such rules of conduct arose from a culture of resignation, of helplessness. But I thought: The Fulani protocols were not born of fatalism. They were born of hope.

Maybe hope comes from our innate memory of the perpetual cycles of relapse and recoupment.

Ousman hitched the calves with handmade rope halters to the calf rope and from among the sundries laid out on the roof of his father's hut he pulled down some hobbles and lariats and the milking calabash made of black plastic. He untethered a bay yearling and it scampered immediately to its mother. Ousman let it suckle for a few beats, then dragged it off the teat by its hind leg and hamshackled its head to its mother's knee so she would let down her milk. He hobbled the cow's hind legs together below the hocks to keep her from kicking and squatted beneath her and squeezed the milk down each of the four rubbery black teats in turn, like the man in the Tassili n'Ajjer painting from thousands of years ago. Like any dairyman, anytime. Warm milk streamed to the long, persuasive nagging of Ousman's long fingers, foamed in the black calabash.

He dipped his fin-
gers in the milk and
moistened the skin of the
cow's teats where it had
cracked from the dust
and the weather and
helped the milk down
the ducts again. Then he
stood up, balanced the
milking calabash in his

right hand, and on his way back to the hut with one smooth and
seamless motion of his left, like a passing harpist absentmindedly
strumming an instrument, he slipped off the cow's hobbles and un-
shackled the calf and unhitched another calf from the reata so it,
too, could suckle. He poured the milk into a larger calabash Fanta
held up with both hands and returned to the cattle, pulled the second calf away from its mother, hobbled that cow, hamshackled the
calf, squatted down to milk again. He did not talk to the cows as he
milked. He didn't have to. He had watered and pastured and de-
wormed them since birth and they knew his touch by heart.

After milking, the cows and the calves stood together in a close
sunlit half loop at the calf rope, at the edge of the circle Fanta swept
each morning with a handful of twigs. Their grassy sighs and the
steam of their manure and the dust they kicked up as they shifted
their big haunches crowded in on the encampment, where Oumarou's family sat close together on mats, quiet and content, waiting
for breakfast.

Breakfast was sweet tea with milk the Fulani called Lipton, and rice left over from yesterday's lunch. Fanta prepared them in two identical round-bottomed castiron pots over the portable hearth of three rocks that framed a fire of dry manure. I knew the pots well. I had eaten meals cooked in them in the strafed deserts of Iraq, in the melancholy foothills of Afghanistan, in the industrial abattoir of Chechnya, in the snake-pit dugouts of Azeri refugees. They were first forged in thermonuclear supernovas that exploded ten billion years ago to fling elements into space and seed the Earth with iron. Some of that iron would pulse in our blood, some would become those cauldrons. Imagine: each morning as the dawn's first light glides westward over the tropic of the dispossessed, from Asia to West Africa to Latin America, women obstinately rise from their sleeping mats and tick mattresses and thin blankets to bend over the same damned star-spawned pot.

The first pot on the fire each morning was to brew Lipton: water, two stringed sachets of Jolly Sun Quality Tea imported from Sri Lanka, a small bowlful of fresh cow or goat milk, and copious sugar. To make sure the sugar was dissolved and to cool down the liquid the women would pour the brew into a tin or plastic bowl and then pour it from that bowl into another and back a dozen times, then slurp loudly, smacking their lips, to taste. There never were enough cups or bowls to drink from, and the family took their Lipton in turns. The first cup, the largest, of scuffed ocher plastic, was always for Oumarou. His youngest grandchildren got the sweet dregs. Lipton was a morning drink only; throughout the day and into the night you drank tiny shotglasses of hot sweet green tea brewed in tiny enamel kettles over wire braziers of wood charcoal, in ceremonies that lasted half an hour or longer. It was as strong as coffee and quenched no thirst.

In the other pot Fanta reheated the rice. She pounded dried fish bones, red pepper, dried onions, and salt into a brown powder in a wooden mortar with a pestle almost as tall as she was and shook that into the pot. She melted a fragrant glob of shea butter in a long-handled iron ladle blackened with ages of soot. She divided the rice between two large and dented aluminum bowls, one for the men, one for the women, and poured the butter on top and the rice sizzled and spat and Fanta clicked her tongue—"Shush!"—and very briefly giggled in satisfaction.

Oumarou Diakayaté had married Fanta Sankari after his first wife had died of some sickness, he did not know which. "We were on the move," he said, "and she became sick and died." He needed a woman to rear his two small sons. Fanta was maybe ten years his junior and had just gotten divorced. Oumarou never asked why. He took her and Mama, Fanta's daughter from the first marriage, and she raised Boucary and Ousman and bore five more children, three sons and two daughters, of whom Hairatou was the youngest. Oumarou and Fanta also were raising Mama's two youngest children: Amadou, who was five and built herds of gorgeous toy cows out of clay, and his sister Kajita, who was seven and could herd goats on her own. All the children and both grandchildren called Fanta "Mother."

Oumarou loved her endlessly. His grandnephews joked that when she was away he prayed not east toward Mecca but in which-ever direction she had gone. She traveled impulsively and all the

45

time. She would hear of a sick relative several days' walk away and in the morning she would wrap a change of clothes in a blanket and take off, alone, and would not return or send any word for a week or two. She could walk thirty miles in a day with a load of milk or millet on her head.

She complained about life in the bush. She complained of excruciating pain in her delicate neck, in her thin-muscled arms and legs, her bony back, her emaciated chest, and as she listed her ailments at each day's close she touched herself gently, pressed her palms to the parts that hurt. Somehow, despite the strict Fulani tenets of forbearance, this was okay. She had no front teeth left and the remaining teeth were rotted and brown. She was narrowboned and gracile and she wore her long gray hair in cornrows woven so that two thin braids ran down in front of either ear and the rest bunched at the back of her head. The tattoo that once had accentuated her whole mouth and blackened her gums had long faded except for an indigo shadow on her full lower lip. She moved like the river. Her beauty took my breath away. Her cooking was divine.

We settled for breakfast in two tight circles on straw mats and on the swept ground, men and women separate but close enough to pass the common bowl of marsh water in which we took turns washing our right hands, just the right—for the left, the unclean hand, must never be used for eating or giving or receiving. Around us the harmattan was drying out the fens and the land around the fens and it carried off loose skullcaps and bits of plastic, slid empty calabashes across the trampled clay, ripped straw out of the huts as if it intended to blow everything away into the Gulf of Guinea. The cows twitched their rumps against its exfoliating gusts and talked softly

46

among themselves. In the thorn trees around us dozens of weavers' nests bounced like miniature upside-down Fulani huts. A French military plane growled over the trees on its way to bomb the desert. Fanta moaned something about her aching calves. In her nephew's hut a malarial nine-year-old girl who looked like a Vermeer portrait was burning up with fever. Or was it the three-year-old? Someone was always sick in the camp. For them, their kin's prayers.

"Bismillah!" Fanta said, and within the men's circle Oumarou pushed down his chin the bottom loop of his faded cotton turban with a gnarled thumb and echoed: *"Bismillah!* Dive in!" Oumarou and Fanta lifted the woven lids off the rice simultaneously and we dipped the wet fingers of our right hands into the edges of our bowls all at the same time to ensure that everyone had the same share of food.

There we sat over two tin bowls of rice: so breakable, so nameless on our uncountable journeys, so inadequate to the pain these journeys laid out before us. Yet our stamina was maddening. We were so tenacious. We were hungry for breakfast.

The rice was scalding and dusted with windblown grit and bits of straw and specks of burnt cow manure from the fire. It was perfect. It didn't taste like survival at all. It tasted like joy.

After breakfast Fanta ducked into the hut and emerged shaking a wood-stoppered gourd with a narrow neck.

"Anna Bâ?" Hand outstretched. It was my time to churn. Hairatou had had a go at the gourd before; Mama would be next. All morning the women churned and churned and churned milk into buttermilk and butter so that when the sun was a palm above the low eastern treeline Fanta could take the dairy to Weraka and Wono.

Cattle belonged to men. Men took cows to pasture twice daily, for several hours each time, at midnight and at noon. A seven-year-old boy was old enough to take out a herd for a day and bring it back. A fifteen-year-old boy was old enough to take the herd on a seasonal migration route alone. When the cows returned to camp it was the men's job to milk them before they reunited with their calves, although women, too, knew how to milk them in a pinch.

Women owned the milk. They decided how much would stay in the family and how much would be bartered for grain or dried fish or sugar or salt or Lipton or lumps of raw shea butter, which smelled like an intoxicating composite of chocolate and human feces, and which could be used for cooking and skincare and sorcery. When they were paid in money they spent it on jewelry or sugar candy or pots or skeins of calico for clothes. When men wanted new clothes or jewelry they sold a goat or a sheep. For the most part the men and the women lived in a premonetary economy and rarely used money to measure the price of commodities they occasionally had to purchase. It was beyond question that there was no truer wealth than milk and cattle.

Manure belonged to no one; it was first come, first serve. Ousman barely had reached the camp that morning when small Diakayaté children ran out to collect dung for their mothers' and grandmothers' breakfast fires. Now two shirtless teenage Bozo girls at the far end of the fen were heaping cow pies into huge thatch baskets.

Fanta looked at the girls. Only two hours into the day and already their shadows had shrunk into hard dark slivers under their feet and the sunlight was the color of quicksilver. It was very hot and getting hotter. Time to get going.

She took the gourd back from Mama and shook it once and knew by the feel of it in her hand that nuggets of butter sploshed inside. She poured the contents of the gourd into a calabash she had whitened on the outside with chalk the night before to make her wares more attractive to her customers. She threw into the buttermilk a curdling stick she had scraped clean with her husband's long broadsword and a small plastic scoop to measure out the buttermilk in five-cent increments, then set the calabash inside another, old and also white and with a long jagged crack patched up with cornhusks and polypropylene string unraveled from a gunnysack. She slapped against her thigh two flat lids that Hairatou had woven out of grass and colored thread, and two ocher puffs of dust shook loose. She arranged the lids on top of the calabashes. She pulled off the roof of the hut a pagne printed with pink strawberries against a limegreen field. She twirled the pagne lengthwise in her hand until the fabric spun a thick rope, pink-green-pink-green-pink, and then with both hands rolled that up into a doughnut and arranged it on top of her yellow and red headscarf. She draped another length of cloth, this with a psychedelic design of yellow and blue and red bubbles, over her head and shoulders like a shawl and wound one end around her neck.

So cocooned in color, Fanta nestled the calabashes on top of her head and set off on the southbound path toward Weraka. She bid no farewells: this was a ritual she performed every other day and it did not merit ceremony. Nor did she ease gradually into her walk. She started right out of the camp at a quick steady stride that never changed until she reached the village. It was the tempo of her last walk, and of her walks before that, and of her mother's, and of all the milkmaids' past recall who had affixed their footsteps to the trail before. She simply picked it up. She would have picked up a dropped calabash that way, or a grindstone she had loaned to a neighbor.

At first Fanta walked with her right hand raised to hold the straw lids so the wind wouldn't blow them away. After a hundred paces the arm and the wrist drained of blood and began to ache. She stopped and shook off her right plastic flipflop and with her toes scooped up from the ground a flat stone. She flexed the right leg at the knee and stood on her left unbending leg and without leaning, without looking, reached behind her with her right arm and picked the stone out of her foot. Neck perfectly straight, the calabashes steady on her head. She had done this a thousand times before. Her bubble-printed shawl flapped against her cheek. She placed the rock on the topmost lid and let both arms fall like a marionette's arms by her sides and walked again. Around her ankles night moisture rose cold from the drying fields. Pied crows hopped in low labyrinths of manure.

When you passed a Fulani woman on a dirt road something strummed within, some liminal memory, an inchoate recognition.

And then you knew. It was the smell of sour milk. The proto-scent.

In Weraka Fanta banged on doors. She banged on doors of reeds tied together with string, on doors of corrugated metal, on doors of corroded tin painted yellow and black, of thick wood. She banged on a door of three metal sheets held together with an uneven black wooden crossbeam that looked salvaged from a busted pirogue. No one behind these doors wanted her buttermilk.

She hallooed no villagers she passed but she did pause to clasp hands with other milkmaids who had come to trade from Somena or from other camps near Doundéré. They greeted one another by asking whether their journeys to Weraka that morning had gone well and whether they and their cattle were in good health. They traded family gossip and accounts of richer pastures and births and deaths, and stories they had heard thirdhand about the war and all the airplanes and the Fulani marabout Amadou Koufa, who once had gathered congregants in numbers that not even Djenné's Grande Mosquée could accommodate and who now was in the Sahara, call-ing upon his nomadic disciples to join the new jihad. This was how the nomads got their news. This was bush radio.

For an hour Fanta circled through the village. From door to door sidestepping sewage puddles that sloughed from trenches dug under compound walls and hemorrhaged one into another in odd phos-phorescent curlicues. She sold nothing. Then she walked south past a large open courtyard where men sat weaving long thin strips of

unbleached homespun cotton on several large foot-treadle looms and she walked below a single twined doum palm that clacked its loud fronds like bones very high above and she walked past all the handslapped mud walls of Weraka and across a fallow millet field in which a halfeaten carcass of a goat that even black kites no longer wanted stank in the sun and into Wono, where a Bozo woman with a stern broad face called, "Hey, Fulani!" and motioned for her to step through a gate soldered from flattened tin oilcans.

Fanta entered a large courtyard. It had been swept recently and in the far corner under a mango tree a preteen girl in a LOVE PINK t-shirt torn at the shoulder was gutting a basinful of small carp. Closer to the gate three women in calico boubous and matching headwraps were pounding millet and rice in three tall wooden mortars, clapping their hands at each bounce of their long pestles, beating out a rickety village waltz. When they saw Fanta they stopped pounding and rested their thick forearms on the tops of their pestles. They spoke in Fulfulde.

"What do you want, Fulani?"

"A woman told me to step in here, said there might be business."

"What do you have?"

Fanta approached the women and set the calabashes on the ground in front of them and lifted off the lids. Eight or nine yellow dollops of butter floated in sour milk bubbles. Magnificent sun crumbs. One of the women pointed at a low stool hewn out of a palm trunk.

"Good. Grab a seat."

Soon the shoeless children of Wono crowded around Fanta with bowls of unhulled rice and plastic cups of dry millet. All the grain was dusty and pebbled. From her stool Fanta poured the rice grains into the larger calabash and poured the millet separately onto a ripped black plastic bag she had borrowed from the women of the house and spread on the ground by her side, and she blew into the emptied cups and bowls to clean them of grain dust and deliberately measured buttermilk into them. Three scoops of buttermilk for a half kilo of rice, for a kilo of millet. She asked each child in turn if they wanted butter. Butter was extra. A woman came with an empty purple lunchpail stamped with yellow and white and pink hearts and the inscription I ♥ AFRICA and paid for her butter in coins that Fanta accepted without counting and tied into the corner of her headscarf.

"Where'd you get the white woman?"

"It's my white woman."

"Eh?"

"Get outta here!"

"Sly Fulani!"

"It's true. She is staying with me."

"Where are you from, white woman?"

What to say? "Home is too mystical for me," says a character in a J. M. Coetzee novel. It never has been easy for me to identify mine. "Where are you from?" my hosts in an Afghan village would ask,

53

my hosts on a farm in Iraq, in the velvet mountains of Indian Kashmir. Defenders of their ancestral homes from foreign armies, from their own abusive governments, from cataclysms and manmade devastations. What could I tell them? I had grown up an outcast in a country that no longer existed, in a city that had since changed its name. An underweight and sickly specimen of a despised minority, a Soviet Jew. I had moved away, and I would move again, and again. My point of departure was never the same. I was transient, in transit: the Wandering Jew. Ahasuerus. The defender of no claimed geography. It made for relatively effortless travel. It made for uncomfortable silences, odd hesitations.

Georges Perec, the relentless scrutinizer of alienation, the French orphan of immigrant Polish Jews killed in the slaughterhouse of the Second World War—he on the battlefield, she in a camp—suggested that we have two options: "to carve the place that will be yours out of space, and build, plant, appropriate, millimetre by millimetre, your 'home': to belong completely in your village . . . or else to own only the clothes you stand up in, to keep nothing . . . and change towns, and change countries . . . to feel at home nowhere, but at ease almost everywhere." The latter was the Fulani alternative.

"They are regarded everywhere as 'the other' or 'the stranger,'" wrote the Dutch anthropologist Mirjam de Bruijn. "They are always the people who come from far away." The Fulani never asked me where my home was. They were hereditary outsiders who appropriated all the space their cows required at any given time but never more than that, and they had mastered the response.

"What's your name?"

"Amadou."

"Where are you from?"

"We are here now."

"Eh, white woman? Can't you talk? Can she talk? Where are you from?"

"She's with me," Fanta repeated. I had walked with her from near Doundéré, she said, yes, yes, absolutely, go ask anyone there, I was staying in her camp, I slept on a straw mat beneath a thorn tree hung with weavers' nests, I was family. I was Anna Bâ, Fulani Bâ, I was a white Fulani woman who had traveled from somewhere on the other side of Mecca, wherever white people were, maybe France, so I could be with her. I was with her, I was hers, I was spoken for. Points of origin did not matter: I belonged.

We walked back along washboard fields. Lotus flowers shone waxlike in bright green swales. A pied kingfisher hovered in one spot over the water, hovered, hovered, hovered, hovered—then plunged, crested headfirst, and recovered a breath away from the surface with a disappointed squeal and banked on flecked wings into yellow waterside reeds. The harmattan blew a gale. The land was flat and endless and without shadow and somewhere upon it an invisible cowbell chimed. The sun took up the whole sky. It was very hot. Fanta swayed snakelike under her pyramid of grains and complained.

"I am so tired, Anna Bâ. Ay, ay, ay. My legs are tired. My neck is tired. My back is tired. My head is tired. My load is heavy."

"Let me carry it."

"It's heavy, Anna Bâ."

"Let me carry it."

It was heavy. Fifteen pounds of rice and millet, maybe more, one covered calabash balanced upon the other. I pressed the lot to the crown of my head with both hands. They went numb in no time. I could not wipe the dust the wind drove into my eyes. I could not see the grooves in the path. I could no longer feel my hands upon the woven lids of my load. What if I tripped and dropped it? The family's breakfasts and lunches and dinners for the next two days would strew the fields. Some maybe would take root in the dung-smeared glop of a marsh's edge. Birds and goats would take the rest. There would be nothing to eat at the camp.

"Tired, Anna Bâ?"

I wasn't tired. I was petrified. We kept walking.

Fanta bragged.

"I gave birth to six children and all of them are still alive. Three girls, three boys."

She counted them off in the order of their age.

First came Mama, whose husband had divorced her because she was always sick, took another, healthy wife, took Mama's eldest son to boot, and left. Because she no longer had a husband, Mama shuttled from one relative's camp to another and could not impose upon these relatives her small children. That was why Oumarou and Fanta were raising Kajita and Amadou.

Then Bomel, the mother of Mayrama, a baby so tiny her nickname was Skinny Butt. Bomel the obliging one, with buck teeth, who was married to one of Oumarou's nephews and lived in a village, not in the bush.

Then Drissa, the taciturn teenage boy who already had memorized the Koran and now was studying to be a marabout at a madrassa in San, a bigger city than Djenné that had paved streets and a football stadium with floodlights and that lay on the main bus route to Bamako. San was the biggest city Fanta ever had seen.

Hassan, the earnest seventeen-year-old who would drive Oumarou's cattle during transhumance in the coming rainy season.

Hairatou, her youngest.

Mama, Bomel, Drissa, Hassan, Hairatou. I repeated the names. That's five, I said. No, six, I have six living children. All right. I tried to focus on the blurred path, to ignore Fanta's blurred arithmetic.

I could not have known about Allaye, who came after Bomel and before Drissa. Fanta had six children but she would not mention him by name. No one in the Diakayaté camp spoke about him at all. Oumarou's prodigal son, his most cherished, his third, the first male child that Fanta had borne, the bright and beautiful boy who had gone to herd cattle one morning the previous autumn and kept going until he arrived in Côte d'Ivoire to work for money and was still gone.

Allaye had left without bidding his parents farewell, without asking their blessing. He had pushed the borders of the imaginable, broken the compact the herders had with the world. The nomad who quit the bush for the city. Who portended that unthinkable end of the ten-thousand-year-old livestock economy that population experts forecast and that the globalized world espoused.

He had telephoned twice: first the day after he left, from Bamako, then a week later, from Abidjan. Because no one in Oumarou's family had a cellphone that could receive calls, he called a family in a camp nearby. Calls were expensive, and Allaye kept his short. He did not ask to speak to his parents. He just asked the neighbors to relay to them where he was. There had been no word from the boy since November, the same month I had last spoken to my missing, missed lover.

Oumarou's heartache for Allaye was so terrifying and so enormous it could not be uttered. He had excised the boy from the prayers he said five times daily for all his other children, dead and alive.

So there it was: the flaw in the hallowed code that championed acceptance of the transience of everything, that idealized stoicism—the hamartia that made us human. Acceptance went only so far. It did not account for love and came apart at loss, became metaphysics. Life shaped out of the friction between our eternal ambition to walk away from woe and our eternal concession that there always was some burden we would be carrying.

When we reached the campsite it was past noon and I told Fanta how afraid I had been of dropping the food. She studied me, frowned, uncomprehending. So what, she said. Things fall sometimes. Besides, they didn't.

◇ ◇ ◇

A few hours later Fanta was on the move again. Now she had to go to Dakabalal. A fisherman in the village owned a chain-driven diesel mill that winnowed chaff from rice. Fanta took the unshucked rice she had bartered in Wono that morning to the mill in a yellow jerrycan.

The winter sun flooded the higher ground and deep ultramarine shadows reached far to the east. The angled orange light carried the distant yip of cowboys driving herds from pasture and Fanta walked toward the sound. Past the hut of Salimata, who came out to greet her aunt barebreasted and eerily thin. Past a hut where Oumarou's nineteen-year-old grandnephew, Moussa, lay sick in a polyester t-shirt that proclaimed BARACK OBAMA PRESIDENT OF THE UNITED STATES OF AMERICA and that had faded from white, red, blue, and black to shades of purple. Moussa had woven a comb of matching purple plastic into his afro for fashion and on his left index finger he wore a heart-shaped silver ring the size of a guineafowl egg. His eyes were closed, his skin ashy. What was wrong with Moussa? How would they know? They weren't doctors. The nearest clinic, in Senossa, was not very far away—if you started to walk after the late-afternoon prayer you would be there by sundown—but it was no good, and the Djenné hospital was farther and expensive. Was the Djenné hospital good? What a dumb question. They weren't doctors. How would they know?

Fanta walked past Moussa's sickmat. Past the dead in their eucalyptus graveyard. Pied crows flew over pooled water in marshes

59

large and small that shone with reflected sunset. Their shadows glided upon the land.

In Dakabalal a heavy woman on a straw mat nursed starveling twins with spooky bellies. Both had strangulated umbilical hernias the length of an adult thumb, as if something were trying to push itself free through their navels. Umbilical hernias were common in West Africa and many children in the bourgou were so afflicted. A handsome middle-aged man with a sickle on his shoulder smiled hello. A teenage girl stared. Fanta strode through the hamlet without acknowledging anyone. She walked into the miller's yard, sat her jerrycan under a mango tree, and admonished something in Bozo at an open door behind which it was dark. Then she turned on her heels and strode out. When she left the village she spat a neat projectile of phlegm onto the ground and said, "Bozo are dirty people."

Among themselves the Bozo described the Fulani as haughty and secretive. The sedentary peoples of the bourgou mistrusted both.

Bourgou legends tell that when the Fulani first arrived here with their cattle only the Bozo dwelled in the Niger's soggy elbow. The Bozo kept the river, the Fulani kept the land. The Bozo would help the Fulani cross the water and the Fulani would give the Bozo manure for their cooking fires and small riverine gardens. They swapped milk for fish, although certain Fulani lineages had retained iterations of the fish taboos they had brought with them from the Horn of Africa, where most pastoralists, just as bone-thin and driving the same zebu cattle or goats, are forbidden to eat ichthyoids. Somali goatherds insult one another: "Speak not to me with a fish-eating mouth." Fanta's family, the Sankaris, had no proscription against fish of any kind, but all Diakayatés who ate catfish regularly would develop leprosy and eventually grow webs between their fingers.

Then some Fulani and Bozo settled, other peoples moved in, farms gridded the land, cattle destroyed precious crops. Acrimony leached into the wetlands. At the end of the previous rainy season, after Fulani cattle once again had crushed unharvested fields at the northern tip of the bourgou, Bozo fishermen helped Bambara farmers drive into the Niger River and drown nearly two hundred Fulani cows.

That afternoon three Bozo boys about ten years old rode two donkeys along a gully past the camp and hallooed the nomads in Bambara. *"Antié!"* They rode bareback on the croups of their donkeys, two of the boys doubled up, and they kept their legs hooked under the donkeys' bellies. Little Amadou, naked by the hearth, became momentarily transfixed by the mounted power and grandeur of these demiurges, and he called a forlorn *"antié"* back and stood to watch them pass. The boys ignored him from their superior heights and age. Fanta yanked her grandson by the arm and ordered him to go into the hut and put on some underwear.

Before dinner, a thanksgiving. Fanta washed her feet and hands and face from a plastic kettle and veiled herself with one of her pagnes and spread another pagne printed with yellow and green fish in the middle of the swept circle before the hut. She shucked off her flipflops and stepped onto the cloth with bare feet and prayed. Her prayers a murmur, her supplications minimalist, concise, as all her other movements. Oumarou performed his ablutions from a large empty can into which once upon a time a worker at a factory in China had packed one kilo of Manvita tomato paste, but the paste had been gone even before the Diakayatés had found the can on one of their itineraries many seasons ago and collected it and taken it for use as part of their housewares. The old cowboy prayed behind the hut on a sheet of black plastic, discreetly and in silence. At the western edge of the campsite a fire of manure and leaves smoked among the cows to keep mosquitoes away, and near that fire

Ousman prayed on a blue plastic prayer mat woven with a faded black ogive of a stylized mihrab. Hassan and Hairatou were still too young to pray.

Outside the hut where Moussa lay sick his teenage sisters and girl cousins laughed among themselves and pounded something in two wooden mortars. *Pah-dum, pah-dum.* The pulse of the Sahel. A long smear of cookingfire smoke stretched from Dakabalal and mixed with the mist rising from the rotting marsh, and above the savannah the replicant smear of a single cloud concealed a pale sunset. In the violet afterglow of the day, Hairatou hummed a chromatic song and ladled out two basins of millet *toh* porridge and two small bowls of pounded baobab leaf dipping sauce. She stacked the bowls into the basins and carried the food to the mats outside the hut. Then the sun died and with it all the day's loud noises and then the quieter sounds of Hairatou's singing, of calves suckling, of hens digging straw nests, until only the startled squawks of glossy starlings losing their balance in acacia spines interrupted the hushed evening. The family ate. There was a flashlight in the camp but the Diakayatés never turned it on for dinner. Out of prerequisite modesty, the Fulani preferred to eat their dinner by feel.

A little later Salimata came to the campsite with her daughters-in-law and some grandchildren bearing half a calabash of fresh warm milk. The women and the children sat and lay down on two straw mats and some of Oumarou's grandnephews came also and sat and knelt around the old man on mats and on the ground. Hairatou brought coal for the brazier and Ousman brewed two kettles of strong sweet green tea. With a delicious moaning the cows knelt in the dust one by one. The evening smelled like burning grass, a winter smell that the harmattan hung between the land and the sky. There was no light apart from the cold diamond luster of stars and the fens around the camp bled darkly into the black.

They told stories. They told of naughty bulls that had trampled farmers' millet and of policemen who had arrested them for transgressions as meaningless as carrying a short sheathed sword and Fanta told stories of heaven and hell and brotherly love and sacrifice. Oumarou said the world had to be very big indeed that it could encompass so many stories and so many people to whom such stories belonged. Someone switched on a flashlight and the shaky white beam picked out the sleeping cows and the people squatted by the brazier and the sleepy children who sat still and upright in their blankets. I lay on my back. Meteors were falling everywhere. When my turn came to tell a story Fanta told me to talk about the sky.

I said the universe was very old and vast and that its origins were difficult to explain because it seemed to have appeared out of an infinitely dense and hot nothingness that nearly fourteen billion years ago had exploded and ushered forth new worlds and galaxies. I said that compared with the unfathomable size of the universe our planet was a round blue bead so tiny it was almost invisible. That the Earth traveled on annular migrations around the sun and that its migrations coincided exactly with the yearly migrations of the Fulani and determined them. That the sun was itself a star that shone off to the side of the massive and ever-expanding group of celestial bodies and gas and debris, a galaxy called the Milky Way. Its lateral disk that very moment adumbrated right above our heads.

I said our sun and our planet and the other seven planets that orbited our sun migrated as well, around the Milky Way, but their migration was much slower and took two hundred and forty million years to complete. It was hard to comprehend such a tremendous span of time. I said the cosmos was so vast that much of it was hard to comprehend but that there were scientists and apparatuses in space trying to learn more about it.

Here I stopped. None of my hosts ever had met a scientist. None of them ever had been to school. None could read or write. Some of the younger men had spent a few weeks memorizing Koranic verses in a madrassa. The Koran proposed that in the beginning heaven and earth had been of a piece until they were cloven asunder and the sky became "as smoke." In my prejudice, I waited for the Diakayatés to laugh, to refute my pagan cosmogony, my heathen blabber.

Oumarou spoke.

He said he had heard that stars were distant suns. He said the roundness of the Earth was news to him. He said it was a well-known fact that things moved within the sky's enormity because every thirteen or fourteen days a new constellation rose—twenty-six, all in all, in a year, though he did not remember all of their names. He said we were four days away from the ascent of the next constellation. He said it was obvious that the world was in motion, since a Fulani proverb said, "Our shadows move, our animals move on the Earth that moves, so why should I myself not move?" He had not heard about the heliocentric makeup of our solar system but conceded that it made sense.

"Good story," he said.

The women rocked on their haunches back and forth in approval and clicked their tongues and said they liked the name, the

Milky Way. They said they never had heard of it, but, looking up now, they could see the resemblance. None of them remembered the Fulani creation myth that had preceded Islam. But it remained within them, interwoven in their stardust-laced bones. It went like this:

In the beginning there was nothing. Then there was a huge drop of milk.

A cow lowed and shifted in its sleep and the nocturnal grass released the day's memories: manure, daydreams, footfalls, whistles of a herder. The Vermeer girl, Mentou, no longer sick, had nestled against my hip and fell asleep and snored lightly.

"Good story," Oumarou repeated. "Go on."

I said I had grown up in the north of our planet, far from the sun, in a cold land that neither I nor any other who lived there had been allowed to leave. I talked about evening gatherings during which my parents and their friends would talk about adult things I couldn't understand and I would drift off to the cadence of their conversations, like Mentou. About the sanctity of familiar closeness on such evenings, the trust created and savored, its powers against depravity.

Fanta wrinkled her nose and said, "Families in cities aren't as strong. Cities are too divided. Besides," she added, "cities are dirty."

Soon everyone went to bed and the women corralled the young children one by one, first calling their names and then rousing them from their blankets by hand and half lifting, half dragging their small limp bodies to their huts. The grown-ups prayed one final time. A perfect crescent swung into the sky: a calabash for milking, the horns of a zebu cow. Then Fanta sat on my mat and took my hand and held it until I began to doze off so very much like the little girl I once had been and then she slipped a folded pagne under my head and covered me with an old polyester blanket. The blanket and the pagne smelled like sour milk. I slept.

Around midnight the cows lowed softly and rose as one. Against the deep sparkled blueblack of the western sky the darker cows stood in full silhouette. On the hides of the piebalds just the chestnut or black patches were visible and the paler spots dissolved into the starry heavens, like constellations. Of the yellow cattle I could see the horns only. Limbs of a bow, lyre arms, arms forever extended either in the gesture of letting go or the anticipation of an embrace.

They urinated long and loud into the dust and some shuddered with only the skin on their thurls and some whipped themselves once or twice with their tails and they headed to pasture. They went on nightherd on their own because they had been grazing in this pasture during the dry season forever and had the route memorized. The older cows led the way. In the morning Ousman would go to pick them up a few miles west of the camp and bring them back and milk them and it would be a new day.

Oumarou came out of his hut with his turban off and his head bare and his chin uncovered, and for a few minutes stood watching the animals go.

On the way back to the hut he paused over my mat.

"Anna Bâ?" he called in a semiwhisper. "Are you warm?"

I was too sleepy to answer. At some point during the night I heard bells. I didn't quite wake and half dreamed of a thousand silver goats flowing to pasture.

A cow is the first to smell when something is bad or wrong or rotten. If a cow smells something it will stop and raise its muzzle and warn its herders. If a wild dog runs through the bush and pisses on a tree a cow will smell that wild dog three days later even during the rainy season and will not stop near the tree because cows are afraid of wild dogs. But snakes are afraid of cows because cows stomp them dead. When the rainy season begins and vipers and adders come out of their pits the safest place to sleep is among the cows.

A cow is the best weapon against the genii that live in the bush. Genii enter people and make them aggressive and make them talk gibberish, but they are afraid of cattle. Once upon a time the hillock on the Bani River where Oumarou had buried his father and two children among doum palms and scrub brush had been the home of a powerful genie. No man or woman could walk on that hillock. But after the Fulani made the fields below it a regular stop on their cycle of transhumance and cows began to graze around the hillock by the thousand, the genie left.

Cows are no use against scorpions, however.

◇ ◇ ◇

In the paling hour before sunup Oumarou stood over me again until I sensed his presence and opened my eyes.

"Anna Bâ? Are you cold?" His eyes smiled in the medieval slit of his turban. He lifted his narrow palms to his breast and pressed them toward me in greeting, then pointed in silence to the plastic kettle he thoughtfully had placed by my mat. The last word before bedtime must be a prayer and the first word of the morning must be addressed to God and the name of God can be uttered only in cleanliness. I took the kettle and walked to a narrow marsh east of the camp and squatted there on hoof-flattened dewy grass facing away from the hut and fanned my skirts about. When I returned the rest of the family was awake and we exchanged proper salaams and Fanta asked me whether I had been warm during the night and ordered me to wrap myself in my night blanket and sit on the mat next to Oumarou while she brewed Lipton and Mama reheated last night's millet *toh*.

I pulled out my notebook. It had been a cold night and it was still cold and Ousman and Hassan and Oumarou sat in their own blankets by the hut and watched me write, and rocked and nodded in encouragement whenever I looked up. The cows were still gone and a small flock of goats whined on their tethers, cried childlike calls of distress. Oumarou reached over and gently traced the callus on my left heel with his fingertips, felt the skin on my ankle, lightly pressed the top of my foot, circled my bunion. He didn't say anything. I guessed he was gauging my foot's worthiness for the transhumance. Then he withdrew his hand and hid it under his blanket again.

The sun blasted into the sky an hour after the morning prayer. A black kite dove for fish in a fen west of the camp and cattle egrets flaked into the hippo grass, rosewinged with dawn light. Starlings fell in and out of the acacia tree with earsplitting screeching. In the tree's tussles hung a butter-colored quarter moon.

It was Monday. On the other side of the fen oxcarts and horse-drawn farm wagons and donkey carts trundled southward on the road on a pilgrimage to the weekly market in Djenné. Ousman and Salimata's eldest son, Boucary, were preparing to walk to town.

Boucary came over and leaned on his staff by the calf rope and rested his right foot against the knee of his left. He had twisted a large cotton blanket printed with orange and purple flowers and wound it around his head like an outlandish sombrero de charro, its brims broader than the young man's shoulders.

"Did you go with the cattle last night, Anna Bâ?"

"Yes, all night I walked."

"How far did you go?"

"To France. To the other side of Mecca."

"Oh, even I can't go that far. But at least I'm young and strong. Oumarou here, he can't herd cattle at night. He's too old and he must stay with his wife so that she doesn't run away with me."

Oumarou scoffed at his grandnephew.

"Fanta won't marry you because you're poor. You have no animals of your own."

"But I'm very handsome."

"A poor man can't be handsome."

An exchange predetermined, almost rehearsed. Prescribed by the ancient laws of *sanankuya*, ritualized jocular relationships that linked kin, families, ethnic groups, and castes and created in West Africa a parallel social structure meant to forestall violence, defuse rage, prevent incest. Some said the origins of the Bambara word lay in the expression for "the easing of everything"; others that it came from the word for the crust at the bottom of a cereal pot: the sticking together, the joining. *Sanankuya* dictated that grandchildren and grandparents of the same gender tease one another, that grandfathers dote on granddaughters, and that grandmothers pretend to marry grandsons. It decreed vulgar jeering among cousins. Some Western ethnographers translated it as "cousinage" but it transcended family relations. It required that all Bâs and all Diallos deride one another as flatulent bean lovers, that all Fulani mock all blacksmiths and vice versa, and it pitted all Bozo against all Dogon in similarly slapstick exchanges of mutual ridicule. It demystified reverence. It mandated laughter. It created an obligation of mock disrespect, and through it, of solidarity. It was another boundary that parted and united the Sahel. At its inception lay unremembered ancestral blood pacts, vows terrible and terrifying issued to conciliate the horrific animosity that forever had suffused the volatile savannah, millennial attempts to bring to order an uncontrollable world.

Oumarou pushed down the turban from his mouth and drank milk out of a white enamel bowl painted with strawberries and red apples and blue grapes. Fruit and berries he never had seen in real life. Little Amadou stumbled out of the hut shy and chilled and half asleep and crawled under his grandfather's fleece blanket and Oumarou patted him there, tucking in the boy's spindly body, smoothing the blanket over him, gently picking bits of straw off the blanket with his long rough fingers. This grandson was too sleepy to tease, or too cherished. Then the old cowboy finished drinking the milk, set the empty bowl on the ground by his knees, pulled up the bottom loop of his turban to the bridge of his nose, and set to disparaging the ways of the young.

"Boucary and Ousman. They are a generation of food. They have to go to Djenné so they can buy snacks in the market. When they camp with the cows they always camp near a village so they can find food. Food food food! I am the generation of milk. When there's plenty of milk you don't have to have rice or millet or fish. When I was young and herded cattle I would go several months just drinking milk. That's why I am stronger than them."

Ousman smiled at his father's diatribe and looked at me with his distant eyes and cocked his head a little and said nothing. It was true that when he arrived in town he intended to buy a small plastic baggie of egg noodles drenched in palm oil, possibly some deepfried dough that sweaty market women fished out of huge black castiron vats with slotted spoons. And yes, he would splurge on some roast goat if he had enough money. But mainly he was going to Djenné to inquire about obtaining something few Fulani nomads had and suddenly, in this country at war, many needed. An identity card.

◇ ◇ ◇

The separatists had charged into northern Mali a year earlier. Stray guns for hire orphaned of land by partitions devised and executed by European colonists after World War II, orphaned of political support fifty years later by a civil war in Libya. Several hundred lordless warriors careening across the desert in looted pickup trucks chockfull of artillery and explosives and rifles they had plundered from the vast and abandoned caches of their slain former padrone, Muammar Qaddafi. They belonged to a nomadic nation of camel herders and raiders whose origin myth claimed European roots, claimed racial primacy, claimed exclusivity, claimed freedom. They came from different families and called themselves collectively Kel Tamashek, the speakers of Tamashek, or Imohag, Free People. In the fifth century BC, Herodotus described them as Garamantes, a standoffish race of men who kidnapped their future slaves on four-horse chariots. Look for their masculine likenesses in the massifs of Tassili n'Ajjer, next to the Bovidian art of the long-ago cowherds. In the twenty-first century the world knew them by their Arabic name, Tuareg: the Paths Taken.

Like the Fulani, the Tuareg often were light of skin and slight of build, wore indigo robes and turbans that concealed the faces of the men, did not require the veiling of the women, espoused Islam, considered themselves a race superior to black Africans, abided by a rigid social hierarchy, recognized no national borders, and bowed to no government. Unlike the Fulani, they had, throughout the twentieth century, fought repeatedly and unsuccessfully for the sovereignty colonial and postcolonial maps denied them. Their tormented statelessness had earned them yet one more nickname: the Kurds of Africa. Legends of their belligerence and valor were manifold. In the nineteen eighties, Qaddafi, at war with the world in the name of Islamic socialism, of which he was the prophet and the tyrant, recruited Tuareg men to be his mercenaries, always dangling before them the hope that one day he would endorse them in the fight for their own independence.

In 2012, Qaddafi was dead, Libya's military training camps were defunct, and Malian government forces were busy fighting among themselves in three successive coups and countercoups in the smoggy hills of Bamako. The separatists crossed the Sahara, swept into the major cities of Mali's desert north, and proclaimed the creation of an independent state they called Azawad: the Land of Transhumance.

The world did not recognize Azawad. But Islamist fundamentalists saw it as a convenient staging post for a jihad from which a new caliphate would rise in the Maghreb. They were mostly Arabs, but also Tuareg, Berber, Fulani. Within weeks they hijacked the rebellion. They flew the black flags of al Qaeda over Timbuktu. They axed down centuries-old shrines and they flogged, amputated, jailed, stoned, beheaded, raped. They reproduced in the Malian Sahara a tragedy familiar from the abattoirs of Iraq, of North Caucasus, of Somalia.

The world's reaction was no less familiar. In January of 2013, the week before I met the Diakayatés, France sent its forces to the desert. By March, small outfits of guerrillas and religious fanatics were fighting a war of attrition against French, Malian, and United Nations troops backed by the United States. Airplanes shelled dunes and dry pastures of scant grass. Suicide bombings tore limb from limb in Timbuktu, in Gao.

Ethnic cleansing marched side by side with the intervention. Reports of summary executions by Malian troops drifted down to the bourgou. Stories of killed nomads. Of men and cattle disappearing. Of fathers and husbands and sons gone missing, then found mutilated in shallow pits. Sand sopped up blood. A practiced task: in another March, in 1591, a Moroccan force of six cannons and four thousand mercenary cavalrymen and musketeers led by the Spanish-born eunuch Judar Pasha had slaughtered in these wastelands the army of forty thousand Songhai warriors. The Songhai had armed themselves with saber, bow, and spear and drove before them herds of cattle. The cows turned out to be gun-shy. They turned and stampeded the Songhai; the Moroccan arquebuses finished the job. This was the Battle of Tondibi, thirty-five miles north of Gao. From there the Moroccans trooped on west to sack and burn first Timbuktu, then Djenné, and the Songhai Empire was no more.

The fighting for Azawad came within forty miles of the bourgou's northern tip. In the rest of the country, Mali's temporary government declared a state of emergency. Checkpoints were everywhere. All nomads were suspect and nomads without documents doubly so. Sometimes gendarmes turned away undocumented cowboys at Djenné's gates. Sometimes they detained them until their identity could be verified, vouched by a *diawando*, or else vouchsafed by a bribe. Fulani herders south of the Niger worried that sedentary peoples angry at the Tuareg would turn on them.

War was the oldest form of human exchange apart from love, as old as humankind itself. But this was a modern, internationalized war, a metastasis of some alien manner of bloodshed the nomads could not grasp fully. It warped time and thrust modernity at the cowherds, threatened to reorganize their lives in ways they could not foresee because fighting of such proportions had no precedent in their teachings, in their oral histories. To protect himself from a government that offered him and his kind no protection in return, Ousman decided to formalize his relationship with the state and reassert his identity in a modern language the state would understand. Documents. Papers. Laminated, stamped, with photographs. He never would be able to read them, but that did not matter. After all, the Fulani were masters of perseverance. They refused to assimilate, but they never ceased to adapt.

At one point Ousman had a voter registration card. It was a strip of paper about two fingers wide, and it had something written on it in ballpoint pen. But the previous summer when he was swimming across the Bani with his father's cattle, the river tore off his shoulder the goatskin bag in which he had kept the paper and carried it away. Now the only form of identification among the Diakayatés was a single frayed cardboard booklet from the tax authorities that listed the names of Oumarou and some of his family members, though not all, and a few of them long dead. The booklet put Oumarou's age at seventy-six. "Suits me," the old man said. "Means I don't have to pay taxes." He himself did not know his age. Like his, most dates of birth in the booklet were arbitrary. No nomad births in the bush were registered, and no deaths. The Fulani passed through the land, shaping and reshaping it, and that was all the account there was of their passing and that was all the account that mattered.

Ousman and Boucary and two of Boucary's friends from the Fulani village of Somena set out for Djenné when the sun was two palms above the east and already hot. Ten fastpaced miles across the fallow rice and millet fields on fast and practiced feet. The men carried their clubbed canes on their necks and rested their wrists on the ends of the canes, and Boucary also carried a black leatherette messenger bag with broken zippers. The men chattered nonstop and so rapidly that I understood very little of what they said. Something about cattle. Something about grass. Flycatchers and egrets sailed shadow-first to pick dainties out of fresh dung. A hoopoe flushed out of the reeds beside a drying marsh and flew off. Sufis in Central and South Asia believed the hoopoe to possess a level of enlightenment unattainable to humans, a sacred knowledge. Ousman and his fellow travelers paid this one no notice.

They passed a laundress bent over her wash outside a homestead, naked from the waist up. They passed and then were passed by and at last fell a few paces behind an oxcart in which several Bambara women and a man and some children lurched in time with the wobbly wheels. Chickens clucked in a cage of twigs and rope. One of the women carried in her lap a boombox that played a cassette recording of Bambara music and for a time the cowboys walked to the beat of kora thumb harps and djembe drums and the soku violin made out of a gourd strung with lizard skin and a single horsehair, until they hooked east across a harvested rice field and the cart kept bumbling south down the rutted road.

Before the first afternoon prayer the men arrived at the bridge over the Bani's torpid arm that seeped past Djenné's northern gate. A Bozo horsecart driver called out to Boucary from the shade of a tamarind tree, "Hey, Fulani, is this your white woman?" And Boucary said yes, she indeed is with us, she is our Fulani white woman named Anna from the family of Bâ, and all the men laughed and I waved and laughed back.

Each Monday cart drivers from the bourgou dropped off their passengers on this grassless hillock next to the town's sole walled cemetery. They waited until the market closed, then they took their customers back to the hinterlands. All day local girls and women coursed among the drivers with coolers full of little plastic bags of homemade golden ginger beer and sweet carmine hibiscus tea and milky baobab juice, all frozen into heart-size nuggets of multicolored ice, and with trays of deepfried dough and spicy balls of peanut paste and cigarettes and oily boiled noodles. Kept the men fed, kept them company by cemetery walls.

Women were not allowed inside the cemetery. The Djennénke said such visits would upset them. But all about under the huckstresses' feet and the feet of the off-duty drivers and the hooves of the draft animals and the wheels of the carts and under the stubbed-out cigarettes and the discarded greasy plastic bags and windblown fishbones and vegetable peels and rotting carcasses of livestock the dead lay in full view.

Human skeletons were everywhere. Inlaid into the laterite topsoil of the hillock. The bones eroded or weathered out of the earth's matrix like macabre filigree, like grotesque cameos in barely raised relief. These dead were not buried on their sides with their heads pointing toward Mecca the way Islam prescribed but were strewn facedown and in fetal position and with arms and legs akimbo and their naked skulls in all directions as if they had been left to lie where death had struck them. Some of their crania were bashed in or missing. There were femurs resting completely ownerless and hand bones severed from the radii and ulnae but otherwise peculiarly intact, the trapezoids and the lunates still in place, as if they had set off on their own, scratching toward water or toward higher ground or toward some fragmentary salvation.

Who were these people? When did they live? How did they die? Had they been buried reverentially in clay jars in the pre-Muslim long ago, jars that then crumbled away with age and wind and flood and vandalism, regurgitating the bones into the light? Or had they been dumped into shallow mass graves that had eroded over time— and during which disaster that had left the undertakers no time to mourn? Or had they been so reviled, disgraced themselves so much among the living, that they had been left to rot and feed the hyenas and the vultures? Did they perish here all at once—struck down by what?—or one by one, shunned and shivering lepers driven beyond Djenné's mote by the fearful townspeople, wasting away in slow agony while the town kept living, slapping laundry, trading in slaves and salt, stewing fish for dinner?

No one could tell me. In *Ta'rīkh al Sudan* the Songhai Empire's chronicler al Sa'adi claimed that Djenné had withstood ninety-nine attacks and yielded to only one, led by Sunni 'Ali, the first Songhai king, who had starved the town into surrender in the late fifteenth century after a siege that lasted seven years, seven months, and seven days. But *Ta'rīkh al Sudan* documented this land's history until only 1613. So many had fallen here since. During the Fulani and Tuareg insurgency against Moroccan rule in the seventeenth century. During the pitched battles against the Bambara of Ségou who pillaged the town and enslaved its women in the eighteenth. During Seikou Amadou's jihad of 1818, the Toucouleur jihad that defeated Seikou Amadou's empire in 1862, the French conquest of 1893. The Malian novelist Yambo Ouologuem summed up his country's history in his parabolic book *The Duty of Violence*: "The crowned rulers, forcing life down the throats of their subjects like the boa gagging on an antelope, rolled from obscure dynasties into those with more sibylline genealogies—each infamy more vicious than the one before."

I asked and asked the elders of Djenné about the dead outside the cemetery walls. No one seemed to know who they had been. I asked learned men, but their expertise lay elsewhere: in the overgrazing of the bourgou's dwindling pastures, in the feckless abuse of water resources, in keeping the town generator running at least six hours a day. I asked the griots. They repeated my name back to me. "Bâ. Bâ. Bâ." We have invented over time so many ways to maim one another, to abandon one another in our finality, but what griots serenaded was life, not death. They had no use for skeletons.

I asked Oumar Tall, a direct descendant of al Hajj Oumar Tall, the Tijaniyya Sufi scholar who had led the Toucouleur jihad. Al Hajj had fought throughout the bourgou against the Massina Empire with bows and arrows daubed with snake venom, with spears and clubs, with broadswords and European firearms; in the three final battles alone seventy thousand men had died. Their bones had laid the foundations of the Toucouleur Caliphate that at its apex reached from Timbuktu to present-day Guinea. They underlay the routes of Fulani transhumance.

My Oumar Tall was the principal of the public primary school that stood on the spot where Sekou Amadou, having spurned the ancient Grande Mosquée as too ornate, had built his own truculent mosque. After al Hajj Oumar Tall's forces had conquered Djenné, the Toucouleur began the demolition of the sheikh's house of prayer. When the French seized Djenné in a battle that killed five hundred and ten Toucouleur soldiers, they dismantled what remained. The French set store in knowledge. After shipping to museums in Paris, for purposes of scientific inquest, the cadavers of some of the Toucouleur soldiers his troops had killed, invading French general Louis Archinard ordered that Sekou Amadou's dilapidated mosque be remodeled into a school. He also, in a bout of orientalist sentimentality or to mollify his new African subjects, ordered for the old Grande Mosquée to be rebuilt. The construction clay for both projects was scooped out of the Bani's floodlands—themselves a composition of so many misremembered dead. A hundred years later the school bore the name of Sory Ibrahim Thiocary, a university student tortured and killed for political dissent by the junta of Mali's second postcolonial president, Moussa Traoré.

Conceived in violence, begotten in violence, baptized in violence. The school's orderly walls of fired bricks may as well have been mortared with blood. Somehow—how? how?—the coagulated ignominy of its existence managed to accommodate shabby plywood desks, cloudy blackboards, acacia trees, a water pump, and a thousand prattling children. Many of the children were sickly. Each year five or six died of malaria, of tuberculosis, of hunger, usually the littlest ones.

Principal Tall was a tall and youthful man with the authoritative paunch of the well-to-do. We had dinner at Pygmée's bar one night, fried perch and french fries and baobab juice under the stars. Fish and chips with the blood prince. He told me of battles and skirmishes that had besmirched the bourgou in the nineteenth century, stories he'd heard from his mentors and grandparents who were no longer alive. The stories sounded fablelike, apocryphal. He ended each with the words: "There were many dead." He did not know whose skeletons lay outside the cemetery walls.

"Maybe there are no fields other than battlefields, / those still remembered, / and those long forgotten," wrote Wisława Szymborska. The whole world was an ossuary. Tamarinds by the cemetery of Djenné contorted their baroque trunks over generations of all the dead and told no stories.

The enormous square before the Grande Mosquée was not large enough for the Monday trade. This was, in al Sa'adi's words, "one of the greatest Muslim markets," and it clogged the square and all the alleys around the mosque and by the mayor's office and in front of the prison and the gendarmerie and adjacent to Oumar Tall's school and tapered out barely a block away from the north gate where the powdered clay kicked up by tens of thousands of feet continued to tongue northward in orange swirls, twisting free of the streets and mixing with the exuberant discord of hundreds of pop tunes and suras and prayers and folksongs and billowing together dust and sound over the earthen bridge outside the gate like something escaped from a freakish foundry. The cowboys kept pace and entered this bedlam holding hands and head-on, the way men enter a stampede.

They threaded their narrow bodies between toppling wagons loaded with calabashes from Blâ and sky-high pyramids of bagged rice from Ségou and women spraddle-kneed on tarps among cornucopias of Ivorian pineapple and cabbage that grew right here on the Bani and girls peddling beaded bracelets that spelled SOURVENI DE-JENNE and LOVE and women in brocade dresses on motorscooters and severe boys with pushcarts twice their size and pharma fraudsters promising larger buttocks and perkier breasts and paler skin and cure from malaria and migraine. They wove around false prophets hawking salvation under flights of mosque swallows, and tramps who grabbed at sleeves with silent fingers. "Reduced to mendicity by old age, blindness, or other infirmities," René Caillié wrote almost two hundred years before of the beggars by the Grande Mosquée. How old the hands of Djenné's alms-seekers?

They pushed past matrons in heavy golden hoop earrings who had strapped babies to their backs with embroidered cloth. Girls bargaining over basketfuls of smoked catfish curled head-to-tail into elegant teardrops. Slender young women carrying dull jewels of gum arabic on pewter trays. Tinsmiths. Pop-up tanneries. They stopped abruptly and oblivious to the exasperated crowd—"Eh,

Fulani, get a move on!" "Eh? Bush clod!" "Goddamn cowherds!"—
to greet other cowboys they had not seen since their last visit to the
market and to flirt in passing with coy Fulani women swaying
under calabashes of sour milk, and under the flapping tarps of the
fabric rows they paused to finger and squint at bolts of indigo and
iceblue and cobalt, because blue was the color Fulani men preferred
for their boubous. They squeezed past onion traders and the women
who spooned tomato paste out of one-liter cans into small plastic
sachets to sell for ten cents apiece and legume traders who rattled
scoopfuls of wormy local beans into calabashes, and past a teenage
girl who was dunking Fulani shoes in a bucketful of suds, rubbing
entire crops of shoes strung together in the soap, then tossing them
onto a tarp where they would remain clean of dust for the next two
minutes. They bought tiny plastic bags of frozen ginger beer spiced
with chili flakes and bit off the polyethylene corners and sucked out
the sugary slush. They inquired from the bootleggers about new
recordings by particular Fulani griots from Burkina Faso and Mopti.
After an hour or so at the market, when his eyes stung from the
dust and his head throbbed with the overwhelming volume of the
city and the olfactory cacophony of freshly cut mint and the sour
nag of shea butter and the sweet piney rot of mangoes and the metallic reek of fresh fish, Ousman strode into a photographer's shop to
the north of the mosque.

A narrow room with no windows. Wallpaper of vinyl photo-
murals nailed onto mud walls: turquoise mountains coned with
piercing white glaciers; technicolor green forests trimming cool blue
lakes that faded into plastic blue sky, in duplicate; a manicured
lawn before a mansion with white columns; a field of scarlet pop-

pies. In the corner opposite the door a bamboo étagère heaped with faded pink plastic peonies. A plastic chair next to it. In another corner, a small printer.

"Yes?"

"I need a photograph for a document."

"What kind of document?"

"A document. Government papers. With a photograph."

"Fulani, Fulani, ay, Fulani. All right. Sit there. Take off your hat."

He sat in the plastic chair by the étagère. He put his conical leather hat on the floor by his feet. He didn't know what to do with his hands. At last he laid them on his knees. His hands were sweating. The photographer pulled down a curtain of dirty white cotton behind his back, blanked out the mountains and the lakes. The photographs were black-and-white and in them Ousman looked startled.

"Enough for today," he said.

He paid the photographer with the money he had borrowed from Afo Bocoum the *diawando* and strode south through the market. The palmshaped sweat stains on his knees dried quickly. He squeezed past tailors, calabash menders, watch repairmen, bakers, jewelers, prayer rug salesmen, vendors of greasy omelet sandwiches. Young talib boys, who lived in communes of peers at madrassas and were sworn to walking only on foot and surviving exclusively on handouts for the duration of their studies, which often lasted many years, extended their empty plastic lunchpails, singing for alms. This was the life of his younger brother Drissa, a marabout apprentice in San, who shared a cinderblock shed with two dozen other boys and spent his days copying the Koran and begging and tending a neighbor's garden in return for food. Ousman had studied in a madrassa himself once, though not for very long. He told the children, "Go with God." He ducked past the crocodile heads and snakeskins and birdwings and herbs and lichen and mottled awful oddities of the fetish market and beside Sory Ibrahim Thiocary School he walked into the alley that every Monday became the center for commerce in small livestock. Fulani herders had been coming here to trade since at least the thirteenth century, before the alley itself ever was. Here they relaxed in their one-legged heron's stance, gossiping, admiring one another's animals, bargaining, chatting. The alley was blue with the flapping indigo and turquoise and sapphire of their boubous.

I bought a sachet of frozen hibiscus tea from a small child and elbowed my way back to the square and sat under the tarp awning of a teashop between the spice row and the tailors. The purple gobbet in my hand iced my fingers nicely. At the teashop young Djennénke men on two wooden benches slurped Nescafé mixed with sweet condensed milk and hot water and watched war porn on their cellphones.

A photograph: an amputated hand lying next to an open Koran on a table or a desk, fingers slightly bent. The cut just above the carpals so clean the whole thing seemed pretend, papier-mâché.

Two photographs shown sequentially: in one, a man with a short beard and shaved skull, buried chest-deep in ocher soil, his right arm raised, finger extended heavenward, in some last request— more time? a drink of water? In the other, that same man, his head and neck and chest limp and red, a circle of white stones blossoming around him like chrysanthemum petals, men in trousers and shirts and turbans pulling him out of the ground by slack arms.

A photograph: a young man on what looked like a hospital cot. Dirty bandages where his foot and hand had been. Peonies screenprinted on his yellow bedsheet. The peonies.

The men in the teashop spoke in French.

"See what they do?"

"Ay, ay, ay. They say it's shariah to punish thieves and adulterers."

"This is not shariah."

"They are not Muslims."

"No. They aren't humans."

"Beasts."

"Animals."

One of the men also had on his cellphone a video. Forty-six seconds, from Gao. A man's body on the ground in a puddle of fresh blood. You couldn't see the face. The body had been hacked in two, top and bottom. The two parts still in place, the sword-cut like a thin red belt. A robed man bent over the body, gesticulated with one hand, trained a cellphone camera on it with the other, recited something. A damnation, a lament, a prayer. Then something happened and the top half of the body, the torso, thrashed a little. Then a group of men were moving the two halves separately onto a blue tarp, maybe a body bag. Were they the men from the stoning picture? Some other men? Were there a lot of men like that in the world—death's janitors?

"It's one of the executioners, a famous butcher for al Qaeda from Gao," said the owner of the cellphone with the video, and the men around him nodded and clicked their tongues and responded that this was a great video, that it demonstrated the mercy of God because the executioner from Gao had gotten his just deserts. They downloaded the video onto their own phones until each had a copy. Then they passed around a tin cup with water and one of the men dripped some for an agama lizard that had darted out of the shade. The lizard caught the drops in flight, before they could hit the dust and curdle like balls of mercury.

I stepped outside.

It was lunchtime and the market had quieted somewhat. I walked a little and came to the threshold of a lean-to that sold fake drugs from Nigeria. I sat there. Past me in a pall of dust and diesel smog and oil smoke from the fryers' vats rolled pushcarts and motorcycles and bicycles and feet shuffled bare and in sandals and in soft leather shoes and sneakers and flipflops and plastic slippers. Some slippers had names: Anna, Ipanema. A man thrust my way a side of veal, tail still attached. My chest hurt. Even on its periphery war corrupted the threshold of dignity, reduced to mendicity the soul. I took out my notepad.

Perec: "To write: to try meticulously to retain something, to cause something to survive; to wrest a few precise scraps from the void as it grows, to leave somewhere a furrow, a trace, a mark or a few signs." To scrape the page with the sharp raw edges of what's broken, to scratch sense into skin.

On the other side of the thinned stream of shoppers an old bearded man in rags knelt next to the wall of a mercantile and with a straw traced something in the dirt between his knees. Poems, maybe. Trigonometric equations. Some madness deciphered by him alone and to him alone meaningful. I continued to trace my own glyphs in the notepad, his mirror image.

For a loss to be monumental, complete, there first must exist a promise of harmony, of some sublime and preordained kinship. My beloved and I had been comrade voyagers before we became lovers, footloose storytellers who shared a supreme reverence for wordsmanship. We filled our notebooks with the beauty and the iniquity with which the world branded and buoyed us. We wished our stories to bring it to some accountability, some reckoning.

We traveled on similar orbits. We met in the spring-green killing fields of Iraq. We passed each other in the minefields of Afghanistan. In the seamy ignominy of hurricane-drowned Louisiana we shared a colleague's kitchen to sleep in. I slept on the floor. He folded his long narrow body onto the obtuse angle of the corner breakfast nook. Years later, after we had fallen in love, we once slept side by side in the lair of a mountain lion, and tall soft grass wove through the stars.

We struck sparks off each other's work. We read out loud: our own writing, the writing of others. When we weren't on the road we were reclusive, and I relished our quietudes, the long physical distances between us. I baked sweets and mailed them in his name to post office boxes time zones away. He sent me books. When we did see each other—sometimes as lovers, usually as friends—we took long walks and held our breath before the same beauty. One time in winter a gale blew sand and sleet along an ocean beach and he shielded my eyes with one hand and with the other led me, blind, out of the wind. One time in summer he collected a bucket of desert rainwater for my bath. "You'll like the suds," he said. He regarded the world magnanimously, from the hip, and when he loved me that was how.

A promise of harmony betokens nothing. He was married. How painful for him were the years of hesitation between me and his wife? I never asked. There were chambers in his heart that were obscure to me because I elected them to be so. He would rush toward me and then pull away, and in my rapture of magical thinking I willed myself to believe his oscillations between intimacy and distance a necessary restraint, a friction integral to the alkahest of our particular love. Such was my desire. Such was my choice. Perhaps it was this very tiptoeing around the fear of loss that destroyed any possibility of a true and viable union.

He chose his wife. Such things happen all the time. He told me we would not speak again. It was late evening, after rush hour, at a trolley stop in West Philadelphia. We strained our eyes into the rheumy dark together one last time, to see the trolley that would take him away. It wouldn't come. Cellophane wrappers blew at our feet, holding nothing anymore: emptiness, emptiness. I touched his sleeve in farewell and left the shelter.

My grief struck me aphasic for months. I knew how to chronicle other people's pain, how to externalize their heartbreak and document loss the way Fulani nomads seared their identity into something else, something apart, the hide of their cattle. I did not know how to contend with my own.

There I sat with it, in the middle of a market square in the heart of the Sahel.

Monsieur Touré, a bitter man warped by arthritis and old age, shambled toward my shelter in disoriented near-blindness. He brandished his walking cane and cursed all the men he saw. They taunted him in response, mocked his doddering walk, his impotent fury. A small crowd encircled him. Someone yanked a cellphone from the chest pocket of his starched skyblue boubou. The prankster held the phone high, out of reach. Monsieur Touré grabbed the air for it, he kicked the ground, he pouted and spat and swore until the thief gave it back and he feinted at the snickering spectators with his cane and they parted and waved him away, the town lunatic, and he walked on, still cursing and mumbling threats. When he came to where I was sitting he stopped. He squinted at the shopkeeper and shook the cane at him:

"Imbécile."

"Coucou," the man responded amicably, and turned away to count money.

Monsieur Touré saw me.

"Madame?" He took my hand in both of his stiff and deformed palms and introduced himself and gave a slight and formal bow. He held my hand very firmly and worried it with his unbending, pained fingers. A keen loneliness passed between us, a pining: his or mine? He wished me a good life. He wished me to be loved. Months of silence had passed since my beloved had left me, and the shock of loss, the anesthesia of it, had begun to wear off, and with my hand in Monsieur Touré's kneading grip I recognized the limitless ache of not knowing whether I had been loved at all. My own love had morphed into an exquisite sorrow and I did not know how to let it go. I began to cry. Monsieur Touré released my hand and walked away and I stayed under the pseudopharma's awning for a long time.

> *Cuckoo your footprints*
> *never were used*
> *for writing*
> —Yosa Buson

By dusk the market was gone. Men draped in white and blue lace filed into the mosque for prayer. Children swept the alleys and teenagers pulled out old foosball tables to play in the orange cones of street lamplight and lizards chased one another in spirals up and down clay walls. The last bus left town with coolers and suitcases and canvas sacks lashed to the rooftop and rimaibe women piled leftover firewood onto their heads and began their return procession to the pirogues that would cross them over to the bush. In their place boys in plastic sandals started a game of soccer. The floor of the square hovered above itself in the lavender dust the market had left behind, and shop owners poured buckets of dirty water on the ground to tamp the dust down. A crescent moon sailed off a minaret and dipped toward the horizon, to grace some other land.

The prefect's office was closed for market day and Ousman's effort to obtain an identity card went no further than the photo session. He and Boucary walked back to the bush and returned to camp in time for the evening milking. I stayed in town and walked to the house of Pygmée the bar owner and sat by myself on the steps that led from the second-floor galleries to the flat clay roof. Night belted forth the grinding of streetcorner diesel rice mills, the monotonous recitations of adult madrassa students two alleys away, Malian pop tunes, laughter. The city smelled like the fish and millet and rice Djenné's ten thousand women and girls were preparing inside their walled patios. Around their cooking fires the town's adobe homes swayed together and fell apart like a mismatched collection of beads on an endlessly coiled string. Above, the low sponge of the sky dripped a billion stars.

Courtyard by courtyard the town cut the black into lopsided rectangles. I walked up to the roof and looked down. An irregular honeycomb unevenly lit by incandescent bulbs, each cell its own iridescence and brightness and shade, and in the center of each tiny human figures reached into the common bowl of their poor-man's evening meal.

That winter astronomers at the European Space Agency released a heat map of the universe as it had appeared three hundred and eighty thousand years after the Big Bang. Nascent buds of future galaxies hurtling into becoming. Around them nothingness, the Beginning. It was hard to create the space within myself to accommodate that kind of infinite life-giving void. I wondered whether the scientists who did also could create some inner space to be more accepting, more curious, more forgiving.

March. The squalls of harmattan were over and dry spring heat was building in the bourgou. The water in the fens fell day by day and in its sunwarmed slug lay the uneaten rhizomes of hippo grass, catfish burrows, cowries blown or dropped here who knew when, strange benthic life. Day and night tipped equal. Gamma Aquarii—Sadalachbia, the Lucky Star of the Tents—had faded from the sky and gave way to Alpha Piscium: Alrescha, the Rope. It was roundup time.

Oumarou's nephew Sita had the family brand. He had tethered seven yearlings to the calf rope he kept staked under the acacia nearest his hut: two tawnies, three fawn heifers, a red bull, a black bull with white flecks on its rump like a map of the sky. On a hot and low fire built with a bucketful of dry manure he heated the iron until he could see the metal's glow even in the bright sun. Then he pulled his broadbrimmed hat of faded red leather and canvas deeper onto his brow and walked up to the reata.

He was in his fifties and taciturn and he had a handsome goatee that was just starting to gray. His full name was Sita Diakayaté but that was also the name of his cousin, Oumarou's other nephew, Salimata's husband, who was almost as old as Oumarou and had no front teeth and whose hair, what was left of it, was completely white. The two Sitas set up their dry-season huts fifty paces apart, to the north of Oumarou's. To differentiate between the Sitas, people at the camp called Oumarou's older nephew Sita Dangéré, Sita of the Crossing, because he was born during transhumance just as his family was preparing to cross a river—though no one knew which river that had been. Because of Sita's age it was impolite to ask. The younger Sita they sometimes called Sita Louchéré, after the village near which he was born, but usually they simply called him Sita because that was easier.

The fourth old man at the camp was Oumarou's uncle Isiaka, a tiny and starveling cowboy who favored acid-green boubous and spoke in falsetto babble. Isiaka was a year or two younger than Oumarou, camped two hundred paces to the south, and had the most cattle of the four men. Although he had grown sons, most of the time he herded his cows himself. He was even more obsessed with the healing properties of milk than Oumarou and steered most con-

versations toward lectures on the subject, and everyone in the camp made fun of him for his shrill rants. But all of them loved him and, in secret, worried awfully about his health.

Sita untied a tawny bull, placed a hand on its rump, talked it nearer the fire. His son Moussa, who had shaved his head to shed his fever and speed his passage from the state of illness to the state of health, pushed the bull down on its left side and squatted next to it and put his weight on its neck. He had changed out of his Obama t-shirt into a blue boubou and was shod in someone else's maroon flipflops with faded plastic daisies on the thongs, and squatting there he quietly told the animal things. Maybe soothing whispered promises of health and a fat hump and a grassy abundance. Maybe threats. Hassan, Oumarou's youngest boy, pinned down the bull by kneeling on its hind legs. Sita picked up the branding iron and leaned over the bull and drew a long stripe from the flank and up the right side to the rump, then retraced it again and once more. Then he seared one small cross into the bull's right shoulder. The animal trembled the first few times the brand touched it, then quieted, breathed shallow breaths. When the boys released the bull it sprang to its legs and ran off to rejoin the herd.

"A Fulani's ID and his passport are the brand on his cow," Afo Bocoum once told me. Sita's brand was a long straight line up the flank and a small cross on the shoulder. Oumarou's a long-stemmed T with short arms, singed from the stomach up to the right thurl, and a small cross on the shoulder. Afo's, three strokes on the thurl. The Petrie Museum and the British Museum in London carried elaborate bronze branding irons from ancient Egypt that dated back to the second millennia BC, the brands themselves cartouches bearing human and animal shapes and the names of pharaohs, but the Diakayatés' simple footlong piece of hooked metal etched into the skin of their cows stories that may have been older even than that. Each line spelled a lineage. A brother who cut his cows out of a family herd added a symbol to the existing family brand—a stroke, a crossbar, a serif. If you could unravel the ideograms, decode the stems and the necks, you could trace the genealogy of a herd to the owner's ancestors, to some of the first branding irons ever to sear a zebu hide. When you placed your hand on a cow's flank the whole history of pastoralist Africa pulsed under your palm.

The iron was graying. Sita dropped it on the fire again and waited till it regained its glow. The boys brought up the other tawny. Then the black. The three fawns one after the other. When Hassan untied the last animal, the red bull, it darted to the side and whammed its flank against the boy's light body—"Hey, what? Stop!"—and galloped off toward the shrinking fen, toward Doundéré—"*Ya Allah!*"—and Hassan started to laugh and Moussa gave chase, laughing also. Soon the entire camp stood outside their huts and laughed as Moussa grabbed and grabbed for the jinking bull, the boy bald and too skinny after his illness and tripping in the borrowed flipflops like a desperate rodeo clown and the frightened animal bucking and dancing in circles and kicking up clumps of red clay with its hind legs and the boy cavorting around it—

"Go get him, Moussa!"

"Left left left—*left, from the left!*"

"Go go go, Moussa—no, the other way!"

"Eh, Moussa, save the dancing for a wedding!"

—and Moussa in his distance-darkened blue kaftan like a giant glossy starling afloat in the field of crushed straw, until at last he grabbed the bull's tail and then caught its hind leg and by that leg and tail he dragged the animal back to his father's branding fire. The bull tossed its head and its three other hooves grooved long lines into the bourgou. The boy threw the animal on the ground downwind of the fire and so close to the heat its eyes went white and wild. Sita retrieved the redhot iron. The bull groaned once, twice, and then was quiet.

"Beautiful bull," said Sita.

Oumarou had branded his cattle the day before. His yearlings had already forgotten the pain. At the dying breakfast fire young Kajita, Oumarou's seven-year-old granddaughter, squatted in hand-stitched blue underpants with crude white basting showing and watched one of them lick rice crusts from a pot.

By the sixth millennium BC the relationship between man and cattle along the Nile was sacrosanct. The earliest ritualistic burial of cattle, at Nabta Playa in the Nubian Desert, has been carbon-dated to 5400 BC and contains a complete skeleton of a female cow. Around that time, a prehistoric artist painted on the granite and sandstone slopes of Jebel Ouenat, a mountain on the crossroads of present-day Libya, Sudan, and Egypt, an image of two children suckling from a cow's udder. Two adults—the children's parents?—are standing by, content. In another painting archers are fighting for a cow. Arrows are flying everywhere. Some men look dead. The cow is just standing there, as cows are wont to do. Probably chewing cud.

In his 1902 book *Affairs of West Africa*, the British journalist Edmund Dene Morel recounted a story about a French officer in the Sahel who had commandeered some Fulani cattle, penned them, and posted sentry a light cavalry recruit from North Africa. Around midnight the sentry woke the officer,

> informing him with much solemnity that it would be necessary to slaughter the black bull at once. "Are you mad?" cried the astonished Frenchman. "Not at all, Lieutenant," replied the soldier imperturbably; "it is the cattle that are mad, for the Fulani are calling the bull—listen." Stepping out into the moonlight the officer listened. Presently from a neighbouring hill came the sound of a plaintive chant. At the same moment a violent disturbance took place among the cattle. The officer hurried toward the pen followed by the sentry, the chant meanwhile continuing in a cadence of inexpressible melancholy. The commotion in the pen increased, and before the Frenchman could reach it, one of the beasts was seen to clear the enclosure at a bound and crash through the bush, following the direction of the sound and bellowing loudly the while. It was the black bull. He had broken the halter which bound him and leapt a palisade five feet high! With the disappearance of the bull the chant abruptly ceased. Next morning the Fulani were nowhere to be found.

Poor French lieutenant. He should have known: Africa's nomads have been retrieving their livestock from cattle rustlers forever.

Cows have changed little since Nabta Playa. Nor has the mystical connection between cowboy and cow faded. In the early twenty-first century, pastoralists across Africa decorated their cattle and sang their praise songs as they had done for thousands of years. Ousman and his friends stored dozens of such serenades on their cellphones. "My bull is the fattest bull to cross the river," they went, and "my cows and I climbed a mountain before it even began to rain / and my tawny bull carried all the ropes," and "I'm the Fulani cowboy who herds the red bull, / so all the other cowboys should just shut up." At the beginning of each rainy season, Hassan paid a marabout to make gris-gris that would help his father's cows get very fat and protect them from evil spirits, from cattle thieves, from breaking into farmer's fields, from getting lost during transhumance. Hassan kept secret the name of the marabout and where the marabout lived, because giving away such information would have lessened the power of the spells. Of a good cowherd, the Fulani said: "He will be buried with his cows."

On the afternoon of the roundup a young heifer calf broke from the herd and planted her two front hooves on top of the mat where Oumarou was sitting with his legs tucked under him. This was not something cows did. Cows stayed within their trampled circle beyond the calf rope.

"What?" Oumarou said. "No. *Shht!* Go away."

The calf stood. Without rising Oumarou reached with both hands and pushed against her chest and neck. But almost on their own account his hands began to wander and caress the animal's neck, massage her cheeks, pet her hard ears. Pitying their grandfather's inability to discipline his cows, Kajita and Amadou came over to help.

They hit the calf: Kajita with her small fists, Amadou with an empty plastic water bottle that he had been trying to kick over the roof of Oumarou's hut. The old man reprimanded his grandson sharply.

You never hit a cow with anything but the clubbed shepherd's staff. It was best if you did not hit her at all. You massaged the folds of loose skin under her chin, here, you see, where it was the silkiest, and you pushed her away with both hands against her neck, like this, tenderly feeling for ticks in the process, and you touched the rhinarium with the inside of your palm to check if her rubbery skin was dry, to check that she wasn't ill.

The calf liked that. She leaned deeper into Oumarou's arms with great bovine pleasure and then she stepped onto his mat with all four of her hooves and lastly she lay down on the mat and rolled over to her side and arched her neck.

"Hah! In all of my life I have never seen a cow behave this way, Anna Bâ!"

And the old cowboy and the children and I leaned over her to caress the satin of her dewlap, the long cool crest of her snout beneath which the nasal conchae accumulated the secret recognition of milk and grass and man, the dry leathery nostrils, the bristle on the side of her ears. We felt and squeezed the warm little horns, hard and barely an inch long and storing the day's heat. We played with the soft fat of her hump and marveled at its curve.

"Amadou, see? When this cow is older and it eats a lot of grass and it likes the taste of that grass it will grow a huge hump. All of us in this camp won't be able to eat the entire hump of a single bull that's eating well. We won't even be able to finish the marrow from one of its legs! When this cow becomes an adult and eats well it will walk and its hump will sway left and right, from side to side, like so." Oumarou fishtailed his right hand before him for a long time, savoring the sway of it, swimming in that imaginary abundance. Picturing the journeys the cow would take and the tall sweetgrass it would eat to grow such a hump. Probably picturing, too, his own paths following the cow on such journeys and maybe also remembering all the paths his narrow feet had walked already, following other cows with swaying humps and udders full of milk. Then he said: "A cow without a hump is not beautiful."

The calf then turned onto her back and lifted her left hind leg the way a dog would, begging. Oumarou scratched the coarse hair on her stifle. He rubbed her stomach. He petted her hind flank. The bottom loop of his turban was pulled down to his chin and I could see: the old man was smiling.

After dinner little Amadou stepped with purpose through the dark and entered the circle of cows and approached one and stood next to her. He had spent much of that day playing with toy cattle he had molded out of clay. Horns and humps and all, each cow no larger than a thumb. Clay cow figurines much like Amadou's smattered the ancient town of Djenné-Djenno, the Iron Age excavations in Daima in northern Nigeria, the settlements of Tilemsi Valley near Gao, where, in the fossil deposits from the Eocene, archaeologists also found the forty-five-hundred-year-old signature of the earliest domesticated pearl millet in the world. Perhaps Stone Age cows, too, trampled Stone Age farmers' millet. Perhaps their owners petted them as well.

Amadou made his toys mount one another and suckle. He made them slumber together on the corner of his grandfather's black plastic tarp. Here the cows left the tarp: they went to pasture. Here they were returning, single file. Here they were gone again, but not all—the calves remained on the tarp, so that their mamas could lactate. Amadou was not old enough yet to help Hassan take the cows to pasture, but in a couple of years, after he turned seven, Oumarou would trust him to herd cattle on his own during the Hoping, when the cows are familiar with the daily itinerary and know where to graze and when to return to camp. That was something to look forward to. Oumarou also had promised Amadou that if the boy played with toy cows a lot he would grow up to own a very large herd.

Now Amadou stood next to a real breathing cow, dwarfed by her mammoth body. This was the cow that calved on the day I first met the Diakayatés. Most cows were named after the color of their hide and this one was called Gunel—Murky, Dark—because when she was born her color was unclear. He ran his hands along her jaw. He rose on tiptoes and touched her horns. He flattened his feet again and fondled her dewlap, flapped it like a heavy curtain. He reached up and fiddled with her shrunken hump. He caressed her coarse flanks. He felt up her front leg and found a tick and studied it a moment and flung it away. Then they just stood together, boy and cow, the boy's nose to the animal's shoulder, his hands on her dewlap. In the starlight they appeared metallic blue, almost translucent.

At the edge of the fen one evening I knelt in the mud and watched a cow the color of burnt sugar lower her nose to the spot where the wetland met the red soil in the thinnest film of water. Without ever lifting her muzzle the cow ripped intently at small blades of hippo grass and quivered with just her skin, which had bald patches where some other cow had nicked her with its horns, and from her black and polypous lips thin silver threads of saliva flew through the setting sun. The air around her smelled of some intrinsic remembering. She exhaled noisily and moistly into the water through her nose so that the water bent in two perfect narrow sprues and I loved being present for her gorgeous and trusting warmth.

Around midnight, before the cattle moved to nightherd, a bull gingerly sidestepped my sleeping mat on his way to the low grass shelter in which Fanta kept her chickens at night and chewed on the roof awhile.

At the end of March, Pygmée came to the bush on his beat-up Toyota motorscooter to help me with translation. Before dinner his cellphone rang. He looked at the number and answered in French.

"Oui, mon général!"

He spoke for a minute and hung up and relayed the news to the Diakayatés. Two bandits armed with machine guns had entered the cattle market in Moura, a large village north of the Niger River, and opened fire. A Fulani man was wounded. That's all he knew.

Cattle raids have been part of Africa's pastoral life for millennia—long enough for Neolithic artists to paint them on the granite of Jebel Ouenat. But until recently the raiders had used bows and arrows, spears, machetes, or simply stealth. Twenty-first-century rustlers were performing the ancient rite with automatic weapons, an inheritance of modern, mechanized wars. Scores of men often died in such raids.

"Ay, ay, ay," Fanta said, and licked the back of the ladle to taste if the rice she was cooking had enough salt. "Even the way people steal cattle is new because of the war in the north. We are not used to this." But Oumarou said: "That's on the other side of the Niger. Here it is safe. Don't worry."

Fanta brought from the fire the dinged aluminum basins with rice and spicy baobab sauce and the men and women bent over the food in two small circles. I thought that a longer conversation about the war in the Sahel would follow but none came. Rinsing her fingers after the meal in the rusty tomato paste can, Fanta said, "It's strange that in this world it can be night here and day someplace else."

And Oumarou replied, "The world is very big. It is impossible to understand most of the things in it."

After dinner Ousman squatted before the front wheel of Pygmée's motorbike and caressed the spokes with gentle fingers. He was lonely because his wife, Bobo, was with her parents in a town a two-day walk away, recuperating from the birth of their second son. The baby's name was Afo, after Afo Bocoum the *diawando*. Their first-born was named Hashem, after Oumarou's father, who had died when Ousman was a small boy. Because Oumarou's father had made a pilgrimage to Mecca and young Hashem had inherited his name in its entirety and inclusive of all honorifics, the toddler was sometimes called, and responded to, "al Hajj." Ousman missed his boys, and he missed sex with his pretty wife.

"Can you ride a motorcycle, Anna Bâ?" he asked.

"Only as a passenger. Can you?"

"The same. Can you ride a bicycle?"

"Yes."

"I can't. All I know is how to herd cattle."

"That's more than I know. Will you teach me?"

I had come to study. Weeks earlier, in Djenné, I had hired an English instructor to teach me Fulfulde. Monsieur Koulibaly was a small, wasted man with insulin-dependent diabetes. The antiquated blood glucose monitor he had bought years earlier on a rare trip to Bamako was unreliable and he was often very sick. He had almost no teeth. He was forty-seven and looked sixty. I met him at a mercantile in front of the Grande Mosquée. His English was immaculate, careful, slow. We held our lessons whenever I came to town. He was a perfect teacher. He spoke only Fulfulde in class, demanded faultless pronunciation, tolerated no mistakes, and admonished me for slacking off on homework. I had middle-school anxiety dreams about flunking out. Monsieur Koulibaly said: "I will be glad to give you the knowledge I have. Amadou Hampâté Bâ—do you know him? A great writer!—he said, 'Knowledge is the only thing you can give away without losing any.'"

Ousman said he would teach me to herd cattle and to milk cows, and Fanta, who lay on my mat, said: "White people have a lot of knowledge. We Fulani are red people, almost like white people. The Bambara people and the Bozo and the rimaibe are black people. Black people are dirty."

Where does bigotry come from? The Polish journalist Ryszard Kapuściński, who worked in Africa for decades, told an audience in Kraków in 2003: "I the Self can exist as a defined being *only in relation to*; in relation to the Other, when he appears on the horizon of my existence, giving me meaning and establishing my role."

Bisecting the world into the Self and the Other is a primal need, our most rigid Manichaean impulse. At some early point of our history it may have been a matter of survival. We probably needed it to limit our impulse for empathy and compassion to extended family, immediate kin, ourselves. Bigotry may have kept a prehistoric mother from starving her own child at the expense of her neighbor's. It preempted generosity that would have endangered the giver. It underlay ownership. "Me and my clan against the world; me and my family against my clan; me and my brother against my family; me against my brother," goes a Somali proverb.

In the twenty-first century bigotry found its ultimate outlet in borders, points of tangency that allowed superstitions to swell to magnitudes of statehood, that bound real or perceived economic hellholes to imagined lands of plenty. Prejudice blossomed on both sides of the partition, took the shape of desire and envy on one, vigilance and pity on the other. Masked militiamen guarded theological divides. Frontlines delineated perimeters of life and death. "Three possibilities," Kapuściński said in another lecture, "have always stood before man whenever he has encountered an Other: he could choose war, he could fence himself in behind a wall, or he could start up a dialogue."

"I'd like to tell a story," I said, and the Diakayatés sat up to listen.

I said that the first anatomically modern humans appeared around two hundred thousand years ago, in Africa. That these humans were the ancestors of us all—of Fanta and all the Sankaris, of Oumarou and all the Diakayatés, of the Bozo fishermen and of the Frenchmen who flew airplanes, and of me and my parents and my son.

Oumarou nodded.

"Go on."

I said that between a hundred thousand and sixty thousand years ago some of us stayed in Africa, and others passed through a strait between Africa and Mecca called the Gate of Tears and trekked north and east on journeys that themselves took thousands of years and that took the travelers far to the other side. That our skin pigmentation and hair texture and eye color changed gradually and much later because of those journeys, as some of us had to acclimate to the sunless winters and bracing winds of new lands—that skin tone could change over a hundred generations—but that any two people anywhere in the world, regardless of the shade of their skin, were almost identical in their human makeup and could trace their origins, our beginning as a species, to a tiny group of the same shared ancestors in one single place.

"Where's that?" asked Ousman.

"Ethiopia."

"I knew we came from Ethiopia!" said Sita, and Oumarou said: "That's what I heard as well. Ever since I was very little the elders have been saying the Fulani came from Ethiopia."

Oumarou didn't know this, but sixty years earlier, when he was a young teenager, the molecular biologists James D. Watson and Francis Crick had made public their discovery of the double-helix structure of DNA that had allowed men to begin mapping the history of our common journey. Since then, geneticists had pinpointed the origin of the Y chromosome of the Fulani haplogroup—called, under the deceitfully bland nomenclature of science, E-V38—to North or East Africa between twenty-five and thirty thousand years ago. One of the haplogroup's two basal branches, E-M329, was found almost exclusively in Ethiopia.

Fanta wrapped around her shoulders the strawberry-print pagne she was using as a shawl that evening and said, "Hah! Good story. We should tell Hassan."

"Yes, yes," said Oumarou. "Hassan would love this story. He really likes stories about the old times. He likes all the stories from the Koran." Of all Oumarou's sons, Hassan was the only one who would not study in a madrassa. Like his father many years earlier, he was too busy herding cattle.

I did not know where in their vast collection of knowledge about the world the Diakayatés shelved my unverified accounts. Did they

incorporate them into their own origin myths, along with the ornate allegories of Islam, the griots' incantatory oral histories? Did they file them into the realm of fairytales, alongside fables of trickster hares, parables that traveled on transatlantic slave ships to the New World to become tales about Br'er Rabbit? Was there, in this birthplace of magic realism, any difference between the two? Did it even matter?

"Before us, our first task is to astonish, / and then, harder by far, to be astonished." So ends one of Galway Kinnell's poems. The Diakayatés listened to all stories, mine or any other's, with an eagerness to be astonished that stilled me. Uncynical, devouring, enthralled. Their universe was at once scrupulously ordered and immeasurable, and it always had room for the unknown.

One day Rabbit crawled into the deep den where Hyena had hidden her newborn cubs. All day for many days Hyena would hunt and scavenge, return to the den, drop the food inside, and go off into the bush to hunt and scavenge some more. Each time, Rabbit would snatch all the food before Hyena's cubs could get to it.

After a while Hyena decided to see how much her cubs had grown. She came to the den and ordered them to come out. They staggered out skinny as death.

"What happened to you?" Hyena asked.

"There is someone in the den with us," her children replied. "He eats all the food you bring."

Hyena was furious.

"Come out, whoever you are!" she barked.

"All right," said Rabbit. "But, if you don't mind, can you please help me by taking my sandals first?" And he stuck his long ears out of the den.

Hyena thought the ears were sandals. In her rage she yanked at them with tremendous force and tossed them as far as she could behind her into the bush.

"Thanks for the lift!" called Rabbit, and was gone.

Back when Oumarou was a young man there were a lot of hyena in the bush. There were lion and cheetah. The cowboys had to stay awake all night guarding their cattle. But for decades most large carnivores had been gone, and the only reason to keep an eye on the cows at night was to make sure that they didn't destroy any farms during the wet season.

As for cattle rustlers, it used to be that broadswords were protection enough, but that no longer was the case. The cowboys were outgunned. Few nomadic families owned firearms, and those who did usually had single-shot muzzle-loaders that bush blacksmiths welded out of car and bicycle parts and sold for twenty or thirty dollars apiece. They fired pebbles, not bullets. No one in the Diakayaté camp had a gun.

The Moura cattle rustlers had not been cattle rustlers at all. They were rebel fighters from Mali's north. There were two of them and they were young and they carried FM 24/29 light machine guns. They didn't want cows. They wanted cash.

Moura had no police force. The district gendarmerie, which was headquartered on the southern bank of the Niger a dozen miles downstream from Moura, in the compact port town of Kouakourou, led a brief and cursory inquiry into the incident. It concluded that after the French had begun to bomb the Sahara that January the pair had made their way southeast toward the northern bank of the Niger, toward Moura, where a few settled Fulani and two dozen rimaibe families lived in the low houses that knuckled out of the desert in dusty bas-relief.

One of the men got a job herding cows for a villager named Ambari Tiembiti, a father of seven. He lived in the desert with Ambari's cattle and he introduced himself to Ambari as Allaye. He told some other villagers his name was Samba. Once or twice he came to Moura to dine on rice and fish at Ambari's house. The Mourari said that he was a Fulani himself. It was possible that he was casing the town's Sunday cattle market. Rebel groups across the Sahel targeted cattle markets because it was common knowledge that cattlemen came to such markets with wads of cash. Cattle were expensive. In Djenné a healthy bull could fetch between five hundred and a thousand dollars, a year's wages of an average Malian government worker.

It was possible, too, that Allaye-Samba simply was taking a break from the war and the idea of robbing Fulani livestock traders came later.

No one in the village remembered seeing the other man before the morning of the attack. The cattlemen who saw the pair together in the market—the men who eventually killed them—said they seemed close friends. Neither carried an identity card.

Moura's cattle market was a large banco corral at the southern edge of the village, where two deep, wide wadis rushed toward each other, toward the Niger. In early spring the wadis rippled with loose sand and gave the horizon an urgently convex feeling, as if the village were its own tiny planet, the Little Prince's asteroid, as if it were about to slide off.

Six days a week the corral stood empty. On Sundays Fulani men in cowhide hats and indigo turbans filed through its single wooden stock gate and crammed it chockfull of animals, mostly calves and bulls. To cut cattle, cowboys walked through the pen in elegant zigzags and called with peculiar politeness: "excuse me excuse me excuse me excuse me." Women with coolers full of hibiscus slushies made their timid way around all the men and cows, and boys perched on top of the walls to watch the slow minuet of the traders.

On the last Sunday in March two dozen men and about a hundred cattle had packed into the corral when the two gunmen walked through the gate and closed it behind them. They pointed their weapons at the cowboys and ordered all the men in one corner, all the animals in another. They ordered the men to empty their pockets.

Ambari Tiembiti recognized his new cowherd. He asked the young man to put away the gun and go home, go back to the bush, mind the cows. He told fellow traders to ignore the gunmen. They were just dumb kids, he said. He said he would not budge from

where he was standing, smack in the center of the pen. At that point one of the gunmen—no one was sure whether it was the youth who had worked for Ambari or his buddy—raised his machine gun and fired and hit Ambari in the thigh. When Ambari did not fall, he shot him again. Ambari sagged to the dust and the gunmen ran out the gate.

The cowboys gave chase. In the square outside the corral a villager driving a horsecart saw the commotion. He put his horse at a gallop and aimed for the strangers with the guns. By the time the crowd of cowboys caught up with them, the gunmen were lying trampled and bleeding.

Someone telephoned the gendarmerie in Kouakourou. The district prefect, in turn, telephoned his supervisor in Djenné, who told the prefect to send gendarmes to Moura and kill the gunmen. The prefect gave the order, then telephoned Pygmée with news of the attack. By the time his gendarmes arrived in Moura, the mob already had dragged the gunmen's bodies to the patch of dirt in front of the mayor's office.

When I came to the village a week later, a Mourari named Amadou Tamboura described the lynching in fast, clipped sentences. "They were on the ground. They couldn't get away anymore. So the crowd clubbed them. I certainly clubbed them, too. And I had my hunting rifle with me, so I shot one, but by then he was already dead. Then the children stripped off their clothes."

Boubou Koïta, a young rimaibe villager, showed me a video he had taken with his cellphone after the gendarmes had arrived. Two bodies on two straw mats, brained, faces pulped, one naked from the waist down, crotch and head sprinkled with straw. Civilian men and gendarmes in uniform are standing around. The gendarmes are taking notes without touching the bodies or turning them over. Everyone looks grave.

"The men clubbed them so badly you couldn't tell where their faces were anymore," said Boubou's aunt Kumba. "It was horrible how they killed them."

In a trice Moura had become a village of murderers. War does such things.

The gendarmes took Ambari Tiembiti, wounded in both thighs, for treatment to a Malian army garrison a two-hour drive away. Before they left they ordered the villagers to bury the gunmen in the desert.

On my way to Moura I had stopped by the Kouakourou office of the district prefect, Sheikh Oumar Coulibaly. The prefecture was a single-story concrete box uphill from the river. Linoleum tablecloths covered two shabby desks, tin shutters shaded a glassless window. A corrugated roof sagged through a ripped-up drywall ceiling. On the unpainted concrete wall behind the prefect's plastic swivel chair an old brown leak stained the wall. A memory of the last rainy season, or of several rainy seasons past. There was no electricity, the humidity from the Niger clung to the skin, and the prefect was sweating in his Western suit. He called the gunmen rebels.

"This is the problem of the North," he said. "It's all the war in the North."

The prefect was frustrated and overworked. We spoke for about an hour and all the while old men from the bush kept filing into his office, asking for papers, for solutions to land disputes, for money. Some carried their market purchases: smoked fish, new plastic mats, goat and cow skins they would use as prayer rugs. Many were Fulani and spoke no Bambara or French. The prefect spoke no Fulfulde. His backwater appointment exasperated him. He rode his motorcycle to Djenné as often as he could and spent long nights at Pygmée's bar drinking Castel beer and watching music television.

"The rebels from the desert, some of them come south," he said. "They rob the Fulani. We don't know who they are. We don't know where they are. We just know they are in the area somewhere." He closed his eyes. "C'est la guerre, n'est-ce pas?"

Amfala Koïta, an out-of-work tour guide from Djenné, took me to Kouakourou and Moura on a borrowed motorscooter. Amfala was in his early twenties, tall and handsome and sweet. He smoked a lot of weed and volunteered unwanted backrubs and pouted at rejection. His friends in Djenné called him High Life. Kumba Koïta and her clan had descended from his family's slaves.

Kumba's grandparents had grown grain and vegetables and cotton to supplement the pastoralist economy of Amfala's ancestors. Now the rimaibe were free by law and had a subsistence economy of their own, their own cattle and chickens and rice fields, but their deference toward the Fulani Koïtas remained. And it was hard to tell whether their emancipation, enshrined in Mali's constitution, had been total. Some of the Fulani families in Djenné told me they owned slaves. In the second decade of the twenty-first century at least a quarter of a million Malians who were in bondage to Kel Tamashek had advocates championing their freedom in Mali and internationally. The rimaibe had none. Nor did anyone count the number of people who remained in Fulani servitude. Nor was there any punishment for slaveholding.

The instant Amfala rode into Moura the family began to cook, sweep, unroll mats in shady spots for him to lie on. Old men came by to shake his hand and bow and ask after his respected father and uncles. Teenage girls set to sharpening kitchen knives on concrete thresholds and boys ran to the fishmonger and returned with a Nile perch the size of a small goat for Amfala's dinner.

Kumba allowed me to sleep on a mat outside her house. But first she led me by the hand to a roofless nook behind her kitchen. Afternoon sun leapt in a bucket of cool well water. She handed me a tin cup. *"Bismillah,"* she said: Welcome. She smiled and stepped out and lowered an oily burlap curtain over the doorway. I stripped and draped my headscarf and pagne and t-shirt over a shoulder-high adobe wall. There was a breeze. A procession of rain-

less clouds drew across the sky. A doum palm above the washroom fanned them on with its fronds. The light was magical and beyond the shadow of the lynching outside Kumba's walls and beyond my own heartsickness I felt my wonder stir. I hummed a ranchera about an infanticidal madwoman and poured cupfuls of sunlit water over my head.

At dusk I took a walk through one of the wadis that ran past the livestock market. Its thalweg was ankle-deep dry sand. In a few months fish would jump here, spawning in water sixteen feet deep, and the only way to Moura would be by boat. Until then, anyone could come to the village. Bandits, thieves, halfbaked griots. I sat down in the sand upwind from a dead goat and watched stars appear in the openwork fleece of cloud. A crescent moon dipped and surfaced, dipped and surfaced, dipped and surfaced.

A cliffside motorcycle ride east from Moura delivered Amfala and me to a sandy beach across the river from Kouakourou. The Niger was bright turquoise, warm, briny with the smell of fish. In a leaky redwood pirogue a latter-day Charon was poling twenty people and three motorbikes and two bicycles our way. We swam while we waited, then sat on the sand to dry. The boat beached. A young Fulani woman stepped ashore first. She wore a lowcut fitted brocade dress and she had cowries and gold coins woven into her braids. I salaamed her. She stopped and asked me where I was headed.

"Djenné."

"Where are you coming from?"

"Moura."

"What's your surname?"

"Surname?"

"Your last name. What is it? Mine is Diallo."

"Ah! Bâ. My last name is Bâ."

"Eh? You eat beans, Bâ!"

"You eat beans yourself, Diallo." Casual mockery mandated by *sanankuya*. We laughed.

"Okay, Bâ, go with God," she said. She turned to labor through the sand away from the river and I took off my sandals and waded to the pirogue. Amfala and the scooter were already aboard.

The boat was drawing water through a gash by my feet. The boatman tried to suture it with a rag, then gave up. Everywhere the river sparkled and sweated and by the southern shore, below the neat hillside market rows of Kouakourou, town boys dove and splashed and beckoned like small mermen and when we approached they helped drag the boat to a sandy mooring where other pirogues rolled lightly in the current.

Before we left Kouakourou I met an oracle. His name was Moussa Bâ. He was an old man in a soiled boubou and an indigo turban that did not cover his hennaed beard, and he lived in town fulltime while his sons herded his cattle. He sat me down on a bale of fabric in his friend's shop and told me he knew nothing. Then he raised a hand for me to wait and closed his eyes and recited to me the list of the constellations that formed the matrix of the Sahelian year. It took him more than an hour to list all twenty-six and explain which weather each brought to the bourgou and how the bourgou had to respond. Coming up: al Butayn, al Sirrah, Aldebaran.

The Little Belly, the Bellybutton of a Female Horse, the Chaser of the Pleiades. Hunger, heat, desiccation . . . Al Han'ah and al Haq'ah, the Brand and the White Spot, when it still rains very little . . . Al Izrah, the Loincloth, when it must be raining all the time . . . Al Jabhah, the Forehead, a lock in Leo's mane, the only star of the twenty-six that lingers in the sky fourteen days instead of thirteen, the last star that allows farmers to plant . . . Dhat al Kursi, Cassiopeia, her hair drizzles some water on the ripening fields . . . Al Kalb al Akrab, the Heart of the Scorpion, when cows begin to return to the half-harvested bourgou and trample farmers' rice . . . Sadalachbia, the Lucky Star of the Tents, Gamma Aquarii, when the Fulani pitch their grass huts in the dry-season pasture . . . A small crowd of men had gathered around us. They were impressed, and waited for more. When he was done with the stars Moussa Bâ asked my first name and the first name of my mother—"Marina! Beautiful!"—and closed his eyes again, and after a quiet moment announced that I was born in a time that was very windy but very dry, under Sadalachbia.

He was wrong. I was born in autumn, under Aljabana, Denib Algenubi, when fall ticks stop bothering cattle. In my land it had been the time of heavy rains, and on my birthday there was a deluge. All of Leningrad's ninety-three rivers and canals flooded their solemn granite embankments. It was my sister who had been born in the time of high winds—in a hurricane, in fact, which had ripped out centennial trees and carried away tin roofs—but that was in July, and then, too, it rained. I was almost thirteen, and while the wind lashed the birches and oaks outside our summer cottage I wrote my newborn sister a letter full of answers to be read when she was older, but later I misplaced the letter and forgot the answers, or even to which hypothetical questions they had rejoined. But I did not tell any of that to Moussa Bâ. I bowed to him, and hit the road.

Laryngitis, runny nose, achy bones. The fetish market in Djenné had treatment: crocodile heads, skin of wild dog, cow femurs, tinctures of lichen. I stayed in the bush. Unparsed horizon, sketchbooks, sticky shotglasses of strong green tea. My eyes were running. I went walking and stumbled into a cow.

A fever was sweeping through the camp.

Salimata was laid up with some malaise on the reed pallet in her hut and a tawny week-old goat pranced around and chased its tail and upturned her calabashes, uncaught. In Sita Louchéré's hut young Mentou lay in her mother's lap, sick again, her breath hot, her sinuses congested, her eyes dull. Fanta and Mama were suffering from migraines. Ousman was gray and thinner than ever and suspected he had malaria. Hairatou was hawking a frightening, deep cough. She coughed when she stood half awake in the doorway of her parents' hut to squint at the first morning light and she coughed when she walked to the marsh with a water bucket and coughed when she filled it and coughed when she carried it back. She coughed when she pounded millet for the morning milk porridge, her father's favorite, and she coughed when she spat onto her palms the better to grip the pestle. She coughed when she stood sideways to the wind and poured rice from one calabash into another over and over, her arms far apart to let the wind winnow chaff and dust from the falling stream of grain. Rocks would remain. We would taste them on our teeth for lunch. She coughed at the hearth where she squatted to cook family meals. Rice millet rice millet rice. When we would slot together on mats after dinner for storytelling and tea I would feel with my palm her small lungs gurgle through her ribs. Her parents said her cough was nothing special.

"Hairatou?" The millet cream was boiling over. "You take that thing off the stove *right now!*"

Pygmée came to visit with a busted tire and a splitting headache and Fanta made him cover his head with a green turban, swept bits of straw and dry leaves with the side of her right hand from the ground in front of his mat, dropped some hot coals in the middle of that space, sprinkled a pinch of dried leaves from a black plastic bag, and ordered him to inhale the smoke. The leaves were gigilé, *Boscia senegalensis*, a caper Fanta had picked on a Thursday during the rainy season by the Burkina border. Gigilé was good medicine, and it grew in abundance in the highlands near the border, but it worked only if you picked the leaves on a Thursday. Thursday was the day of the spirits.

The rest of us shared my bottle of ibuprofen. What was a pain-killer against malaria, against pneumonia? A placebo. A kind of helplessness returned to me, an acute sense of inefficacy before the suffering of others. I recognized it from years of tramping through the Old World, through wars. But it really was an expression of my own self-pity, my vanity, because no one in the camp was looking to me for help.

In fact, Isiaka declared that all of us were sick because there was not enough milk. He, too, was not feeling well. He sniffled and refused to eat. He was a stick figure under his absurd bright green boubou, an unreal modern blot in this oldest setting, skin taut over bones, and he ranted in his squawking voice.

"Milk and yogurt and butter—if you have it every day you'll never get sick! Rice constipates you. That's why I'm not getting better, because of the rice. If you look at a boy who drinks milk and a boy who eats rice, you'll see the difference. The boy who drinks milk is much healthier."

One of Isiaka's teenage daughters rolled her eyes. She'd had enough of his rants. She'd had enough of the bush.

"Tell me," she asked Pygmée, "is there a good job for me in Djenné?"

"Your job is to stay here and feed the old man tasty rice," Pygmée said.

But Isiaka fluttered his skinny arms. "I don't care for her rice! I don't like rice! I just want milk! But there isn't enough! Because this is not milk season."

It was al Butayn, the Little Belly, Delta Arietis. An evolved giant star in the constellation of Aries, one hundred and seventy light-years from Earth, twice our sun's mass, ten times its radius, forty-five times more luminous. It proclaimed the beginning of the hot season, the hardest time of the year. The hot season, the Fulani said, lasted two months. That year, it would last three.

"The beginning of the waiting for rain," Moussa Bâ the oracle had explained to me in Kouakourou. The sun shone hotter, brighter, longer, and at night mosquitoes filled the ears with their thin song. The swales around the Diakayaté camp held shallow membranes of tepid water or no water at all. Day temperatures hovered around a hundred and twenty degrees Fahrenheit in the shade, but where was the shade? Even the clouds that now gathered in corners of the sky each day seemed to cast none. The Diakayatés spent more and more time in the heated crepuscule of their huts, coughing at the dust that sieved from the thatch. Acacia trees had begun to shed their feathery pinnations. Each time glossy starlings lifted off their spiny perches the leaves would petal down into Fanta's cooking, upon the cattle that grew thinner behind the calf rope, upon the straw mat where I was nursing my malady.

Last year's harvest was almost gone, and in markets and villages grain was expensive. From the country's north and south trickled stories of families broken, displaced by war and hunger, starving in refugee camps and in overcrowded homes of relatives. When they heard such stories the nomads would change the subject. Hunger was merely a state of living. When you didn't have enough to feed your children you farmed them out to someone who did. Pygmée, for example, was raising his own four children and two nephews and a niece whose parents could not afford to provide for them. Besides, it was just a matter of months before there would be enough milk again.

The Sahelian moonscape was hammered out of cycles—

nanorhythms of breath drawn and released, circadian processions of darkness and light, weeks of killer heat and absolutions of rain, droughts and famines alternating with years of plenty. The Earth turned, inexorable, impassive. Agama lizards went on clicking and ribboning the world into Möbius strips of their courtship circuits millions of springs old, and the first mangoes ripened in the groves south of the bourgou.

"Anna Bâ!" said Oumarou. "In your France in America is it also very hot and dry?"

It had been snowing when I had boarded the plane in New York. But Fulfulde had no word for snow. *"Galaas,"* I said: ice, a loanword from the French. I said that in the place where I was born there were entire months that were so cold that ice fell from the sky instead of rain, every day, and stayed on the ground for weeks at a time, sometimes knee-deep.

For once I had told a story the Diakayatés' anthology of the world could not accommodate. Everybody laughed. Impossible! Then I worked it out: my hosts were picturing the only ice they knew, the scarlet and orange frozen slushies of hibiscus and ginger and baobab juice they sometimes bought in the Monday market in Djenné. Paisley fields of sweet and sticky fuchsia and daffodil and pale yellow. Savannah glacé. And I laughed with them.

A vermilion sunrise on a Monday. A wide sky unspooled in puffy lace of cirri, and in the foreground a small yellow weaver lifted off a thorn tree branch and the branch sprang back up, bounced, halted. In Djenné at dawn all woke and began instantly to move, mate, go, do in an uproar of movement and sound: donkeys brayed, rock pigeons with their redrimmed eyes mounted one other, roosters clucked and crowed, women called out to neighbors over banco walls, talib boys begged door-to-door, motorcycles revved and belched black ash, pancake vendors lit fires under honeycomb griddles, children ran up alleys to borrow and deliver fire, matches, salt. In the bush, every sound, every thing, stood out in precious starkness because for everything there was space enough. When a flock of turtledoves rose from the fallow millet fields on blue wing, each individual wingstrike sounded.

The litany of morning greetings. A silent Lipton ceremony with last night's milk. Distant rattle of early market-bound carts. Smears of red dust on the horizon where cattle slogged back from nightherd. Fanta was preparing to visit her younger sister, whose daughter had died of malaria the day before. Sad news traveled fast in the bush. The girl had been fifteen, the same age as Hairatou. Three days earlier Fanta had walked all day to pay condolences to a niece who had just lost a two-year-old son. He had been coughing and he had been very hot to the touch, and then he died.

His death, too, pealed through the bush.

"May God protect us all," said Fanta, because that was what you said at times of death.

"Sometimes children die," said Oumarou, who knew.

Children in Mali died more often than those in any other part of the world. At night Djenné's chief pediatrician rode his motorcycle to a riverside bar, where there were Ivorian hookers and Malian beer and groves of eucalyptus to block out the heartbreak and helplessness of his days. Healthcare experts cited malnutrition and communicable disease as the two main causes of child mortality. The Fulani also named two causes. One was disease. The other was the witchery of an owl. Fanta said it was an owl that had killed her grandnephew.

The owl lives at the cemetery. At night it leaves its roost and picks up clawfuls of dust from the graves. If you are an adult and you sleep outdoors during the months when it is cool enough for people to pray inside the Djenné mosque, the owl will sprinkle you with cemetery dust and you will become very sick.

The owl flies over villages and nomad camps, listening, listening. If it hears a child cry in the night, it gives that child malaria or pneumonia. Such children almost always die and then the owl takes their souls.

An illness inflicted by an owl is "perceived to be untreatable, particularly with modern medicines," wrote the anthropologist Sarah E. Castle, who studied child mortality among the Fulani in Mali. But no one can tell whether a sick child has fallen prey to an owl until that child dies. Only then does owl sorcery reveal itself, to old men and women and to traditional healers who know such things.

If you eat owl meat, you and your children will be protected from killer owls for the rest of your life. The hitch: such owl protection is more effective if passed down by the mother, not by the father, and women rarely can afford to eat owl meat because the hunters who sell owls at the fetish market charge a lot for it, though slightly less than for a pied crow.

Once in spring I watched the Diakayaté children stone a Pel's fishing owlet. It was only slightly larger than my hand. Led by young Amadou the children took turns throwing at it lumps of shit, dirt, straw. The bird panted. Yellow riverine eyes blinked asymmetrically. It fluffed its flightless wings, then hopped away, rotating its head all the while toward its molesters, stunned by their cruelty. It dragged a crippled rufous left wing away from the camp, toward the green grass of the withering fen. Adults and teenagers watched from the shade of a thorn tree. At last Amadou daringly stepped forward, grabbed it by the wings, carried it a few steps, slammed it against the goopy ground. Soon it was dead.

After Fanta left on her condolence call I hiked to Djenné. Monsieur Koulibaly was waiting for me at Sory Ibrahim Thiocary School. On Mondays all Djenné schools were closed, to give the students an opportunity to earn some coins in the weekly market, and we could hold our lesson undisturbed. We sat beside a plywood desk in a deserted classroom, out of the sun, and practiced simple dialogue.

"Are you healthy?"

"*Al ham du lillah*, I am healthy."

"Your daughter was sick yesterday. Is she healthy?"

"She is very healthy now, *al ham du lillah* . . . Excuse me,

Monsieur Koulibaly, how do you say in Fulfulde 'She is not very healthy'?"

"You don't. If you say 'She is not very healthy' or 'She is still sick,' it means 'She is on her deathbed, she is dying, she will not recover.' Even if that's the truth you cannot not say it. It means you have given up hope."

Giving up hope was an infraction against the omnipotence of God.

I looked out the glassless window into the vast school courtyard. Empty. I thought of the schoolchildren who were very healthy now, *al ham du lillah*, and then they were gone. I thought of the children I had seen that afternoon in the market on my way to the school. A preteen boy who tripped and fell in the dirt road choked with motorcycles and draught horses and donkey carts and bicycles and pushcarts, and lay there eerily motionless until a tall young woman

passing by in silver heels and a glittering and richly embroidered long dress bent down and grabbed him by the forearm and yanked him up and steadied him somewhat vertically and kept going, leaving the boy to fumble in the dust with his feet for his blue rubber flipflops.

"Fulfulde," Oumarou told me once, "is the hardest language, because it has so many nuances and meanings."

In the afternoon I joined the Diakayaté men on the mound of unclaimed skeletons at Djenné's north gate and we hired five spots in a horsecart back to camp. The two Sitas sat up front, next to the driver, legs dangling off the cart, talking incessantly. I sat on my backpack behind the driver, my back against a sideboard. Across from me a teenage Bozo girl with Down syndrome clutched a pink plastic doll with fuchsia hair. The girl's face and neck were very dirty and her teeth were very white and straight. Our toes touched. To my right a young woman in a fish-print dress, the teenager's mother or sister, gripped with her thighs a naked toddler girl who wore strings of blue and white beads around her neck, wrists, and waist. Gris-gris against the evil eye, genii, sickness, poverty, life. In the back of the cart an older woman, probably the toddler's grandmother. Next to her, perched on a sideboard, Boucary and Ousman. Ousman held by a leash a gray nanny goat. From time to time the teenage girl sank her fingers painfully into the goat's side and twisted. Ousman pretended not to notice. The horsecart jolted and shook. Sita Dangéré's bony left buttock drilled into my left foot, the driver's leather whip stroked my arm and neck on each backlash, and the hot metalwork on the cart's sideboard sawed into my back. The naked toddler sang a wordless ballad of bumpy roads. In the sweet yellow haze of sunset, cattle in the swales moved like water. Somewhere Fanta was walking back to camp from her mourning duty in torn flipflops until at last she took them off and balanced them on her head and walked the rest of the way on the treebark soles of her bare feet.

Before midnight I woke and couldn't sleep again for a long time. My chest shrank with anger and grief and unresolved longing—for all the dead, for my lost lover, for the simpleminded village girl in the horsecart. I lay under the insatiable African stars frustrated with myself. I had been expecting from the magnanimous vastness of the Sahel some pronounced and palpable deliverance, heartfill, even an epiphany, but all I got were stronger legs, skin sore from the sun, and thicker foot calluses. I was no wiser, no less vulnerable, no less heartbroken.

In 1973, Peter Matthiessen traveled through the remote mountains of Nepal on a quest for something ineffable—a rare animal, closure after the death of his wife, mysticism, serenity, self-forgiveness. In the book about his journey, *The Snow Leopard*, he called it "a true pilgrimage, a journey of the heart." But if the heart cracked open at each encounter with pain or beauty, then what?

In the early days of our ill-starred courtship my beloved had given me a beautiful brass pocket compass. He'd had the lid engraved with *"Solvitur ambulando,"* the Diogenes aphorism that promised walking as a cure-all: a lodestar, or an unintended portent of the separation to come. Now I thought: Diogenes was wrong. The walking didn't stanch the bleeding, did not alleviate the hurt. You could not really hike away from sorrow, nor did callus grow over love.

Around me Oumarou's cows rose colossal against the far sky. Night magnified each sound and thought. A brocklefaced cow ambled up and exhaled in my face and licked the ground around me and I drifted off thinking that I might never again be able to fall asleep any other way.

The next morning before dawn a white goat came to stand on my knees, the better to reach an acacia branch under which I was spending the night. It was a young goat; only one of its horns had come in. A unicorn, I thought, not quite awake. A good omen.

On the Bani right after sunset brown frogs pecked insects out of the heat. At that hour the tranquil river was the same color as the sky, the color of pearl. Freshwater oysters shone dully on the strip of green riverside grass. The water exhaled a metallic tang and fishermen poled their pirogues across time.

A large Bozo man pulled his boat ashore next to me. The pirogue cut into the grassy bank with the soft sound of skin caressing skin. In the bottom by the bow lay a small heap of silver fish, toothless garras that liked to nibble the bare ankles of laundresses. Western foot spas used them for pedicures. The man caught me looking at them. "A small catch for a small net," he explained. He said his name was Mohammad Kayantau. He did not ask mine. He wiped his palms on the seat of his canvas pants then on his mudcolored t-shirt and shook my hand and stepped on the grass.

For a time we didn't speak. He sat down crosslegged next to me and prepared to roll a cigarette with a piece of graph paper. I shook a Gauloise out of a pack and held out the pack and he nodded, took one cigarette, crumbled some tobacco out of it into his paper, added a pinch of dried marijuana leaves from a narrow plastic vial, and handed the half-gutted cigarette back to me. He rolled his joint, lit it with a match, tossed the match into the river, exhaled. We listened to the hiccupping loops of cicada symphonies. Then he spread a plastic gunnysack on the grass and emptied onto it a small cloth pouch of cowrie shells and read to me my fortune.

He said I had a good heart. Said I had traveled for work. Said I should stay out of cities and sleep in the open. Said to sacrifice one white bird. Said to give someone I liked ten kola nuts.

"You can give them to anyone, even me," he said. "I will be very happy if you give them to me."

Mohammad Kayantau finished his joint, collected his cowries, picked up the gunnysack, and stood up.

"Who is the genie that advises you?" I asked.

He shook his head.

"Not a genie. Genii are bad. I listen to the wakula."

Then he left. Bats came to blot out the Milky Way. Night in the bourgou.

The world is divided into the above and the below. Below lie the anabranched rivers, the swales and the floodlands, the lakes and the blind creeks. Above are the dry bush, the dunes, the highlands where the Diakayatés take their cattle on rainy-season pasturage. Genii live above and below; they both control the flood and the rain and the drought and are controlled by them. They meddle with time. They enter humans at whim and turn them into healers or madmen. Sometimes they kill humans altogether.

Wakula are lesser creatures in the genie world. They have magical powers, good and bad, but they control only the mundane—objects, material wealth. They are sprites, about the size of a four-year-old child, and they talk gibberish in high-pitched voices. They are invisible to most humans, but there is a marabout in Djenné who can summon a wakula named Samirou with some alcohol and snuff.

Wakula are untrustworthy tricksters, fond of mischief. When you fight a wakula for the first time he will let you beat him easily. He will do so to trick you into fighting him again. When you fight him a second time he will say: "Wait, wait, I'm not ready yet!" That is a trap. If you wait till he is ready he will kill you. If you fight him right then without waiting you will pin him to the ground after some struggle and he will say: "I will give you whatever you want." You then have to wait for him to grant your wish while you are still holding him down, because if he gets up he will break his promise. After you receive what you've asked for, you have to test whether it is good or not without releasing him. Only then, if you are satisfied, can you let a wakula go.

Wakula wear funny pointed hats. If you get a hat of a wakula your life will become very easy. But it is very hard to get one, harder even than pinning a wakula to the ground, harder than catching a pied crow alive.

In 1986, Jean-Marie Gibbal, a French anthropologist and poet who studied magic rites in the Sahel, set out down the Niger River to witness and record the summoning of genii by genie priests called *gaw*. During one ceremony, Gibbal felt "overtaken by waves, vibrations, and shaking that had me participating physically in a rite whose meaning partially escaped me . . . I had the feeling of a strange presence." He suspected the *gaw* had tried to test him, perhaps even draw him into a trance, and likened his experience to the "assault by magic or sorcery" upon his American colleague Paul Stoller, who, as a young anthropologist, became a sorcerer's apprentice in Niger.

"I am well aware that I can produce no tangible evidence of this," Gibbal recalled in *Genii of the River Niger*. "I sometimes seem to tip over into a different reality."

Gibbal did not enter a trance during that possession ceremony. But the slim lyrical gem of a book he wrote after his journey is full of the quiet wisdom of a wanderer at ease with traveling on the brim of things:

"Void is added to void; we only pass, incapable of retaining anything of our passing. These moments of abandon—are they not the finest? And then to let oneself be overtaken, drunk with useless movement."

All night the wind blew from the north and shook down stars. The goats woke at cock's crow, at the chromatic calls to prayer that gusted first from Weraka, then, louder, closer, from Doundéré. The bush smelled of old firesmoke, sour milk, manure, sweat. The smells of ten thousand years ago. I washed my face with tepid water from the tomato paste can.

Oumarou greeted me from the dark. "Anna Bâ?" The sleepy salaams, the goodwill of forward-turned palms. We sat on our mats and quietly watched morning fill the Sahel.

Fanta came out of the hut and prayed and moaned the lament of all aging women with bird-hollowed bones—"my knees, my joints"—and walked in small barefoot circles tidying up her camp. A slow morning ballet. She picked up a rag with the toes of her right foot, bent her right knee, reached with her hand behind her back for the rag without looking, shook it out, deposited it onto the roof of her hut. Another rag. A cooking stick. A box of wooden matches. Never stooping. She picked up a ripped black plastic bag and tossed it to the wind and it blew east toward a marsh. Then she swept. Then she collected all the flipflops and plastic shoes mismatched in last night's after-dinner dark and paired them and stood them in a row at the entrance to the hut. Pedestrian monuments to human presence. Next to the hearth a white newborn calf with brown ears, a female, unsteady on its day-old legs, took in its first morning.

A blue mound outside Ousman's hut shifted and rose and became Ousman. He stumbled to the fen, squatted to piss, washed, prayed, stretched, walked over. Shivering and clutching around his skinny shoulders a polyester blanket with scarlet tulips on a yellow and blue field.

"Papa? Was your night peaceful? Mother? Anna Bâ?" He found

a pair of plastic shoes in Fanta's row that fit him and bent to put them on. In the east the sky turned red, then livid-yellow with cloudy sunrise. It was time to bring the cows back from nightherd.

Ousman walked fast through a land cupped in sifted golden light, a land doubly illuminated: from without, by a sun made soft by flaky cirrus clouds, and from within, by yellow trampled straw. Fifteen minutes west of the camp he spotted the contour of his father's cattle in a fallow millet field, a swelling bunting that rose out of the ground in overlapping layers of powdered clay and legs and bodies and projected skyward in the curved tapers of horns. The herd was still moving slowly west, away from camp. He kept his pace and approached until he could tell each animal by the coloration and pattern of its hide, and he hooked around the herd to the south so he could see every cow at once in the early light and there he came to an abrupt stop. He took them in. Fewer than fifty head, ten in milk. He appraised their stomachs with his eyes. The rumens big but not full. They could stand another hour or two at pasture. He strode ahead of the cattle and when the distance between him and the front of the herd measured a hundred or so paces he stopped short again and sat down on dry turf in one downward motion like a marionette collapsing. He watched the animals drag heavily toward him. When they passed he could hear them crop sparse shoots of sharp couch-grass, breathe against the dry clay, against the minced straw. After the last heifer, a yellow, had caught up with the rest he stood up in the same easy marionette flow and overtook the cows again. He knew their destination: a lotus marsh a mile or so farther west that still held two feet of water and some hippo grass rhizomes. He walked briskly, leaving the cows far behind. The banks of the marsh were green. In the hummocked sod there were drops of dew yet unburned by the dry sun of April and in that cool damp Ousman sat down again and leaned back on his elbows and after a few beats lay down on his back completely and closed his dreamy eyes and drew a corner of the tulip blanket over his face. He waited for the cows. He slept.

Did the cows know this route from men, or did the Diakayatés learn it from the animals? For as long as Oumarou could remember— seven decades of transhumance—his father's cattle always grazed in the same place during the dry season. Herding cows during the dry months never had been a matter of taking them to pasture. Rather, it was a matter of trying not to tamper with the course they had inherited from all the cows that had walked here before.

That fall, during the Diakayatés' slowpaced return from rainy season pasturage, Ousman's little brother Hassan would doze off on nightherd at a campsite by the Bani River and the cows would run off at a trot toward Doundéré, a day's walk away. The boy would spend the morning looking for them, and ultimately would find them a quarter of the way to the bourgou, in cattle pens of thorn-brush and daub beside a village of rimaibe millet farmers. The villagers, alarmed for their unharvested grain, would demand a five-dollar ransom for the animals' release, and Hassan would have to trudge two hours back to his father's camp, report to him the price, return with the money, and drive the herd back again.

"When my father sees me he will beat me," the boy lamented along the way.

But Oumarou said only: "It's the cows. They knew the rainy season was over and they were impatient. They were craving some sweetgrass."

A Fulani anthropologist in Bamako told me: "Old cows know the way. When an old cow wakes up she starts going where she knows." His name was Abdoul Aziz Diallo and he ran, from a small office on the second floor of an apartment building, a pan-African association that worked to preserve Fulani culture and heritage. Most of what he said sounded like proverbs. Then again, a lot of things people said in the Sahel sounded that way. Precise, workmanlike tags, born of living in a frugal and unforgiving landscape.

"The Fulani are losing old knowledge. Before they would get sick a lot, they'd die a lot. At night they used to only drink milk. No tea or food. No tobacco. There were many different wild animals in the bush that would attack humans and there were no flashlights. Life was harder. Today there are roads, villages, telephones, cars, motorcycles. Now they are learning in schools. But they are forgetting the traditional ways!"

So lamented my godfather Babourou Koïta from his perch in Djenné's market square. Babourou and Ali the Griot and three or four other Fulani elders from the town sat swapping newspapers that had arrived by bus from Bamako the night before. *Maliba Info, Le Zénith-Balé, Info-Matin, La N'velle Patrie*. They smoked one another's cigarettes and shook their heads and swore at the news. The provisional government in Bamako insisted on a presidential election in the summer. Chad deployed troops to northern Mali.

Secessionist Tuareg factions in the north celebrated the anniversary of their unrecognized independence; festivities included camel races. A thousand French troops were searching for terrorists outside Gao, where almost five hundred years earlier Songhai forces had lost a battle and an empire to Moroccan mercenaries. Suicide bombings, corruption, refugees. New knowledge. New dispensations.

Babourou went on.

"In the past a Fulani would sell a cow and buy a horse. Now a Fulani sells a cow to buy a motorcycle. Some boys sell their cows and come to the city and eat meat and sleep with women and they lose their cows and they leave the bush for good. In the past people didn't know about months or hours of the day, and now they do. But they are losing their knowledge of stars.

"For example"—he pointed—"look at this one!" An old man in a white boubou had dismounted a Toyota motorcycle and was shaking hands around. "This one here"—Babourou grabbed the man by the wrist—"he is my cousin. He is a Fulani but he sold his cows to marry a second woman and buy a television. He is a very stupid man!"

Ali the Griot perked up.

"He has nothing now, just his penis."

The man snorted at such clumsy *sanankuya* jokes and bent down and pulled a cigarette out of Babourou's chest pocket and turned to Ali for a light. He exhaled the smoke through his nose and said: "Babourou! You're not a man because you only have one wife." The prescribed exchange of vulgarities was thus complete and the men went back to their newspapers.

Babourou himself didn't know much about stars. His ancestor, the *diawando* Diabourou Koïta, was one of the seven Fulani nobles Sekou Amadou had requested to remain in Djenné as part of the Massina Empire's new ruling class two hundred years earlier. That *diawando*'s descendants stayed put also. Babourou did not herd cattle and he lived year-round in a clean banco house that had electricity whenever the town generator was running. He wore a watch and on a wall in his house he displayed a Gregorian flip calendar that had photographs of cows in it, a different kind of cow for each month. He rode a motorcycle and read newspapers and books when he could lay his hands on them and he sent his children to school. Someone else took his massive interbreds to pasture each morning and brought them back to town at night. He did not trust the bush with his cows. They were not many, but they were much more expensive than the zebu and the amount of milk they gave was astounding. Once a year he hired merchants to take some of them to Côte d'Ivoire to sell or trade. He took me to see them one time, in a small corral at the end of a labyrinth of adobe alleys in east Djenné. He walked among them and touched each one on the flank with reverence. "Métises," he whispered, awed. "Ten liters of milk per cow!"

The venerable opinion of the educated men in town notwithstanding, the Fulani in the bush saw no threat to their expertise or lifestyle at all. Millennia on the hoof had taught them to absorb whatever was of use at any juncture—slaves, plastic tarpaulins, flashlights, motorcycles—and to cast aside whatever was not, to combine the old knowledge and the new in an optimally advantageous fashion. Their communion with their cattle remained unchanged.

The first thing a Fulani cowboy learned was the itinerary: where the cattle went to pasture and to water. He learned to identify the hoofprint of his cattle. He learned to tell from the depth of the hoofprint in the mud by the side of a swale whether the animal was running or walking. On dry land he learned to interpret the movement of small rocks, to infer the cow's pace from how far the animal had flung stones from its path. He learned to tell whether the cows were thirsty by the height of the veil of dust in their wake. He learned to tell apart the drool of a cow that was near labor and the drool of a cow that was sick. He learned the difference between trees, and which fruit were edible for humans and for animals and which leaves could stanch the bleeding if a cow got hurt and which could cause or ease bloating. He learned the different names for the hippo grass, which was the most delicious, and the nutsedge, which was an anti-inflammatory and helped contain diarrhea, and the thatching grass, which animals rarely ate, and the short hot-season couchgrass and the translucent grasses that grew on the granite cliffs of the rainy-season grazing land near the border with Burkina Faso, and the pale delicate lovegrass that appeared on some pastures at the onset of rain.

He learned the ancestral complexities of the relationship between farmers and herders, the reciprocal animosity and the mutual respect. He also learned where the sweetest grass grew, even if it happened to be on a farmer's land.

He learned the different ways to talk to the cows. *"Ay!"* meant the cowboy was calling them to come close to him. *"Shht!"* meant he wanted them to stay close together. *"Ay, shht, oy, trrrrrr, uh!"*

meant he was taking them out to pasture, and *"jet jet jet!"* or *"jot jot jot!"* meant he was taking them on a long journey, on a stretch of seasonal transhumance. He learned by being with cattle, by watching his father and brothers and cousins, by listening to their fireside talk.

He knew all this by the time he had turned seven. All Oumarou's sons had grown up with such knowledge, and when their own sons were old enough they would carry it with them on the old paths of countless herders.

As for stars, it was simply impossible for Fulani cowboys not to know them—maybe not all, but some. They had to. Without such knowledge, Oumarou explained, they wouldn't know to avert their eyes on the night the Pleiades first sprayed into the eastern sky. Only three creatures could look at the Pleiades on the first night of the constellation's heliacal rising without harming themselves: a black horse, a strong cow, and a black addax. But if a man saw the constellation on that night, he would die.

The sun was high by the time Ousman drove the herd to camp. The Sahel bent in the heat. Within six weeks farmers would get ready to plant and pasturage would become limited and the Diakayatés would have to buy cottonseed in the market to keep the cattle fed, one fifty-kilo bag each week. Already some land around Doundéré had been turned and farmers had burnt footwide strips of straw along the perimeter to discourage cows from ambling into the fields to graze.

Ousman passed a Bozo woman from Dakabalal who was pulling behind her a turquoise plastic basin on a rope like a sled. She bent down now and then to pick up dry manure and drop it into the basin. Beside a lonely thorn tree across the fen from the camp, two of Afo Bocoum's calves lay on the ground in quarantine. One, a black calf, made to rise but stumbled, and Ousman steadied it with both his arms. The calf shook gently. Small flies buzzed about. "Malaria," the man said. "That one, too." He clicked his tongue. Afo had entrusted the calves into his father's care and now Ousman would have to walk to Djenné and trade a goat for the injections he himself would administer.

But that would turn out to be unnecessary. By noon both calves would be dead, and pied crows and black kites would feast in the shade of the thorn tree.

The cows arrived at the camp lowing in waves, like ocean swells rolling ashore. The cow that had calved the day before came up to the thorn tree and stood over her calf and licked and licked it.

Oumarou walked among the herd. Making sure the animals had had enough food. Making sure they had been properly watered. Making sure none got lost or mixed with someone else's cattle. Young people could bring cows back, he grumbled, but they didn't always know their father's cattle from someone else's. Ousman bore the insult in silence. He knew that in just a few hours he would be eating beef, and that exhilarating prospect made it difficult to focus on any parental offense for a meaningful length of time.

◇ ◇ ◇

A Fulani nomad would slaughter a cow under two rare circumstances: when the cow was deathly ill or when a boy in his family was getting married. The day before, the tenth of April, marked the first day of the Fulani wedding season, and at nightfall a wedding party had screamed up the road past Doundéré: four carts, music blaring, men yelling, horses at a reckless and random-footed gallop. Most weddings in the world share the same ecstasy of promise, if not for the betrothed then at least for the guests. At the sound of the procession, Isiaka's son Yaya—twenty-three years old, heavy silver and agate rings on almost every finger, a purple plastic comb in his afro, a long sheathed sword in a scabbard of etched leather across his back, and dangling on leather lanyards from his neck a cellphone, a remote key for a motorcycle he didn't own, a lighter for the cigarettes he didn't smoke, a small mirror, and a medicinal pouch for gris-gris—danced through the camp yelling: "Wedding tomorrow, meat tomorrow, dances tomorrow, it will be crazy good! Tomorrow-tomorrow-tomorrow is the day of the young! Tomorrow will be awesome!" The next day, Sita Dangéré's son Allaye was scheduled to celebrate his wedding to his cousin. The couple had married the previous summer but had had to postpone the nuptial feast because by then most of their relatives already had begun their rainy-season transhumance.

Allaye was twenty-four, broad-shouldered and short like his father. His bride was a leggy girl a head taller than him and seven or eight years his junior, with a ready smile and large breasts and a runway walk. She had arrived at the camp a week earlier.

"Fanta, what's the girl's name?" I asked, forgetting that Fanta was the bride's grandmother and the rules of *sanankuya* applied.

"Pain-in-the-Ass," said Fanta.

And Oumarou said:

"Her name is Kajita, and"—here he raised his voice—"if Allaye doesn't bring me the hump of the bull they kill for their wedding feast I will marry her myself."

The bull slaughtered for a wedding feast had to be healthy and fat, to demonstrate to the guests that the family of the groom blessed the union openheartedly. The slaughter had to be performed by a marabout or a respected butcher. One hind leg and a kidney had to go to the mother of the bride, to compensate her for the loss of a cook, a fetcher of water, a collector of firewood, a seller of milk. Another leg, a kidney, the liver, the lungs, and the heart were to be cut into chunks and mixed and taken to the relatives on both sides of the family, men and women, to ensure a strong union in marriage. The hump went to the eldest male relative of the groom. The ribs and two remaining legs were to be grilled and eaten by the groom's male peers and their older brothers. The head and the hooves were to be handed over to the women at the camp, who would cook them for dinner by narrow moonlight. The young boys of the camp had to steal some meat from their older brothers, who had to fight them off with broadswords and staffs, allowing, however, for enough meat to end up in the youngsters' bellies. Such were the ancient edicts of a Fulani wedding. The Diakayatés observed them as best they could.

On the morning of the feast Allaye and Yaya and other young men their age cut a tawny yearling out of Sita Dangéré's herd and led it to the slaughter. Sita and his sons had agreed the night before to sacrifice this specific bull, though the young men made a show of picking it and seeking the formal approval of Boucary, who, as Allaye's older brother, represented his elders. Boucary nodded a self-important assent and the boys walked the bull a few hundred yards north of the camp to spare the women the trauma of watching the slaughter and stopped at a dip in the land around a fen's bend. Cattle egrets tiptoed in water filmy and bubbly with frog eggs. Black kites stood motionless and low in the sky in anticipation of a feast, and farther north four Dakabalal donkeys bent into their reflections and drank. Pied crows stood on the donkeys' backs and surveyed the land, Napoleonic. The boys crowded around the bull and waited for someone to come and slaughter it.

By midday no marabout or butcher had shown up. Perhaps they had forgotten the invitation. Or found the place too far to reach, or the customary pay—the neck, maybe some organ meat—too insignificant. The boys in the groom's wedding party, nauseated and agog with anticipation of meat, laid the bull gently on its left side and prepared to kill and dress it themselves. But who would do the killing? For any of them to slit the bull's throat would have signified his subservience to the rest of his age set. At last the set's leader stepped forward. His name was Adama and he was a striking twenty-year-old who during the dry season pastured his animals near Somena. His impeccable complexion and clean boubou and new leather hat bespoke a particular wealth in milk and cattle. Not even the slavish act of slaughtering a bull for someone else's wedding could diminish Adama's standing among his peers.

Blood pulsed from the animal's neck and its legs sprinted along the wilting grass, miming one last feeble run through the bourgou. When it quit moving, the rest of the men pounced to skin and dress it with their dull short swords—

"Hey, you dumbass, don't take the meat with the hide!"

"Cut here!"

"Pull harder!"

"Why don't *you* do it if you're so smart?"

"Stand the other way!"

—and when they loosed the organs, the bull's heart was still beating and the men hushed when they saw it.

And hushed again when they got to the testes.

"*Wallahi!* So tiny?"

The wedding guests were all young men. Three boys in their late teens arrived on foot from Somena, wearing identical knee-high soccer socks in black and white stripe and identical Elvis Presley sunglasses with giant white plastic frames. One of them carried a cassette deck on a rope halter around his neck. More came by motorcycle. A few came from Senossa and some from the outskirts of Djenné. They juggled their staffs and their swords and smoked one another's Liberté Blondes cigarettes and put them out in the fen and drank its rancid water. Several boomboxes were blasting at once and some men also played music on their cellphones: go on, go on, go on, go on, go on! They were dressed in their usual billowing nomad blues though some wore jerseys that said LIVERPOOL and BARACK OBAMA—YES WE CAN! and MICHAEL JACKSON and ETIHAD AIR-

WAYS and they inquired about the roads their friends had journeyed and about their families and animals and they constructed a grill out of some dry mud and sticks. They shared the earthy pink lobes of a kola nut, and hawked bitter orange spittle with numbed gums, relishing the nut's sweet aftertaste in the back of the throat, its mild high. Kites swooped down from the sky for bits of rumen. Higher still, an invisible French bomber went to war.

By midafternoon most of the meat was cooked medium rare and the young men loaded it onto a tarp and carried it away from the grill and divided it among themselves. They added no spice or salt and the meat was cooked unevenly. It was the first beef most had tasted in months, even a year. Boucary in his extravagant blanket-hat was wielding a whole femur and was taking bites out of its pink flesh. He had severed the bull's tail from the hide and wrested off its hairy skin, which he spent much of the afternoon stretching onto the wooden handle of his sword. Someone's younger brother darted to the tarp and made off with two ribs and carried them to the grill, where a dancing and ecstatic crowd of teenage boys clubbed one another with bones and slapped one another with bloody offal. Hassan, Oumarou's youngest son, usually taciturn and serious, whooped the loudest.

After they had finished their portion of the meat the party guests retreated in waves to drink cool *chobbal* of pounded millet and sour milk and hot pepper and well water in Boucary's hut. A toddler came by in bright oversize plastic sandals that squeaked with each step. They had been made for larger, industrialized toddlers, presumably to encourage them to walk. In the bush, they could fit a seven-year-old. A seven-year-old in the bush would be herding cattle on his own.

A man walked in carrying on his hip a naked baby boy, a son or brother or nephew. He sat down and lit a cigarette and with the index finger of his free hand gently and absentmindedly flipped the baby's penis until it was tumescent. The erection put the baby immediately to sleep. The men laughed. It was very hot in the hut. The baby snored lightly, clutching in his sweaty baby hand a piece of gummed red meat.

Young Mentou perched on a waterjug by the door to study the men in silence. A blue plastic pitcher sat upside down on the cracked plastic plate that covered the jug.

Yaya said: "Give me some water, or else I won't marry you."

Mentou turned and reached for the pitcher and lifted the plate. Then she thought about it, pouted, let go of the plate, put the pitcher back, and left the hut without a word.

Allaye the groom could not attend his own wedding party. After his friends and brothers had chosen the sacrificial bull, he took the rest of his father's cattle to pasture. He would eat his portion of the ribs and offal with his dinner. Kajita, his bride, was hiding from the sun in Oumarou and Fanta's hut. She sat on the edge of the couple's pallet of wrist-thick beams draped with six layers of reed and thatch mats and gossiped with Hairatou in giggly whispers and ate her wedding beef and laughed from the taste of it on her tongue. The vaulted entryway framed, in middle distance, a murder of pied crows picking apart the carcass of Afo's dead calf.

The guests left in late afternoon. They had to round up and milk their herds. The music and the dancing ceased and the family circulated through the camp slow and satiated. Oumarou had eaten his hump alone in the privacy of his hut and now he reclined on a gunnysack his family used as a mat, a prayer rug, and dry manure storage and dispensed truisms his family knew by heart. "Three things make a person have good blood: milk, honey, and the meat of a fat cow that has never had malaria." "A real Fulani doesn't weigh more than fifty kilos." "The best oil is butter. After that, fish oil. After that, peanut oil. Then shea butter." He would eat beef twice more this year, and neither occasion would be joyful.

Darkness came and the Big Dipper hung from a thorn tree, empty and dry. Cows stood to shit, then lay down again. In the morning a waxing crescent would mimic their stately horns. One cow rose again and stood guard to the camp. The Diakayatés were drinking evening tea. The conversation turned to weddings.

It cost sixty dollars to marry a woman from the border with Burkina Faso but three times as much to marry a woman from the bourgou. Those amounts did not include the two or three years of engagement during which the groom's father had to buy his son's future bride presents for Eid al Fitr and Eid al Adha each year: two or three sets of clothes, shoes, shea butter for her skin, the cost of braiding her hair.

"You spend many years courting a woman, you spend a lot of money," said Oumarou. "That's why bourgou men can be thirty years old and not yet married."

"Marrying a rimaibe woman is cheaper," said Ousman. The bride price for a rimaibe girl was ten dollars. His own wife was from the bourgou, as was Fanta.

Mama moved hot coals about the brazier with her bare fingertips and looked at me. She knew that I, like her, was divorced. I had told her nothing of my heartache.

"Don't worry," she said. "One day you'll meet someone and you'll also marry."

"And you too, Mama."

"We'll all dance at your wedding."

"Thank you. Oumarou, would you slaughter a bull for my wedding?"

"Sure! We'll slaughter Anna Bâ!"

Everyone laughed. You slaughtered a bull when your son got married, not an adopted strange woman.

Marriages in the bourgou were arranged. They followed years of elaborate inquiries by the parents of both the bride and the groom and years of betrothal and were intended to be failproof. Nor did Islam condone dissolution of marriage. Why, then, did some Fulani get divorced? Fanta and Mama laughed some more. Oumarou said:

"People get married but their ideas about life are not the same. So they separate. Sometimes it's the woman who decides to get divorced, sometimes the man."

"But it's always the woman's fault," added Ousman.

"Anna Bâ, Anna Bâ, don't ask them!" Mama tossed her chin, squinted. "They don't know anything. They don't live with people, they live in the bush with the animals." She seemed to speak not only of her stepfather and stepbrother but also of all the cowboys unseen now in the night. "But I'll tell you. All the problems in life are because of men."

Distant flashlights drew sudden arcs in the black, catching batwings, silvering them. Children lay asleep all around and Mentou was cuddled against my knee. She was naked except for a short pagne and her herniated bellybutton pushed into my shin. The protrusion looked somehow indecent. I covered her with my headscarf and rested my hand on her back. Such a skinny girl. A little heart beating inside, warming her, warming me. I felt that we were helping each other breathe.

By the door of Oumarou's hut the newlywed Allaye squatted in the blue light of his cellphone screen. Some young men crowded around him and looked at the screen and moaned quietly and clicked their tongues. There were no women nearby. I thought the men were watching porn. I stood up and shuffled over to take a look. They were looking at photographs of cows, fat cows with enormous udders and tall humps standing in bright shoulder-high grass.

Abdoul Aziz Diallo, the Fulani anthropologist, said:
"An old man told me that in the Sahel the world belongs to three things: the frog, the cow, and the Fulani. When you hear the frogs crying in the river, in less than a week you will also hear the lowing of the cows. When you hear the lowing of the cows you will also hear the laughter of Fulani women. When the frog stops crying, you will stop hearing the lowing of the cows, and the laughter of the women. The Sahel will be silent until the next rainy season."

Frogs had come to the evaporating marshes of the bourgou but the rest of the land was bone-dry and nothing to laugh about. Everything in the bush was hungry and everything survived and nothing complained. In a way the Hoping already had begun. At night the pearly lightning bolt of the Milky Way dripped shooting stars from the sky and charged what was left of the frog-ridden water with its light and from my sleeping mat it looked as though the meteors that fell down simultaneously bubbled up from the marshes. I imagined each egg in the lumpy buildup of frog roe a tiny star.

Homer said that we ride into the future straddling the horse of time backward, our eyes on the past. Oumarou walked into his future on foot, and his eyes were pinned to the sky. He was looking for the West African trade.

The West African trade was a wedge of weather five hundred miles long that pushed northwest out of the equatorial Atlantic Ocean in mid-February and slammed into the coast around Liberia and Côte d'Ivoire at some point in March. By late April an occasional sprinkle usually would bless the Sahel and sizzle in the hot-season dust. The Fulani called such fine rain Mango Rain or Rain of the Trees and the Birds because it did not revive the pasturelands, nor did it herald more immediate precipitation, but it sweetened the mangoes ripening on riverbanks and cajoled some new leaves and allowed passerines to bathe for a few minutes in globules of rainwater. By the second week of June, if all went well, the downpour would begin in earnest, delivering to the bourgou the cooler temperatures, the first smooth lancelike shoots of millet, the migration of the herds. By October, the weakened monsoon would circle back south, completing its annual cycle of rebirth.

The rain's journey was millions of years old. As far as geological time went, its magnitude and its schedule never had remained set for long. Deposits of eolian hematite dust from the Sahara in the Mediterranean Sea and marine sediment core in the Gulf of Guinea and pollen in West African rivers and lakes show fluctuations in the monsoon's patterns over time. Millennial oscillations. Stingy sifts of mist to tease the land and then nothing—for years and years. Or deluges on a biblical scale, recurrent Geneses.

In the early twenty-first century, the bourgou and the world that surrounded it were changing once again, this time through the doings of man. A meteorologist showed me a chart: since the nineteen seventies Mali had become twelve percent drier and nearly two degrees Fahrenheit warmer. "Consequences are enormous!" an environmental engineer in Bamako shouted at me. We had met at a bistro; he was rushed and interrupted our meeting twice to take cellphone calls from his wife. I couldn't tell whether to attribute his terse English pronouncements to his hurry or to the urgency of the subject. "Migrations! Droughts! Deep poverty! For us climate change is not a question of adaptation. It's a question of survival!"

Nomads in the bush never had heard about climate change but they could describe with scientific precision its symptoms. They talked of how in recent years the wind had grown hotter and stronger and laden with more sand from the Sahara. Of how rainfall, never reliable in the first place, had become more fickle. Of droughts, always to be reckoned with, that now whammed the bush in rapidfire succession. Of seasons once attendant to the stars that now mostly ran off-schedule. During the famine of the nineteen eighties the Diakayatés had had to dig wells to water the cattle for the first time, and they'd had to dig wells again two years before we met.

But if the nomads doubted the stars, they did not show it. Nor did they accept a new identity as people who got water for their cattle from wells. Sita Louchéré's wife, Hairatou, the mother of Mentou and Moussa, found the very idea to be a great insult.

"Rain—that's our well!" she said. "If it rains over there tomorrow, we move. If we hear there's food for our cows in Guinea, we go to Guinea. If we hear there's food for our cows in Burkina Faso, we go to Burkina Faso. We rarely spend a night in the same place, so what's a well to us?" But that year she and her husband and children would spend more than seven months in the camp near Doundéré.

An almost unbroken pattern of cumuli lidded the Sahel. The rare sunrays fell on the savannah in angled white beams. Oumarou greeted a succession of gritty yellow dawns outside the hut, hands hugging his knees under his tartan fleece blanket, little Amadou cuddled against his shins naked and with the distended stomach of hot-season malnutrition. Each morning the old cowboy would look to the south. He watched the southern horizon for the portent of the monsoon, and he divined the wind-punished land for a sign of how his animals would fare until the rains fell.

One morning Oumarou said:

"It rained somewhere last night."

"How can you tell?"

"I can tell."

Oumarou saw in the sky a military plane sail north between layers of cloud.

"Haven't the rebels been finished yet?"

"No, there is still fighting in the desert. Now there are Americans helping the French fight the insurgents."

"May God protect us!"

"Amen, amen, amen."

"It had been years since we'd seen a plane and this year they fly over the bourgou almost every day. How big is a plane? Is it as big as a bus? How fast does it go?"

"Some are much bigger. And they are very fast. If you get on a plane in Bamako in the morning you can be on the other side of Mecca by night."

"*La ilaha il Allah!* I've never even been to Bamako. I've never been inside a bus."

"I've been on a bus to visit Drissa in San," said Fanta. "And I've seen a boat from Bamako on the Niger River once. It was really long and it went *ji-ku, ji-ku, ji-ku, ji-ku.* Loud! It had a roof. I would be afraid to step onto that kind of a big boat."

Indeed, boats were very dangerous. A man had told Oumarou once that when a boat entered the sea all people onboard had to prepare to die. He himself believed that people from the bush had no business venturing into the sea. But legends told that in the year 1311, Abu Bakar II, the sultan of Mali who preceded Mansa Moussa—the richest king in the world's history—sailed across the

Atlantic Ocean with a large fleet provisioned with gold and a year's supply of water and food. Some said he arrived in Yucatán two hundred years before Hernán Cortés and was worshipped by the Aztecs as a god.

Oumarou saw a black kite swoop down for one of Sita's chickens and make away with it. He shooed Fanta's chickens into the grass shelter. Not out of care for the birds—he did not eat chicken or chicken eggs, because chickens would eat anything, even human sputum—but out of respect for his wife. Fanta kept them for cash: a good-size chicken would fetch in the market as much as two full calabashes of buttermilk, even more. A different story altogether were guinea eggs with their flinthard shells. Guinea eggs were better for a man's blood than honey or beef, and almost as good as milk. *"Kural doktooro,"* Oumarou called them: an intravenous drip, a shot in the vein, a prescription drug. But Fanta did not keep guinea hens. They were too much trouble. They laid only when it rained or when you sprinkled water on them with a straw besom and they were very loud and tended to wander far from camp.

That afternoon Ousman returned to the camp from Wono, where he had spent the night drinking tea and gossiping with friends.

"Last night where I was staying there was a tiny bit of rain," he said.

And his father said, "See? I knew it."

A week later a massive lightning storm rolled into Bamako from the south, rimmed the capital with darts of electric discharges. Gusts pushed into the city the distinct smell of wet dust and ozone. The storm did not reach the bourgou.

◇ ◇ ◇

Days and weeks progressed in miniature migrations. The morning rounds to greet the Diakayaté relatives. The twice-daily walks to pasture and back. The hikes for water. The walks to sell buttermilk. The walks or cart rides to market.

Mama went to Bamako by oxcart and truck to look for a cure for her migraines. In her stead her younger sister Bomel came for a long visit with Mayrama Skinny Butt, the small and whiny ten-month-old with giant eyes. Ousman sold a goat in Djenné to pay for a vet who arrived one morning by motorcycle and squatted to drink a calabash of fresh milk courteously proffered and vaccinated Oumarou's herd against rinderpest, foot-and-mouth disease, bovine pleuropneumonia, and anthrax. There were other callers. Afo's herder Kiso, a hired hand of such storied skill that other cowboys said he'd have to be buried with the cows when he died, limped by to fix his plastic shoe with the help of Fanta's paring knife and coals heated on a tea brazier. Two young cowboys, one from Somena and another from Senossa, rode through camp on a motorscooter inquiring about the goats they had lost. A distant relative stopped for an afternoon bowl of leftover millet cream on his walk from Kouakourou to a marabout school in San. Within such movement, near and far, passed the month of May.

June delivered low thick blue and brown clouds and clammy cool air and swarms of mosquitoes. It rained to the south, in San and in Ségou and in Bamako. It rained to the north, in Moura and Kouakourou. Strong wind blew moist rumors of the monsoon, and the Diakayatés could feel in the coolness of the breeze rain falling someplace else. The bourgou remained dry. It had not rained there for ten months. Yet hopeful farmers had begun to stake out territory. They hoed neat wrist-deep pits for millet seeds that overwintered in giant straw thimbles and they burned fields to prepare them for rice. At night the pink flares of their fires lit the horizon around the camp; by day uneven patches of soot blistered the yellow savannah. The pasture was dwindling, and the moon grew fuller and rose higher into the sky and then it, too, dwindled once again to naught. The cattle grew thinner each day. There was little milk and Fanta's trips to Weraka became rare. There was no more grass, only the sharp yellow weeds out of which the women wove mats. Cows had eaten the grass shelter in which Fanta had kept grain and chickens.

The Fulani were leaving the bourgou. In horsecarts, in donkey carts. In wagons pulled by cadaverous bulls. On foot. Astride burros saddled and bareback. They carried calabash pyramids and burlap mounds and cylinders of thatch. They carried babies and fowl and kid goats and newborn lambs. Some of these emigrants rumbled north to the Sahara, some west, to where the Niger's sandy banks were less farmed, some east, toward the granite highlands on the border with Burkina Faso they called Hayré: the Stones. They fanned out from their singed promised land in caravans and in tandems and in single trundling equipages. They sent ahead of themselves their sons who drove to transhumance skeletal cattle with deflated humps and empty rumens. They did not know whether there was grass where they were headed, only that there was none where they were coming from. Their wake always was faintly perfumed with sour milk.

This was Hassan's first season to drive cattle all by himself. An ageless coming-of-age rite. The boy was very proud. He had saved up the spending money his father had given him for tea and sweets and used it to pay a marabout for amulets that guaranteed extra protection for the cows and he hung the gris-gris on long woven leather strips from the cows' necks and horns. At the beginning of the third week of June he told Oumarou it was time to move. The cows, he said, wanted to travel.

There still was no news of rain around Ballé, the village on the Bani River near which the family herd would stop on its way to Hayré. Ballé was a full day's walk away from Doundéré. The old man ordered Hassan to wait. He waited. He became restless. He wanted to prove that his acumen with cattle and the gris-gris he had bought were sufficient for him to take the herd on the first leg of migration, to know when it was safe to go. On the fourth Monday of the month after the scant morning milking he took the cattle to grassless pasture and then hazed it east and drove it to the riverside grazing lands outside Ballé without his father's consent. He had seen other men's teenage sons do the same thing. He left behind a single cow in milk because he knew his father would become very sick if he had no milk at all to drink.

Several hours later, a horsecart carrying passengers from Djenné's market paused on the northbound ruts outside Doundéré. A tall Fulani man in a brand-new indigo boubou jumped off and strode toward the Diakayatés' campsite. Lean and lightfooted, he carried a small black faux-leather shoulder bag. It was Oumarou's long-gone son, Allaye.

The greetings were cordial but subdued. There was no celebration. No words of acrimony, no inquiry into Allaye's betrayal.
No interrogation at all of his absence other than the prescribed
polite question that the Fulani asked all arrivals: "How was your
road?" The nomads were used to long separations. The strictures of
their transhumance, its very uncertainty, demanded restraint. Allaye was here now.

He unpacked his shoulder bag in his parents' hut. A cellphone.
A charger. A frosted glass vial of knockoff cologne labeled BOOS.
Three yards of sequined dark blue fabric for a future boubou. A
black plastic bag holding several silver and agate rings. After the
boy had stuffed the shoulder bag and its contents behind one of the
reed hoops that formed the hut's skeleton, Oumarou told him to
milk the goats. That night he included Allaye in his prayers again.

I once had complained to Oumarou about my teenage son.
Alone in Philadelphia he had misbehaved and I was seething for
hours. At his indelicacy, at my helplessness. At my guilt for being
so far away from him.

"Anna Bâ!" the old man said. "God created children so they may
try the patience of their parents. But if we are angry with them for
more than a moment we only punish ourselves. So it's better for you
to stop being angry with your son now."

When a small child did something very wrong—hurt or endangered another child or someone's animal, or played dangerously with a sword or fire—Fanta would wallop the delinquent once and firmly say, "Don't!" Then the disciplining would end. There was no endurance to her annoyance, no lingering resentment, no prolonged berating. Maybe because in the bush there always was too much work to be done, and protracting a punishment for any transgression made no sense. Or else she knew how to let go of her anger once she had expressed it into the world, how to step over it the way she stepped over a furrow, or a rock, or a thorn on her path.

Oumarou never struck his children or grandchildren. Sometimes he'd tell them, "You have let me down." Or, "Don't do this again." Often he would say nothing at all and keep to himself for a minute or two of quiet displeasure.

Ousman said his father's disappointed silences always shattered him the most.

The sky broke two days after Allaye's return. Not a torrent at first: a steady silver drizzle. Enough to spot the campground dust, to pool in the shallow depressions of abandoned flipflops, to streak a wooden pestle. Wind shook leafless thorn trees that the sun had bleached to fishbone spines. It thundered.

Then all of a sudden it rained hard. Gusts harried dense gray diagonals across the gray plain. The rain gathered into large milky puddles in the clay and hammered out of them liquid crowns, staccato marks, temporary coronae. Amadou and Kajita stepped barefoot from puddle to puddle, curious, savoring the wet.

"Cold!" said Kajita.

"Cold!" mimicked Amadou, and laughed.

By midafternoon it was blowing a gale from the southeast. The women of the camp gathered inside Oumarou and Fanta's hut and wove straw mats and grass calabash lids and kept the brazier going with charcoal and boiled endless pots of tea. Raindrops sprinkled into the hut and the hut's reed frame rasped in the wind where the reeds were slung together with pagne strips and rope. From the horizontal loops of the frame hung curdling sticks, an unfinished sequined straw lid with a large sewing needle stuck in it, some ladles of wood and plastic, a couple of blue plastic cups, a king-size mosquito net, a black plastic bag holding something small, another bag with dry pepper flakes, a scouring mop, a kuffiyeh wrapped around a pouch with Oumarou's cardboard tax document, a pair of turquoise flipflops, Allaye's knockoff cologne. Bomel reached for the vial and sprayed the perfume at Hairatou's drawings on the clay wainscot, at the palm of her left hand, at the reed pallet. She sniffed in wonder. The scent mixed oddly with the buttermilk smell of the hut. Young men and teenage boys walked in and shucked off wet sandals in a puddle by the door and leaned their staffs against the thatch and talked about the water and the grass it certainly would bring. Yaya invented tales of falling asleep on nightherd and being carried away bodily in his sleep by a mischief of mice; of harnessing a hippo in the Bani and riding it through the bourgou; of conversing with lions. Isiaka came wearing a faded pink L.L.Bean puffer jacket with ripped armpits over his bright boubou. He sat down on the earthen floor, sniffling.

"Are you healthy, Isiaka?"

"I have stomach problems."

"Did you eat something bad?"

"Yes. I ate food and I should be eating milk instead." The cowboy's eternal refrain. Everyone snickered. Allaye teased his great-uncle:

"You're sick because you're older than all of Mali."

"I'll sell you," Isiaka squeaked back. "For money, though you're not worth much. I'll sell you and buy milk for me."

Mentou arrived, wrapped in something that looked like house insulation. Her skull had been newly tonsured and the remaining hair coiled in tight thin cornrows around the crown. She looked regal. In the dusk of the hut she sat down next to me on a bit of burlap sacking and then she touched the hem of my skirt and took my hand and held it. Then her mother came by and she let go instantly. She had cheated on her mother. I knew such treachery. I once had been a little girl who had believed in sudden escapes from tedium, a besotted child who had imagined that life with my mother's friends would have been somehow more magical. I don't know if my mother ever noticed, but to me such fantasies had felt sinful.

The Diakayatés watched the rain and watched the world in the rain. The downpour turned to drizzle and back to downpour. The sky was a gray and darker gray scape of multistratic clouds. In the clouds there were rifts and valleys and tall upside-down mountains and it thundered all the time and the light that fell through the clouds was the color of mercury. Somewhere above, pockets of low pressure were sucking in air, inhaling the Sahel's hot breath. Shadows became faint and cast at unfamiliar angles, as if the atmospheric war had rearranged the very course of the planet's journey. In the rain someone's herds moved on transhumance in moaning and fuzzy dark lines. Three Dakabalal boys galloped their donkeys bareback across the measly fen to the west and through the multiple prisms of falling water they seemed like genii riding magical beasts loosed by the tempest. Gusts blew away wet slippers. Above it all a sole swallow struggled against the wind.

It rained all day. A group of bare-breasted teenage girls and two older men came out of Dakabalal to feel with their hands and toes for catfish in the muddied marsh. In the Diakayaté camp toddlers ran naked outside until they shivered with the cold. Their parents and older siblings toweled them off with pagnes and blankets.

Oumarou had gone in the morning to the district hospital in Djenné to visit a sick friend and returned to camp in the gloaming. He strode across the muck on his thin long legs shod in turquoise

plastic Fulani shoes and he wore that day a boubou in blue and white stripes and he looked from a distance a peculiar windwhipped marshbird. His trip had been in vain. His friend had been released from the hospital the day before with pneumonia, for which he would receive a traditional treatment of chest massage with shea butter at his own campsite.

Oumarou shook off his shoes

and sat on the sleeping pallet where his relatives had made room for him, and said:

"This isn't the real rain."

"How do you know?"

"I just know."

He said that while that particular day's rain was plentiful it was no indicator of how the season would go or whether there would be enough grass for the cattle. He said it would have to rain this way every day for weeks on end for the rain to make a difference. That only when a cowboy driving cattle to camp for the evening milking saw no dust rise at the heels of his herd for weeks on end could it be said that it had rained enough.

The old man had been in a sour mood for days. He had been studying the land as if he had to decide what to do with it, though he had no jurisdiction over it whatsoever. Nor over the rain, nor over the farmers' planting schedule. Not even over the itinerary of his own cattle, now that Hassan had obstinately taken it to the next camp.

If one were to truly accept and embrace uncertainty, as the canon of transhumance enjoined—if one were to give up the very human urge to govern the ungovernable—then perhaps within such an acceptance one could discover control of a higher order, a triumphant subjugation of wanting and attachment. And since greed and desire and fear lay at the root of sin one could, conceivably, conquer all sin, become the most enlightened and powerful marabout. But Oumarou's journey to such a level of serenity remained asymptotic. Sometimes it worked. For the most part it was an aspiration, a splendid theory. Right now he was terribly worried.

He also was irritated after his wasted five-hour roundtrip to Djenné, half of it on rain-slicked clay. He ordered the noisy younger children out of the hut and announced that his family would break camp and head toward his cattle outside Ballé in six days, the following Tuesday.

By nightfall the wind died down and the sky settled into long hoar-colored streaks, like an echo of the rainstreaked and pulpy Sahel below. Sita's cattle lowed in a crowded semicircle at his calf rope. Where Oumarou's cows once had stayed there was a sodden gap. A fine calm mist fell upon the bourgou and then stopped, and the pink lightning of the receding storm flashed along the horizon to the north. At the very last minute of the day the clouds in the west parted and for a few heartbeats a barely pink strip of sunset lay doubled in the narrow remains of the marsh, like a parting caress. Then pale blue, then gone. Dark earth steamed into the dark. I made my bed in the mud from a sheet of blue tarpaulin. Fits and starts of frog song. Bedtime whispers. The rapping of a goat's ears. Thunder somewhere. Quietude of the soul.

That night crickets fell from the sky and the next morning steam rose in the slanted dawn and all the winged termites hatched at once and glittered blind and disoriented like fragile spalls of fool's gold. Goldrimmed mare's tails squeegeed the bright blue sky. The rain had pushed snakes out of their hiding places in the ground and saw-scaled vipers traced looped infinities in the damp ash of farmers' fires with their pale bellies.

The termites drifted in windblown columns and settled on my skin. The land smelled like doused-out fire. Bomel woke on a mat next to me and walked a few paces away and there squatted and looked up smiling at the sunrise as she peed. In the distance everywhere cattle flowed in endless groaning herds.

Her husband's cattle gone and with it the manure for her breakfast fire, Fanta was left to gather sticks. She wandered around the camp looking for deadwood and talking to her granddaughter Mayrama, whom she had strapped to her back with the strawberry-print pagne.

"Life in the bush is hard, Mayrama," she cooed. "No manure, no wood."

Oumarou heard that.

"There are some people who don't want to live in the bush. They stay in villages or in towns. We migrate. If someone doesn't like to migrate, they should stay."

Where did it come from, this obdurate devotion to movement? "The romantic image of nomads as aimless wanderers, free spirits, is a fantasy," wrote Thurston Clarke in *The Last Caravan*, his melancholy ode to the Kel Tamashek camel herders of Niger. He called his nomads prisoners "of a seasonal rhythm determined by the monsoon" who moved "to escape threats and seize opportunities." Yet migration itself was a daunting obstacle course, not relief itself but rather a search for relief, an anticipation of something better—taller grass, fuller udders, larger humps. Oumarou's transhumance was not mindful meditation, wasn't Wordsworth's blessedness. It was hard work.

"Even though the bush is difficult," he said, "people who grew up here prefer it because this is what they've learned from their fathers and grandfathers."

A toil prescribed by the dead. The indigenous Australians in Bruce Chatwin's book *The Songlines* came to my mind, travelers who followed a geographical score sung into being by their totemic ancestors at the era of creation they called the Dreamtime. Chatwin theorized that the first humans had sung their way across the world, that the poetry of their songs was the original *poïesis*, creation. The Diakayatés, according to such a theory, followed the paths chanted into existence by the early nomads. This meant that I, crossing borders and cultures and continents, was trespassing, eavesdropping. I felt like a cuckoo, left to try on other people's routes and from such wandering, from the multiple scores of the world, to piece together my own song-map, forever poking for some ancestral Dreaming track that had been lost to me in advance of my own birth, when my migrant forefathers finally settled in shtetlach on the Black Sea. Settled and kept on singing in place, those stubborn badkhens.

For an instant the thought—the notion that I somehow needed to affix my traveling lifestyle to some overarching, grander, older meaningfulness—made me feel exceedingly solitary. Then it felt like a conceit. Because here we were, warming our bones on mats soggy from the year's first rain, and Fanta had found enough firewood to heat up a runny *sombi* porridge of rice and goat milk and the chili flakes I had pounded in her wooden mortar, and little Kajita was lacing her thin fingers through mine, and in the thatch by the entryway to Oumarou's hut a busy potter wasp was sculpting a clay nest, unaware that in a few days that thatch and that hut would be gone. Simply, it was morning, I was with friends, and it was good.

Oumarou continued:

"When I was very young there were no farms between here and Senossa, only grass for cows, and very few people. Now, as you see, there are a lot of people, a lot of rice farms. The country is changing, so I do believe the people who say in a hundred years we will have to live in towns." He paused. He slurped his *sombi* out of a scuffed purple plastic bowl.

"On the other hand, when my brothers and I were growing up we heard stories that the time would come when all of us would move to the town and the cows would just move on their own. So it is a very old story, Anna Bâ. And we are still here."

The next day Sita Dangéré walked to Somena to farewell some friends and came back with a small black plastic bag full of laminated identity cards about the length of a thumb. The Diakayatés turned the cards in their hands, puzzled over them. They could not read what the cards said. They could not understand what the cards meant.

I read out loud.

"RÉPUBLIQUE DU MALI. UN PEUPLE UN BUT UNE FOI." One people one goal one faith. The Diakayatés sniggered. Eh? How could they have the same goal as the Bozo, the same goal as the Bambara who were about to drive them out of the bourgou for a whole season?

"Go on."

Below, the name of the bearer and of the bearer's parents, the date and place of his or her birth. Profession: cattle herder. Domicile: Ouro Ali, the district to which Doundéré and Dakabalal belonged.

"Ouro Ali? What? Our domicile is the bush. We are nomads! The government is so stupid, it knows nothing. Go on."

Fingerprint. Gender. Photo.

"Look at this!" Isiaka held up a card. "This doesn't look like my wife at all! What does it say, Anna Bâ?"

"Mayrama Sankari. Born 1963. This means she's fifty years old."

"That's not even my wife's name. Her name is Fatoumata. And she can't be fifty. How could they get both her name and her picture wrong? How would they even have her photo? My wife has never had a picture taken in her life!"

Bomel pointed at the corner of a card.

"What's this, with different colors?"

"It's the flag of Mali."

"Mali?" said Oumarou. "I keep hearing people say Mali, Mali, Mali, but I don't know what that means. I know that when I herd my cows and I end up in Burkina Faso I am no longer in Mali. I know Côte d'Ivoire is not in Mali. I know that here it is Mali. But tell me, what is Mali?"

"*Mali* is the Bambara word for 'hippo'!" said Yaya. And so it was.

Sita Dangéré said:

"What do we do with these cards, Anna Bâ?"

"You use them to vote for president." After a year of coup d'états,

Mali was holding a presidential election in July. To ensure a turnout that would legitimize the next president, the interim government in Bamako had ordered that the cards be issued to everyone on the books, free of charge. Ousman did get his ID after all. But Sita Dangéré was displeased.

"Vote? Why do they want me to vote? If they need me to vote they have to give me something. They give me something and I'll vote. But they aren't giving me anything. The candidates only want us for the votes. When they become presidents they never come by to say hello. I don't like that."

"When's the vote?" asked Oumarou.

"Toward the end of Ramadan."

"Well, we'll be far away by then."

"God willing, we will."

The Fulani were virtuoso escape artists. No government-issued laminated piece of plastic could contain their identity.

Oumarou laid out his plan. First he and the family would travel to Ballé, where Hassan was waiting with the herd. It was an easy place to live. There was a river for the cows to drink, and, after it rained some, grass. It was a four-hour walk from Djenné, where the women could sell their buttermilk. But after the rains began in earnest the cows would not be able to stay near Ballé because they would get stuck in the mud and drown, and, on top of that, there were many farms and many mosquitoes. Oumarou planned to stay near Ballé for two or three weeks. When it became very wet he and his family would move to Hayré and spend the rest of the rainy season there.

Hayré was at elevation and had no natural waterholes. The market was far away from the campsite. So was the well. But there were few farms the cows could trample and no mosquitoes and the women could trade buttermilk in nearby villages. The villagers in Hayré, the farming people called Bwa, were not Muslim. They were animists, fetishists. They ate dogs and donkeys. They ate pigs. Some even made fetishes out of humans. You could not go into their villages at night because they would kill you and eat you.

Amadou and Kajita listened to their grandfather with their mouths open, stupefied and enthralled by the outrageous and exciting horrors that lay ahead.

The family spent the last days in the bourgou in preparations for the move.

Ousman went to check on his father's animals outside Ballé and returned with a report, in order of importance: A cow went mad and stopped allowing her calf to nurse. Another calf refused to let its mother go, which made it difficult to milk her. A bull gored a heifer and he and Hassan had to stitch a piece of a calabash into the cow's belly to prevent the guts from spilling out. There had been no rain in Ballé and still no grass but some Fulani already had begun to arrive. Oumarou's younger brother al Hajj Saadou was there and in good health, *al ham du lillah*, and looking forward to the reunion.

Sita Dangéré's son Allaye, the newlywed, had arrived in Ballé safely with Sita's cattle.

Fanta walked to Weraka and Wono to shop for a hundred kilos of rice and fifty kilos of millet with which to feed the family during the early weeks of transhumance. She returned from her trip noshing on a small smoked fish she had found on the ground on her walk home, but otherwise empty-handed. Just like the nomads, the bourgou's farmers had been studying the sky, and they clung to last year's harvest because they were not sure there would be any this year. Eighty miles to the north, international relief agencies were distributing bags of sorghum and rice seeds, but there were no distributions of the kind around Djenné. Fanta found the farmers' reasoning inadequate. "Black people are like cows," she snapped. "They know nothing." She told Ousman he would have to walk all the way to Senossa or Djenné to buy grain. Then she stretched out on a mat and rested her right arm across her eyes and fell asleep immediately. Oumarou looked at her with concern and disapproval at once.

"She tires quickly. I always tell her: As you get older you mustn't work very hard and walk very far."

"But you," I said, "you yourself just hiked to Djenné and back in one day, and you're older than her."

"Because I know I can."

I walked to Somena and bought a large honeycomb from an itinerant rimaibe tradeswoman and borrowed a lidded enamel pot from one of Fanta's distant relatives who lived in the village to carry the honey to the camp. The land stretched in steamy pastures and diffracted in mirages and in the foreground grasshoppers clicked in and out of tall charred grass that flanked quadrate fields. The road was barely dampened by rain but milky puddles stood where the clay was hard and unabsorbing. There were snakes. The people I greeted in the village and along the road all asked the same question: "Has it rained where you are coming from?" "The same as here," I told them, and we clicked our tongues in empathy and communal worry.

The day before departure Ousman's father-in-law brought on his motorcycle Ousman's wife, Bobo, and their two sons, and everyone at the camp wondered at baby Afo, how plump he was, how big. Afo Bocoum, too, stopped by to bid the Diakayatés farewell. Both men were dispatching their herds to the desert border with Mauritania with hired hands, and they sat on mats drinking tea with Oumarou and Sita Dangéré and fretting about the unpredictable world around them.

"The marabouts say the year will be good."

"Yes, but the marabouts never say that any year will be bad."

"Last year the rain began on the sixth of June," said Afo. He was an intermediary between the ancient and the modern, and knew how to express time in both idioms with equal ease. "This is already the first of July and the rain still has not begun. We're all worried."

"Yes, and also we are very worried about the war. I've heard stories of rebels up north confiscating cattle from the Fulani."

"Everybody is worried about the war and the rain."

"It would be better to have guns."

"Guns won't help you if there is no rain."

"If al Nashira comes and there isn't a lot of rain on the first day, it means the year will be pretty dry," said Bobo's father, who had a beautiful salt-and-pepper beard and wore clean new clothes and spoke delicately, with the easy elegance of wealth. Al Nashira, Gamma Capricorni, a giant star whose Arabic name meant "the lucky one," "the bearer of good tidings," was beginning her thirteen-day tenure in the sky that Friday.

"Yes. God willing it will rain on that day."

Two years earlier, a drought had pushed more than eighteen million people in the Sahel to the brink of starvation. Tens of thousands had famished to death. The Fulani in the bourgou had fared decently that year, considering. Some relatives had died but people died every year, such was God's will. Bobo's father had spent four hundred dollars—the price of an average bull—on cottonseed to feed his cattle. The men talked about whether they would have to buy cottonseed this year and how much the cottonseed would cost. The price kept going up. Then they talked about the first time they had ever had to buy cottonseed, during the drought of 1985. Bobo's father said many of his cows had been so weak that year he'd had to pry open their mouths and palm the cottonseed onto their tongues to feed them. He had lost a hundred cows then. Ten had died in one day after a light rain, of hypothermia.

Oumarou, who had lost most of his herd during that drought, hundreds of cows, said nothing. Ousman had driven the last milch cow to Ballé two days earlier, and without milk the old man felt lightheaded, dizzy, untethered from the land that he had learned by heart and by feel but that was always changing. He stood up and shook Amadou out of his blanket and walked off to relieve himself. On the way he tripped on a stick Fanta kept by the hearth to use as a poker, or to throw at goats that ambled too close to her cooking, and it rattled on hard clay a lonesome warning, like a gong.

Above the men the sky churned with indecision. It contained distant stormcells and billowing low rainclouds and mare's tails and high-pitched blue, like blown glass, and, to the west, a golden sun prying open a lidded blackness, and a few fingers above that the whitest whirl of nimbostratus. In the east a double rainbow arched. The Fulani name for a rainbow was the Road of Fatoumata Bintou ya Rasoul Allaye—the road of Fatima bint Mohammad, the beloved daughter of the Prophet, the mother of his only descendants. A road before the road seemed to be a good sign.

The women had begun to take things apart. Fanta packed the makings of future matting into a gunnysack. Bomel and Bobo, who walked around in a dress torn at the chest so that her right nipple showed, were fitting plastic and tin bowls into blue and black plastic bags. Hairatou pounded millet to mix with curds and hot pepper into the dry makings of *chobbal* for the family to take on their journey and dilute on the road with whatever water they could find. Then she turned a castiron cooking pot upside down, sprinkled it with sand, climbed on it in green plastic shoes, and shuffled, balancing, engrossed, hiking up her skirt to the knee, polishing away the soot.

Sita Dangéré had dismantled his wife's kitchen shelter to fashion out of the reeds a cage for her chickens, and Sita Louchéré had pulled down the thatch to fortify his own hut against rain. Oumarou and Sita Dangéré would travel to Hayré together with their families, but Sita Louchéré and Isiaka and their kin would stay for a few more weeks and then travel north, to the Sahara, or west, toward a town called Sin, twenty-five miles away. The decision would be Isiaka's, because he was older. I asked him if he had a preference.

He said: "I'm like a bird, perching, waiting for real rain, waiting to see where the best place will be. Where it rains better, there I will go."

No one in Isiaka's or Sita's family had a cellphone that worked to make or receive calls. For five months, the Diakayatés would have no contact, no news of one another, until—and at this speculation the men evoked God's name—they reconvened on the narrow knoll near Doundéré and Dakabalal the following December. All across the Sahel Fulani families were studying the sky and plotting the routes of their rainy-season transhumance. That month all the no-mads would disperse from the bourgou, splitting kin from kin, scattering across rivers and deserts until the end of harvest.

That evening I cooked a stew of fish and tomato paste for everyone in the camp. Fanta helped me peel two dozen tiny garlic cloves and tossed some in the fire, to keep the campsite safe from the evil eye. Garlic was particularly effective as protection for the very young. When I squatted by the hearth to feed to the fire long knotty sticks of kindling, Bomel came over and smiled at me.

"Are you missing someone, Anna Bâ?"

I started.

"Why do you ask?"

"You're singing."

I was? I was. I hadn't even noticed.

"They say when a woman sings, she is missing someone." She squinted at me. "You sing to yourself a lot, Anna Bâ."

We ladled the stew into extra bowls and dispatched the food with small children to the huts of Sita and Sita Dangéré and Isiaka. In return, Oumarou's relatives sent calabashes of milk. We dined in the dark and afterward we ate wild honey with our forefingers straight out of the pot. A menacing red pall trimmed the land to the north where farmers were burning their fields again and to the southeast stars darted across the sky before a coming lightning storm. Ousman lay on his back with his right foot resting on bent left knee and played songs on his cellphone. The phone was called Tiptop Power for Life and had no SIM card; Ousman used it to listen to music. Now a man in the recording sang: "Because sometimes Fulani cut tree branches to feed their cattle / the Ministry of Forestry and Water Resources persecutes the Fulani."

"When I was young," Oumarou said, "there were no phones. When I wanted to listen to music I'd go to the griot and I'd reach into my pocket and suddenly there would be a lot of money there. I would sit down in front of the griot and command: 'Sing very well. Sing for me from here to the sky!'

"Sometimes my friends and I would pitch in and organize a party and hire a griot for the night. Those griots, if you were to meet them today and ask them about me, they'd say, 'Oumarou Diakayaté, son of Hashem al Hajj,' and they'd tell you the story of my whole family. Except I think all these griots are dead now. I don't know if there are still griots anymore."

One afternoon in the Djenné market square Ali the Griot chain-smoked my cigarettes and complained about his life. "I am Griot Number One!" he said. "But no one wants to pay for my stories. So now I am Goldsmith Number One." No one wanted to pay for his jewelry either. Afraid of the war in the north, Western seekers of the exotic no longer came to Djenné. The town's tourist-based economy had collapsed. Several millimeters of dust and grime coated every-thing in Ali's workshop and his massive display table heaped with silver rings with geometric Tuareg designs and goldleaf Fulani hoop earrings and ebony bracelets inlaid with silver and bronze was a uniform beige bas-relief, like an anthropological dig, a recently dis-interred burial site.

Ali complained and I took notes.

"For what?"

"So I don't forget things. To tell the story accurately."

"You will tell the story of how Griot Number One sits in the square all day?"

"*Inshallah.* If that's okay with you."

"*Wallahi*, Anna Bâ. You are a griot, like me."

After the music had quieted we could hear thunder and we also could hear invisible herds on the move. In the ash of the hearth a goat had nestled like a giant horned hen, warming its belly.

In the night it drizzled lightly, then the wind kicked up to a heavy storm. I ended up the seventh adult jigsawed into Oumarou and Fanta's hut, jostling for room on the floor cemented with a blue paste of crushed acacia beans and manure ash and clay beneath Hairatou's artwork, on halfpacked sacks, on mats not yet rolled up for travel. I rested my head on a bundle of coiled pagnes, sinking into its buttermilk scent. Outside the wind shrieked, and squalls thrashed the hut with wet sand and rocks. Frogs began in unison, then stopped. Anxious goats whimpered. Fanta's chickens peeped by the wall. A mouse ran across our bodies. Then there were more frogs, and goats again, that ancient Sahelian rondo.

But first, at the very end of their last evening in the bourgou, after Hairatou had finished pounding millet and rattling aluminum bowls, after the adults had prayed the final time and baby Afo had dozed off by my side on a polyester mat, the family sat in the dark and drank the milk that Isiaka and Sita had sent over. They drank from two calabashes, slowly and in complete silence.

THE
RAINY SEASON

❖ ❖ ❖

Traveling. . . .
The illusion of having overcome distance, of having erased time.
To be far away.

—GEORGES PEREC

The cart was large and tall and had no sideboards. It had been nailed approximately together from wide boards of unfinished wood. Its two wheels had been filched from a sedan. Its underslung metal axle and single shaft were painted canary yellow. A massive and rusted eye lag screwed the tip of the shaft to a heavy yoke carved out of a tree trunk to harness two oxen, but instead the cart was hitched with three donkeys. One of the donkeys was round with pregnancy.

By the time the two rimaibe boys from Senossa drove the cart into the camp most of the Diakayatés' possessions lay on a single reed mat. The calabashes, stacked one into another. The wooden ladles. The woven straw lids. Two mangoes, one halfeaten, in a calabash. A plastic bowl holding a small bag of peanuts. A green plastic bucket with smaller baggies of spices and medicinal herbs. A tall sack with mat makings. Three large blue plastic bags with something. The kettle for ablutions. Ousman's own black polyurethane knapsack with a broken zipper, inside of which were the family brand; two muzzles—one studded with thorns, the other with iron square nails—to discourage yearlings from suckling their mother cows; a plastic bag with sugar and tea; a blue enameled teapot; a mostly empty vial of Amitraz 12.5 percent emulsion, an acaricide and insecticide for livestock; a sewing needle; a spool of black thread; his SIMless cellphone. Next to it all lay the mats and blankets and reeds of Oumarou and Fanta's marital bed, rolled one into the other, a single thick bundle of future rest.

Oumarou and Ousman untied the bits of rope and cloth that for nearly seven months had held together the old man's hut. They pulled down the thatch, two heavy mats they would take with them to use again. Loose grass flew and dust billowed and Hairatou's fingerpainting fell to the ground and vanished forever.

The boys from Senossa loaded the mats and rolled-up thatch first, then the heavy bags of rice and millet, then the blankets and the clothes. Cookware and utensils wrapped in pagnes. The mortar. Loose cooking sticks. Then they ran down Fanta's chickens one by one and tied their legs with strips of cloth and Fanta stuffed them into a netted fishtrap she had found somewhere on her wanderings. The boys hung the fishtrap from the back of the cart, and they tied the tall wooden pestle to the axle with strips of torn pagnes. Sita Dangéré and Oumarou's son Allaye had left at dawn, driving goats in two separate herds toward Ballé, and cousins were helping Boucary load Sita's belongings into Sita's own two small donkey carts. A sheet of clouds had come in and the wind was picking up again, and it blew away tethers and loose matting and it blew from the south the antediluvian whoops and yelps of unseen cowboys ushering their cattle on transhumance.

A hearty meal of millet porridge and fish sauce, for the road. The cart drivers ate with the men. After one more spot of tea Fanta swept the campsite for the last time, out of some sense of rectitude. She tossed to the wind spent teabags, broken flipflops, slivers of cracked plastic. They would tumble into a fen, create a second, industrialized bottom. Frogs would spawn in them. The heavier jetsam—broken veterinary syringes, cracked calabashes, vials of dewormers, smashed flashlight batteries, ripped plastic shoes—snaked in a broomed stria where the calf rope had been. At the beginning of each rainy season the entire bourgou was charted with such tidelines, the markings of nomadic comings and goings. Rain erased them. When I visited the campsite three weeks later the only thing I saw was a patch of tramped dirt.

After she finished sweeping Fanta stood in front of her husband and informed him that she was not coming with him that day to Ballé.

Her elderly brother was very sick. She had learned about his illness from a migrating friend the night before and she had made up her mind to pay him a visit. There was no telling if he still would be alive when the Diakayatés returned to the bourgou after the rainy season, she explained. Or if she still would be. Her brother lived north of the bourgou, on the Niger River, two days away on foot. She already had bound some spare pagnes and a little *chobbal* into a knot, to take along. Bomel would tie Mayrama to her back and walk with her mother for a couple of hours, then schlep half a day to the west, to the village where she lived with her husband, who was also her cousin, the son of Oumarou's youngest living brother, Allaye.

Oumarou sat for a while and considered his wife's announcement in silence. Then he said:

"When will you join us?"

"God only knows."

"Amen, amen, amen . . . It's far."

"That's true."

"You'll be tired."

"I'll be fine."

"Don't go."

"I'm going."

"All right."

To show disapproval would have been to demonstrate defeat. "If I need her I'll tell her to come back sooner," the old man said. How? Neither he nor Fanta had cellphones. "Oh no, don't let Oumarou get a cellphone," warned Boucary, the teasing grandnephew. "If he has a cellphone he'll call all the women in the bougou and marry them all!"

The sun was a full palm above the horizon by the time the three carts slowly pitched across the dried-out fen crazed into large polygonal flakes. The passengers rocked toward the southbound road. In the front Oumarou, young Kajita and Amadou, Hairatou with a sick skewbald week-old goat in her lap. Ousman, Bobo, and their two sons following. Boucary with his wife, Abba, their three small daughters, his mother, Salimata, and his newlywed sister-in-law, Kajita Pain-in-the-Ass, barely fit into the last cart. Their relatives who were staying behind walked alongside the procession, calling out last-minute instructions, tightening slack ropes, holding hands of their departing kin—holding left hands, to ensure another meeting, after the harvest.

To hell with the etiquette of stoicism. Hairatou was openly bawling. All the Diakayatés, disciples of unattachment, Buddhists of the bush, were in tears. Even Yaya. He had walked the farthest after the carts and waved goodbye the longest. After he turned away at last he wiped his face with both hands. Then he lifted the little beaded mirror he wore on one of the lanyards around his neck and checked his eyes.

Boucary's cart was the slowest in the caravan. The donkeys trotted for the first few miles, then tired and slowed to a trudge. I walked beside them. Boucary whipped the animals and called out the names of things he saw on the road and asked me to name them in English. Horse. Field. Hut. Sky. Cow. Like Chatwin's Aboriginal people we sang the Earth into existence.

By the time the family reached Senossa, the old capital of Sekou Amadou's caliphate, it was almost noon and the wind had picked up and was driving red laterite dust from the east. Lightning sparkled in the haze. We took shelter in the adobe anteroom of the compound of Kola Cissé, the Diakayaté family marabout, the owner of the large cart Oumarou was using for his journey to Ballé.

Marabout Kola had dedicated his life to the mystical pursuit of proximity to God. Sleep deprivation and constant thought had worn him to a thin shadow. Even his mustache and goatee were thin. His head was shaven. His eyes were deeply sunken and searing. He spent most of his days and nights in prayer and meditation over kabbalistic ciphers and equations that triangulated to Koranic verses the specific concerns and family histories of his clients and loved ones. Fifty years earlier or more he had studied the Koran with Oumarou's younger brothers, Allaye and Saadou, in a school operated in this very house by his own father, who had lent his spiritual advice to Oumarou's father and his kin. Now his father was dead and he himself ran the school. He had taught, at different times, three of Oumarou's sons—first Boucary, then Ousman, then Drissa.

In the Inner Niger Delta memorizing the Koran has been the cornerstone of Islamic learning for centuries. When Ibn Battuta passed through circa 1352 he extolled the locals for making "fetters for their children when they appear on their part to be falling short in their learning of it by heart, and they are not taken off from them till they do."

Seven hundred years later marabouts no longer manacled their students. A dozen or two young boys flitted in and out of Kola's house at all hours, and the marabout taught them when he was not in prayer. The children inked Koranic verses with homemade styluses upon long wooden tablets smoothed over with lime. After they could recite from memory what they had written they washed the boards and wrote the next passage of the text. Sura by sura, an average child took seven years to memorize the entire book. A marabout charged his students not per lesson but per volume of text they were able to recite.

None of them comprehended any of what they had learned because none of them spoke or read Arabic. Only after they had committed the Koran to memory would the students be initiated into its language and introduced at last to the complex stratigraphy of the scripture's expressed substance—by some other marabout, in a different madrassa. That was what Drissa was doing, under the tutelage of one of Marabout Kola's sons, but few students endured that long. The rest would never understand the words of the Koran, and their own calligraphy would remain forever self-contained, a beautiful and foreign cursive script.

Yet how could anyone say that the quintessence of the sacred text was lost on them? For if the Koran was the dictation the Prophet Mohammed took from Archangel Gabriel, who was said to have relayed to him verbatim, over the course of nearly twenty-three years, messages from God, then the students who declaimed the book by rote were enunciating the exact words as God Himself had shaped them. They may have been unlettered, but they were directly partaking of the divine, and Marabout Kola was granting them access to the inviolate sanctity of language.

In Senossa on the day of the move the marabout wanted to talk about journeys.

How far would the Diakayatés travel on that day? And when would the rimaibe boys—his students—return with his cart and donkeys to Senossa? He did not want them to return in the dark. How far had I come to reach the bourgou? What was my religious practice? he asked, using the Sufi term *turuq*—way, path—and upon hearing I had none: Would I like him to guide me?

He led the Diakayatés in midday prayer and then fed them a lunch of rice and dried fish. He gave me a packet of gunpowder tea and some sugar: "For the road." He gave Oumarou a present of some millet and a mango: "Millet for your dinner, mango for your children." Then he led Oumarou outside where the gale had died down and humid sun cast sharp shadows under the donkey carts, the donkeys, a pair of doum palms. The marabout stood in front of the old cowboy in that chiaroscuro world and ordered him to extend his upturned palms and took them with his own fingertips and held them like that at chest level. He closed his eyes and stood silent for some time. Then he recited a quick devotion, spat twice onto Oumarou's hands, and in this way the Diakayatés' rainy-season transhumance was blessed.

By midafternoon Boucary's donkeys were so tired the younger women had to walk to lighten the team's load. They walked in the single file that took them out of the Horn of Africa, the same way ancestors of modern humans walked through narrow clearings and trails a million and a half years ago. They never turned their heads, never craned their necks. Their metronomic arms ticked off the unfaltering rhythm of their journeys. "Instead of roads, there were trails, usually shared by people and cattle alike," Kapuściński wrote of foot travel in Africa. "This age-old system of paths explains why people here are still in the habit of walking single file, even if they're traveling along one of today's wide roads. It explains, too, why a walking group is silent—it is difficult to conduct a conversation single file." Here Kapuściński was wrong. Without ever looking at each other the women talked ceaselessly, exchanging news of the latest ailments and births, rumors, stories. They laughed. They clicked their tongues. Abba with an infant daughter drooling down her back, Kajita on her long legs. Whenever they became tired they would step off the road and out of their flipflops and squat barefoot for a few minutes. Then they would slide their flipflops back on and resume their walk.

White stone-hard land, dry gypsum, rare acacias under bent

sky. A hoopoe watched from a leafless tree, sang the travelers on: quick-quick-quick, quick-quick-quick! Two boys were stretched out on their stomachs under a mango tree. Salimata gasped from the cart: "*Wallahi*, they are dead!" They were not; one stirred when the cart passed him. Outside the northern wall of Niala, a village of rimaibe millet farmers, Boucary steered around a giant baobab that lay on its side.

A baobab could live longer than a thousand years: the tree outside Niala might have stood there when Ibn Battuta traveled through Mali and wrote, in amazement, of seeing a weaver use a baobab as his loom room. Ibn Battuta might have seen that very tree. It was difficult to rationalize the death of something so substantial, so ancient, like thinking of a lost language.

Oumar Tall, the school principal, said that once upon a time there had lived in Niala a giant strongman named Bris who would kidnap village women and children when they went to the well and then trade his captives at the slave market in Ségou for beer and tobacco. This went on for years. At last the villagers conspired to put a spell on Bris. They paid a marabout to hex the giant so that he would be forever barred from entering Niala. Bris moved to Ségou, and went on to kidnap women and children along the banks of the Niger until a local Bambara fighter named Boucary the Big fought and defeated him. When I asked the principal when all this had taken place, he said: "There are no dates for these events. They could have happened anytime."

Boucary Diakayaté whipped his plodding team past Niala and past the rotund granaries of banco and wattle that rose out of the flat sweep of the land at random, with no apparent owners. Past termite mounds shaped like mushrooms and chimneys and thrones, relics of deserted kingdoms. Past swept clusters of neat villages inhabited and past stumps of villages abandoned—in exoduses or die-offs, fifty years ago or five hundred. There were no dates for such events: they could have happened anytime. Abba and Kajita sidestepped the creeping traps of bindweed tendrils that even livestock did not eat, a pair of dark-blue ripped gym shorts, a dead viper.

"Careful! Very dangerous!" said Amadou Gano, the young man who was working with me as a translator during the rainy season. He toed the snake with his flipflop. "If a viper stings you and you don't die you'll become very wise. But if you take that dead viper and grind it up and throw the powder into a well, anyone who drinks from that well will die."

The young women brought their hands to their mouths in awe. *"La ilaha il Allah!"*

"Amen, amen, amen—but! If a woman has mastitis you take a snakeskin, you burn it, you mix the ash with shea butter, and slather that on her breasts," Gano said. The Diakayaté women clicked their tongues. They were intrigued. They only knew to cauterize infected breasts by pressing redhot broadswords to the areolae, scarring glossy flower patterns into skin.

"Next time try this snakeskin treatment. It worked for my wife. Three babies! Though one is dead." His second-born, a boy. He would have been ten years old. Gano kept a digital photograph of him in his cellphone. He showed it around. A handsome long-limbed child with his father's tranquil smile, his responsible and kind eyes.

"What happened?"

"He didn't have a mosquito net when he slept and he got malaria. It was God's will."

He thought a little and offered a clarification.

"We say God did it, Anna Bâ, even though sometimes it's we who did it."

Gano had had another child who had died many years earlier, a son also, with another woman, whom he had never married. The child had died in infancy. "An owl took him. I had eaten owl meat

195

for protection when I was young, but my son's mother had not. She is married to someone else now."

Gano lived in Djenné with his wife and two surviving young children. He was twenty-eight years old, the son of two settled Fulani: a famous actor and musician who had conducted Djenné's first orchestra, which had dispersed after his death a decade earlier, and an actress from Moura, a stunning woman who was nearly deaf and who had been his father's eighth wife. Gano was accommodating, generous, and witty. He had driven his scooter from Doundéré to Niala and now was pushing it, leaning into its weight, walking with us. He liked company. He had strung around his waist a leather cord with three gris-gris sewn into rectangular leather pouches to protect him from penury, the envy of others, the dangers of the road. In his wallet he carried another gris-gris, also in a leather sheath, that could protect from a curse up to five thousand people at once, if they had their hearts open. On the middle finger of his left hand he wore a thin adjustable copper ring his marabout had given him. The marabout had explained that at a time of danger the ring would constrict around his finger, in warning. "I will tell you if it starts constricting, Anna Bâ," Gano promised, and laughed. "I will cry, 'Run, Anna Bâ! Run very very fast!'"

He also carried:

A lemon: "It's my father who told me to keep one with me all the time. It protects you from bad people, bad spirits."

A crystal of what looked like gum arabic but had no scent: "This is from Mecca. It protects you from the evil eye."

A snakeskin in a plastic bag: "Good for a woman."

A ball of resin of African myrrh, *Commiphora africana*, which smelled like burning rubber when you heated it over a flame. "It helps when you have a headache and protects you against being killed by an owl in the night." The resin also was an aphrodisiac and an insecticide, but Gano either did not know this or did not say it out loud.

A ball of dark blue thread and a large needle: "Protects you from ripped pants. You use this to sew them up."

A small bag of *jiminta*, a cloying chewy ball of peanut paste, ground chili pepper, and caramel, wrapped in plastic: "Protects you from hunger. When you're hungry you eat it."

Batteries: "Protects you from running out of flashlight in the dark."

Glass prayer beads, to finger while whispering prayers of protection "from all the other things."

When a wheel came off Boucary's cart outside the western walls of Ballé, it was Gano who unloaded the cart and hoisted the axle onto a wooden pestle and refitted the wheel while the Diakayatés watched in exhausted impatience. He had in his arsenal no sorcery to assist with such repairs. While he was working, the sun behind the caravan began to melt into the ground. In a rotting marsh, low and black, village children played and white statues of egrets stood in mango groves. It took Gano days to clean his hands of grease.

A mile or so east of Ballé the dry land suddenly swept toward the Bani River in a grassy slope where Allaye and Sita were already waiting with the goats. The river was bluegreen. It carried goat droppings, shreds of torn nets, bits of tackle, faint petroleum rainbows. It carried Djenné's sewage and brocade dyers' lye. It carried love songs of laundresses and all the desires and regrets that drained into a watershed three times the size of the Hudson's. From its headwaters in Côte d'Ivoire to the bourgou in central Mali it seamed and sundered the Sahel with oxbows and veins and here, at Ballé, near the end of the six hundred and eighty miles of its meanders toward the Niger, it seamed and sundered the Diakayatés' migration with biannual crossings.

The river was the egress and the access. It divided the year into two seasonal pasturages: the rainy, when it was the gateway to the time of hope, and the dry, when, on a good year, it ushered the Fulani and their cattle into at least a few weeks of sated rest. It sloped its west bank toward the bourgou into which it spilled in late summer months, flooding rice paddies and irrigation canals and swales and sometimes entire villages built carelessly low, and it thrust its east bank up toward the sun. Although it was not very long, the Bani was wide and, during the rainy season, deep and murderously fast, a force to venerate and heed. Twice yearly, in the early days of rain and at the onset of the cold months of winter, the east bank became the point of convergence of dozens of Fulani families on the move, a place of assembly and parting, a staging point for a seasonal mass migration. It was fitting to pause before crossing such a boundary.

The Diakayatés unhitched the carts and right away the donkeys wandered off to graze on tiny daisies. Unmanned pirogues lolled in the shallows. Oumarou sat looking across the water at the east bank, where last rays bronzed a swallow-hollowed sandstone cliff.

On that cliff, at the very crest that caught the first light of morning and held on the longest to the last light of the day, Oumarou had buried his father, a daughter, and a son in a small wood of doum palms. On the plateau beyond the graves was his youngest son, Hassan, and his cattle, and his brother al Hajj Saadou. Oumarou would cross the river in the morning and the reunion would be sweet. The nomads were always leaving, leaving—and they also were always returning, returning.

The land let go of the light at last. Everyone was dog-tired. The men pulled down some matting from the carts and lay upon it. Ousman cradled baby Afo and brewed tea. Bobo mixed handfuls of *chobbal* with river water. We drank.

I wanted to see the world. I walked from Hayré with a friend to the big asphalt road and I took a bus and went to Bamako. I'd heard about Bamako and wanted to see it.

"When I got to Bamako I just spent two nights there. I liked everything. Such a good city! Nice houses, nice clothes, nice people, nice cars, electricity everywhere. I stayed at my friend's relatives' place—I don't know the name of their neighborhood. A nice neighborhood.

"While I was there I heard that I could prospect for gold in Côte d'Ivoire. So my friend and I went there. We took buses, with several layovers. At the gold mine we spoke Fulfulde, Bambara, and Mossi, the language they speak in Burkina, because the owner of the gold mine was from Burkina. We would start at eight in the morning and stop at noon. If we worked for two days in a row we were paid fifty thousand West African francs for two days of work. It was easy. The owner had this machine that took out the mud. Then we took that mud to another machine that pounded and washed, and then we used mercury to separate the gold. When you find a kilo of gold you get twenty million West African francs. I never found a kilo of gold, though.

"I spent one month at the mine. Then I traveled around Côte d'Ivoire because I wanted to see the country. I took little jobs in Abidjan. I ran errands for shop owners. Just small-time retail: clothes, shoes, electronics. I pushed carts with boxes and helped around the shops.

"If I had to choose between the bush and Bamako I'd choose Bamako. I'd move there if my parents agreed. I really like to travel and I'd like to travel to the United States."

Allaye's heavy rings shone dull orange in the orange flickers of the brazier. A slender boy with smooth skin. His identity card said he was twenty-one. He spoke in a half-whisper, so that only Gano and I could hear. He said he had brought from his seven-month sojourn five hundred thousand West African francs: more than a thousand dollars. With that money he could either marry and buy a few cows or buy a house. But he wanted to do both, and he also wanted to hire cowboys to herd his cattle so he could enjoy the pleasures of his wife and of life in a city, and so he was planning to return to Abidjan to earn more money.

"Anna Bâ, next time you go to Bamako, take me with you."

"Don't they need your help here now, during the rainy season?"

"They have three people, they don't need me. That's plenty of hands. I want to earn money. The fifty thousand I earned in Côte d'Ivoire—I've spent nothing of it. I'm saving up for a beautiful life—oops, excuse me!" Allaye spotted his father's and uncle's goats trot west toward Ballé, and he jumped up and dashed into the night in bare feet after the animals to steer them back toward the river. "*Ay! Ay, shht!*"

Allaye had not told his father about his plans, or about the money he had brought. Oumarou had not asked. "I'm studying him," he would say. "I'm waiting." From his mat he watched his son's dancing figure chase the scattering goats and spoke clearly and gravely.

"When Allaye returned last week I saw that he hasn't changed very much. He is still the same Allaye. He's just changed in his body, became a little less weathered. His color became the color of someone who lives in the city. He has a cellphone that makes and receives calls. I have forgiven him. I'm happy to see my son back. I hope he becomes successful. But I will not accept that my sons live in the city. In the city there is nothing for the cows to eat, no place for them. I want my sons to always herd cows. Cows can give milk. If these children who eat money are so hellbent on getting money, they should know that milk can be used for a lot of things, even for money."

The old man stabbed the dark with his long index finger, pinning his sons forever to life on the hoof. A Pel's fishing owl flew out of the west and disappeared over the water.

Late at night the Diakayatés quietly walked to the Bani to wash. They took turns, mindful of one another's privacy. I went last. The water was warm and silty. A strong and soundless current tipped away from a skyful of stars. Darkness deepened the silence.

Above the slope where Oumarou's family made camp that night there stood a coppice of mangoes and doum palms that concealed almost entirely from view a couple of banco huts. The grove and the huts belonged to the extended Bozo family of Kotimi Genepo. The Diakayatés had relied on the Genepos to help them cross the Bani during migration since before Oumarou was born. Back then the Bozo family, too, had been nomadic, moving along the river in boats and stopping from time to time long enough to raise cylindrical cane dwellings on its shores. The Genepos had settled in the grove in the nineteen eighties.

The men poled their pirogues up and down the waterway, one quiet man per boat. They wove and patched their nets and sometimes they tilled with a four-ox plough a small patch of swampland that lay behind their huts. They kept a small flock of goats that fed on refuse and riverside grass. The women, whom Bozo taboos forbade to fish from boats, set fishtraps in the point bar, raised chickens and guinea hens, and traveled to markets in Djenné and Madiama, a large village between Ballé and Hayré, to trade fish and doum nuts and mangoes and peanuts, depending on the season.

Like everyone else in the bush the Genepos fixed their life to the progression of stars. Stars announced the arrival of the blue-tinged Nile perch, of the short-striped daggers of clown killi, of the lunar disks of the Niger stingray. The river was never the same and yet it was, and the fishermen relied on the predictability of each day's haul: the thickheaded catfish for smoking and stewing, the tiny petrocephalus and oily raiamas for deep-frying, the scaly flanks of African carp, a shimmering mess of minnows. But, like the savannah around it, the river was behaving strangely. The droughts that throttled the land were wringing it dry. Flash floods washed away harvests and entire homesteads, altered the relief of the banks and the bottom. Acres of deforested riverbank dried out and blew away. The abrading topsoil no longer kept alluvial cutbanks from slumping into the water. And now big-town markets sold imported, ready-made fishing nets, which Bambara and Dogon farmers and Songhai traders who never before had waded into the water now used to trawl the river, taking what the Bozo believed belonged only to them.

It had drizzled on and off all night, and a thin moon shone sickly through the clouds. At last, a sunrise broke through thunderclouds. To the north stretched a black sky, and on the horizon hung

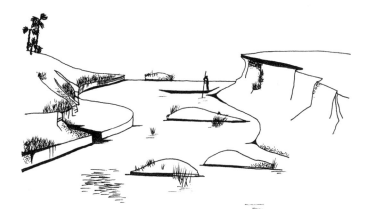

the pink glow of lightning. The cloudline ran over the camp exactly, dividing the heavens in two. The river sparkled with dawn. But within an hour the sun had gone behind black clouds, and the river, too, had turned black.

Gano and Allaye and I walked into the grove to buy some fresh fish for breakfast. But Kotimi just smiled.

"I have very little, and I don't think you'd want it." She peeled back the black tarp over her smoker and looked down at a few handfuls of tiny smoked carp, each no larger than a thumb. She smiled again, as if apologizing for such paucity. The Bani was spent.

Kotimi handed us several doum palm nuts: Bobo and Hairatou would scorch their fibrous and fermenting yellow meat to black strands over the cooking fire and that would be our breakfast. Then she walked us down to the water and waded in. A few steps from the shore she bent down to drown a woven fishtrap, fixing it in place with a fist-size rock. Maybe a catfish would wend its way inside. Without unbending she washed her face, rinsed her mouth, spat a long spurt of water back into the stream. She straightened out. She smiled again. She walked home, up the slope. A ghostly light shone upon the slate river.

Once Kotimi had showed me a cherished souvenir, an aluminum ring with an etching that read: "Inform RIKSMUSEUM STOCKHOLM SWEDEN." And a number: 9247797. A bird ring.

"It came to the river when this one"—she pointed at a teenage boy—"had just stopped nursing. We'd never seen a bird like that. It was diving and flying. It was white and had a big beak."

"We have birds, but we never put rings on our birds. Who does such a thing?" Kotimi's uncle said.

"What happened to it?"

"We killed it and threw it on the grill."

"Oh my God was it tasty!"

"I'd never tasted any meat so sweet in my life."

The boy did not remember the taste of that bird. He had been too young. But he nodded at his mother, and grinned. He had been hearing stories of that legendary feast his entire life. He was wearing a black t-shirt with a stenciled drawing by the American graffiti artist Shepard Fairey. Below the drawing was the word OBEY.

Months later I emailed the number to the museum in Stockholm. "We gratefully acknowledge your report of our bird ring with this number," the museum wrote back. "Osprey *Pandion haliaetus*. Age: Nestling, 2 young in brood. Date: 2003-07-04. Place: SWEDEN, NÄRKE, STORA MELLÖSA, EKHAGEN." For centuries, Närke, a wooded and landlocked province in south-central Sweden, had raised oxen. Until the middle of the twentieth century, its most important industry was shoemaking. It lies at the fifty-ninth parallel. From its cold forests the raptor had flown thirty-three hundred miles to become the most memorable dinner Kotimi had ever had.

The wind rose and the river's surface quivered. Ousman stood on end two rolled-up thatch mats that the morning previous had been the walls of his father's hut, and threw over them a large blue tarp. A pop-up storm shelter. Allaye, Gano, and I walked back west to Ballé to buy from a man who ran a mercantile out of the anteroom of his compound some sugar, tea, and hardboiled guineafowl eggs for lunch, and to pick up their cellphones, which they had left with the man overnight to charge for ten cents apiece. But the mercantile owner said his motorcycle battery had died in the night and the phones were not charged. He said it was my friends' cell-phones that had drained the battery of its last juice and so refused to give the men their coins back. For a few minutes we stood in his messy yard. From the corners shaggy goats and mucoid children and two women watched us in a silence that underscored the impasse. We left. On our return walk we passed, on the eastern outskirts of the village, three or four women stringing neverending threads of homespun cotton around a eucalyptus grove. Later, their husbands would weave the threads into expensive blankets with traditional Fulani black and white geometric designs.

The storm never arrived. While we were gone, the rest of the family had piled their possessions next to the water, and from there Ousman and Boucary were loading two boats, and Oumarou and Sita were bargaining for the boat rental with Kotimi's husband, a stocky gray-haired man in ripped green slacks and a dark-blue-striped boubou that barely came down to his knees, a cellphone in a camouflage pouch on a lanyard around his neck. On his forehead and on the tip of his nose were circles of dirt, unwashed since his last prayer. The Diakayaté women and children would cross the river first, with the mats and the calabashes, then Gano's motor-scooter and the remainder of the baggage, then Oumarou and Sita and Sita's two carts. The young men would help the women unload on the east bank, then return and wade or swim across with the goats and donkeys in the shallows upstream. The women with their bundles squatted by the water.

"Are you afraid, Anna Bâ?" asked Hairatou.

"No. Are you?"

"Of course. The Bozo are people of the river. We Fulani are cowherds. We are people of the bush. The river is no place for us. Of course we are afraid of crossing it."

But in the next few weeks Hairatou would ford the river many times and splash around in the water to beat down Ramadan thirst. She swam like a mermaid.

On the east bank of the Bani Oumarou sat on the knee roots of a thorn tree and waited for his animals to cross. The women lugged everything but the heavy bags of rice and millet onto the bluff, scrambling up the sandy talus of the cutbank in their skirts.

"Bobo?"

The daughter-in-law stopped midbreath, a mortar on her head.

"Have you already been to the camp Hassan made?"

"Yes, Papa."

"Did you see if the calf rope is there?"

"Yes, it is."

"Okay. Then once you have carried everything onto the bluff you may start moving stuff there. Set up your kitchen."

On the other side of the river Ousman and Allaye and Boucary were rounding up the goats, pushing them into the water. The goats bleated wildly. Some ran out of the water and the men hove them back in. Some swam in circles. The river on the far bank frothed white, filled with the shrieks of animals, with the cowboys' oaths. Hassan arrived, greeted us politely, stripped out of his boubou, plunged into the river to help out. Oumarou reminisced.

"Here is where we come every year to cross. Here I buried my father. And two children from my first wife, the boy Adama, who was two years old, and the girl Fanta, who was seven. Here, too, when I was as young as Hassan is now, three white people came to my father's camp and spent a night with us. It was incredible, Anna Bâ—that white people would come to stay with the Fulani! Can you believe it? Amazing! It never had happened before, and it never has happened since."

And who was I? I watched the river.

From the side pocket of his canvas pants Gano produced three hardboiled guinea eggs. Their pink-brown speckled shells were so dense he had to bang them against the metal handlebar of his bike to crack them. He offered one to Oumarou.

"Ah!" The old man took the egg, peeled it, bit into it delicately. "Ah! Just what the doctor ordered. Guinea eggs are very good for your blood."

"What about egret eggs?" A cattle egret stood at the river's edge and studied with one yellow eye the screaming mottle of goats.

"No one eats those eggs. No one eats egret meat."

Egret meat was black and not good for anything—not even for magic. The Fulani did not eat egrets. The Fulani also did not eat foxes, because foxes were like dogs, and dogs were unclean animals, like pigs. But Gano said he would eat any meat. He would eat donkey. He would eat dog. He *had* eaten dog. He even would eat pork. What he would not eat was anything cooked with Maggi seasoning, because Maggi seasoning made men blind and impotent. With that Oumarou agreed.

"That's true. You take two or three of those Maggi cubes, dissolve them in a little water, give them to a bull and the bull will become sterile. I've never done it to any of my bulls but I've heard people tell it so."

After all the goats had crossed, Oumarou's sons and nephews stood wet and shining on the shore and considered the heavy bags the women had left behind. They stood there for a long time. Hauling heavy things was not the job of a cowboy. Such a job was contemptible, ignoble. It was the job of a slave, of rimaibe, but all the rimaibe were on the other side of the river, in Ballé. The men stood around. Someone produced a plastic bag of soggy raw peanuts. Raw peanuts were good for virility. The men ate. Perhaps they were waiting for the loads to magic themselves up the bluff.

At last Gano walked over and offered his help. One by one they hoisted the bags upon the translator's back. One by one he carried them up the steep bank. Then he pushed his motorcycle up the cliff. Then, one by one also, he loaded the bags onto his bike and drove them over to the campsite where the women were setting up their hearth.

But for a man in love, Gano would have been a slave.

His grandmother Djidi was born into a nomadic family of Fulani nobles who lived in the bourgou. The name of that family has since been forgotten. One day when Djidi was a girl she and her older sister walked from their parents' camp to the Bani to fetch some water for their mother's cooking. A group of men rowed up in a pirogue, grabbed the girls, forced them aboard, and took them to slave markets—Djidi to Djenné, her sister to Tie, south of Bamako. One market day in Djenné a young Fulani man spotted Djidi among the slaves for sale. The family tradition went that he instantly knew from her uncommon beauty and stateliness that she was not a slave. Maybe he simply fancied her. He bought her and married her, restoring her to nobility through marriage. He was Gano's paternal grandfather. Years later, the sisters found each other. Gano knew he had relatives in Tie, but he had never met that side of the family.

While Djidi was in captivity her kidnappers refused to give her milk. For weeks she had not tasted it. After that she never drank it. Nor did her son, Gano's father. Why? Gano didn't know, and there was no one left to ask.

Gano's last name was not a traditional Fulani name like Sankari or Diakayaté or Bâ. It was a stand-in for the one that had been somehow forgotten, or misplaced, the one that would have helped griots trace his family roots to Ethiopia. A muddled legacy, a history unremembered. Gano meant "here." As in: we are here now.

The sick skewbald kid goat that had ridden to Ballé in Hairatou's lap had made it across the river. But the swim had exhausted it and when it reached the eastern shore it fell down. Now it lay amid oyster shells and chamomiles in the muddy grass next to Sita's empty cart. Blood was drying around its eyes and nose and horns. Pied crows had pecked it to death.

◇ ◇ ◇

The plateau was colossal. It toyed with the perception of distance: the thick low thorn stubble that seemed to be a few hundred paces off became a sparse grove of century-old fissured acacia trees where the Earth curved out of sight three miles away, and from among those trees more savannah unwound in endless lion-hide splendor. It dwarfed all upon it, man and cow. You could picture mammoths on it. It had been there for more than two billion years. Red, dry, and spare, it was a thing entirely apart from the fertile leas of the Bani's west bank, as if an abrupt desiccation were a necessary preamble to the highland kopjes of Hayré that lay another day's walk from the river.

Nomads already had begun arriving here, on foot, on donkeys, on motorcycles, in carts, driving before them cattle and goats and sheep, carrying all of their earthly possessions, carrying expectations of fodder and rain and reunions. Some built huts. Most squatted in the lath shade of the sparse thorn trees or reclined under their upturned carts, ready to move on once it began to rain steadily. Any day now, they said. Any day now.

By lunchtime a small deputation of men and women and children clustered around Oumarou's calf rope. Sita and Salimata and their children and grandchildren. Oumarou's younger brother al Hajj Saadou, as tall and thin as Oumarou and in clothes as threadbare. Their youngest living brother and Bomel's father-in-law, Allaye, visiting from Gagna, with a new leather hat and the smooth skin of a rich man who drank plenty of milk twice daily. Saadou's wife, Kumba, with a weeping, pustular wound on her right cheek;

in the months I knew her it would not heal. Their two grown sons and their daughter-in-law Djamba, the same age as Hairatou, with silver coins woven into her cornrows. Their youngest son, Adama, who was thirteen and always wore the same black denim leggings and a short green boubou basted with black thread and who, after shaking my hand, whispered to Gano:

"Is that a man or a woman?"

"Can't you tell by the skirt?"

"I can't tell."

"Imagine me exactly the way I am now," I suggested, "but with darker skin. What do I look like to you?"

Adama studied me awhile.

"A Fulani."

"Man or woman?"

"A Fulani woman."

The relatives clasped hands. They sat on mats and stood and walked around in pairs, in groups of three. They asked after the rain in the parts of the bourgou from which their kin had come, and offered guesses as to whether it would rain in two days, on the first day of al Nashira. They asked after one another's cattle and after relatives not present. The young men compared new frippery and gossiped and the girls prepared a large reunion lunch of rice and thumb-size fresh fish and peanut sauce and laughed and teased one another about beaus real and imagined. Hassan gave his father the full account of the cattle drive and the days following: all here, all healthy, *al ham du lillah*, all hungry. It had not rained thoroughly in Ballé and there was not enough grass—there was barely any grass at all. He would be going out to fetch the cows after lunch.

"Did you miss your family while you were by yourself?" I asked the boy.

"No. Because my cows were with me."

The Diakayatés were taking their lunch beneath a thorn tree when they heard the low drone of engines. Persistent, close, closer. They rested their sauce-stained right hands palms-up on their knees and lifted their heads to search in the overcast sky. Where? Where? Then someone pointed directly west.

The warplane rose out of the horizon not two dozen feet above the tree crowns. A heavy belly with no windows, like the belly of a whale. Swept wing, no insignia. The whirr of its four engines deceptively quiet as if it were a mile away. Its hulk was so huge it took up all the western sky, shrank the landscape below. Suddenly we were toy people, toy cattle, toy goats, toy trees. It seemed to move in slow motion, sweeping its gigantic mass in a wide circle around the plateau. You could throw a stone at it and hit it. No one did.

Who were the pilots? What were they looking for? Were they following up on military intelligence that Islamist fighters from the north had chosen the migratory staging area at Ballé to hide, to blend in with other men on the move? What if that intelligence was true, and there were among the nomads mercenaries who wanted to plunge the bourgou into a new jihad? Or was it a misinterpretation, a guess by some remote Western data analyst who saw the satellite images of a movement and assembly she knew nothing about? Was it possible that somewhere—in Bamako? France? the United States?—uniformed men and women strained their eyes at pixelated images of us eating lunch? What did the pilots see? Motionless diners, stacks of gunnysacks, long bundles of matting. Animals. The plane was low enough for them to see the uncomprehending fear on our faces.

An expression came to my mind, the American military slang term for images of humans killed in drone strikes, killed by a push of a button. "Bug splats." Baby Afo crawled out of his mother's lap with a howl. Then the plane submerged behind the low treeline to the south and was gone.

"Praise the Lord!" said al Hajj Saadou. He had pilgrimed to Mecca seven years earlier and possessed knowledge of the world that extended beyond the Sahel. "I thought they were going to drop bombs right on us. Okay, let's eat."

But Oumarou was pensive.

"That plane was looking for something," he said. "I think it was looking for the way back home. It is easy for strangers to get lost in the bush."

After lunch the men made their devotions. They aligned two goatskins, a polyester carpet, a straw mat, and a torn pagne in a mismatched row that faced the immensity of the plateau and took turns washing their feet and hands and faces from a plastic kettle. They stepped upon their makeshift prayer rugs almost in unison. Saadou's son Hassan, in a white boubou printed with tiny images of kitchen utensils, performed his ablutions, spat, took the cellphone on its lanyard from his neck, placed it carefully on a cow patty, and bent down in prayer.

The men were engrossed in sup-
plication and did not notice that at
the hearth Afo stood up and let go
of his mother's skirt and walked toward them through dung and straw
and red dust, brave and unassisted.
A nomad taking his first steps upon
the Sahel.

Later that day Oumarou measured a dozen feet south from a solitary thorn tree nearest the calf rope and, with the heel of his
plastic shoes—light green, with tiny pictures of airplanes and the
molded writing BOEING 767 on the sides: airplane shoes—traced in
hard ground a circle approximately eight feet across. Ousman
watched, then retraced it with his own blue-and-white plastic heel.
This was the circumference of his father's future temporary house,
his shelter until it was time to move on.

Sita's upturned carts were barely visible in a low thicket of dwarf
persimmons more than a hundred yards to the southeast. To the
west, halfway to the river and from Oumarou's campsite appearing
no larger than three grains of rice, stood the three huts of Saadou,
who wintered on the plateau. The physical distance between the
camps did not signal aloofness. It served the symbolic purpose of
respecting one another's boundaries. In the high scrublands of the
Sahel no place existed to sequester oneself, to be completely alone.
When the nomads went to sleep at night they spread mats and plas-

tic sheets near the cattle, with nothing to shield them from one another, from passing herders, from somnambulist cows, from the sequined sky above, from off-course warplanes. But I have noticed: no one ever intruded on the silence of others. My hosts made up for the absolute lack of physical personal space with exceptional respect for the sacred limits of internal peace.

Along the notch marked by his father's heel Ousman began to dig foot-deep holes for future posts. He used his broadsword. He dug a hole, measured a sword's length from it along the scored perimeter, dug again. Later he would forage for the frame among the wreckages of former Fulani homesteads, set up and dismantled during earlier migrations. When he grew tired of digging he handed the sword to Allaye, who dug without enthusiasm and grumbled that the outline of the hut was not perfectly round. But Amadou and Kajita already were running in and out of the imaginary door, pushing against imaginary walls, palming the wainscot not yet there. They shrieked with delight at being the first to populate their grandfather's hut and overhead, in the leafless branches of the thorn tree, twenty yellow weavers shrieked as well.

That morning Amadou had asked Gano to bring him and Kajita a puppy from Djenné.

"Okay," said Gano. "I'll bring you a puppy if you get me a bag to put it in."

"But," Amadou said, "won't the puppy cry in a bag?"

In the reddish glow of the setting sun emaciated herds returned to the campground. Dust rose at their heels in low red waves. Hassan tied up the calves and Ousman strode up to the herd with the milking calabash, shuffled a notch in the ground to steady it, untied a calf, petted it, let it suckle. He milked. Oumarou lay on a mat beside his future hut and looked away, not studying the herd, not taking it in. He had spotted the animals' deflated humps and prominent ribs from afar and he did not want to see up close their crushing hunger. As if sensing her father's sadness Hairatou paused over her mortar, pensive, her eyes stilled at some distant point in the maroon clouds.

The nomads talked for many hours after dinner. They moved in small groups from camp to camp, men and women separately, carrying with them braziers and baggies of sugar and tea. Reacquainting themselves with old friends, new babies, relatives they had not seen for many months. I stayed put. Baby Afo slept against my hip and I floated in and out of conversation as it came and went. Then Hassan took the cows out to pasture into yellow moonset and I fell asleep.

In the night the plane returned. The deep hum of its engines woke me up and I lay in the dark trying to make out its silhouette against the sky. I could not see the plane, or even gauge from the sound where to look for it. I listened and worried. It circled the camp into predawn. The night was cool and humid and mostly still and mosquitoes whined around my mat. My leg was warm where Afo had wet himself and I pulled the heavy polyester blanket tighter around us. When I fell asleep again I dreamed that an American plane had flown in to bomb the camp while we were drinking tea. I had seen aerial bombardment in real life, in wars, and the mechanicals of my dream were precise and horrendous. The dream-plane banked; the first bomb struck the river; the earth jerked and gave way. A fountain of hot dirt mixed with water and tongues of fire woke me. It was just before sunup. Afo was snoring lightly, Oumarou was already awake, Hairatou was squatting by the hearth, and a pot of Lipton was beginning to boil.

So began the last day of al Izar, the Veil, Epsilon Boötis. The next day would be the ascent of al Nashira, the star that determined whether there would be enough rain that year. There was no sign of rain at all. Only the clouds of dust, the chittering of weavers, the rusty clucking of Kumba's guinea hens. In the morning the sky frowned a little, then the sun came out again. At a certain angle you could see the few spots where the laterite had sprouted the finest film of grass. Like patches of oxidized copper. Oumarou's mood was somber.

"This time last year there was grass. This year there is none. This year I am looking at the cows and I'm seeing a big difference since they left Doundéré. They look worse. They were fatter in Doundéré. And there is still dust under the hooves of moving cattle. That's a very bad sign."

With no rain to tamp it down dust blew almost as steadily as during the ocher months of harmattan. Gusts churned columns of debris, pushed them around the plateau. One whirred through Oumarou's camp that morning, picking up buckets and twirling them away from the hearth. It was a good thing that no one was at the

camp just then. Dust devils were very dangerous. If you found yourself encircled by a dust devil you became sick for the rest of your
life. If you threw a stick at it blood gushed from your arm as if from
a wound.

In the afternoon Ousman dragged to his father's camp the skeleton of an abandoned hut he had found nearer the river. He sunk
the beams into the holes he and Allaye had dug and roofed that
frame with the thatch he had salvaged from Doundéré and bundles
of straw he had found nearby. He strapped the bundles to the frame
of the hut with rope and fabric and whacked them with long sticks
into being more watertight. Dust and two praying mantises flew
out of the straw. To the top of the hut he strapped a blue tarp. A
signal flag, an appeal to the sky, a plea for rain.

As for the warplane, the Fulani did not talk about it. It had been
some communal futuristic nightmare, not worth dredging up. They
did not see another so low over Ballé again.

On the first morning of al Nashira fine rain wafted down for a
few minutes. A tentative gray mist. Then it stopped. White
egrets flew. Oumarou settled under the thorn tree to receive and
return the greetings of neighbors, to study the sky. By the time he
had finished his Lipton, all was dry and through a nacre sheet of
clouds the sun shone very bright, solid, unblinking.

"Was your night peaceful, Oumarou?"

"It was peaceful. But I am worried. Before this morning I wasn't really worried but today I am very, very worried."

"We are also worried. The cattle are hungry."

"True, true. But the day is long. God willing, it will rain before the end of the day."

"Amen, amen, amen."

Rain or not, the cycle of chores kept on. Ousman milked the cows and Hassan took them back to scanty pasture. Allaye took the goats to the river to drink and brought them back. Bobo took the dishes to the river and stood ankle-deep, scrubbing them with sand and a sponge made from a fishing net, and schools of inchlong fish dashed about, feeding on breakfast scraps. Hairatou tidied up the camp and set off, with Djamba, to forage for firewood. The hungry cows did not make enough manure to keep the hearth going, and besides, manure would become useless as fuel when it rained.

The girls walked single file upon clay hard and windpolished to a sheen, like the surface of a frozen lake. For thousands of years hyena had hunted giraffe here, and men hunted lion with spears. When Oumarou was young, hyena and lion took weak cattle and infants. Now the land was emptied of large wild predators. Giraffe had been extirpated from most of West Africa by early-twentieth-century hunting and mid-twentieth-century drought; Thurston Clarke wrote that in 1908 French colonial authorities had hired Tuareg gunmen to kill giraffe because the animals' long necks had been ripping down telegraph wires. Elephant were a rare sight. Weak cattle remained. And man: bewildered, hungry, clinging to old ways that seemed to be rapidly losing to new, careening toward self-extinction. Man in a fierce and unwitting battle with himself.

Djamba started a wordless song and Hairatou joined in, and after a mile or so they entered a low coppice of shrubs. There they wound separately through the brush, pulling long gnarls of barkless deadwood out of bramble thickets, using one dry branch to knock inchlong thorns off another, heaping the firewood into long stacks. They tied these woodpiles with strips of fabric, bits of rope, the bark of African myrrh. They wandered apart and came close together again and their song split and spliced, split and spliced. A hunter-gatherers' duet.

It was hot and there were no birds. There was a fairytale quality to everything: the song and the singers on their quest, the crackle of deadwood underfoot, the shrubs contorted to protect themselves from the hard white light. In the long ago, before Ballé became the staging point for migrating cattle, genii had lived in each of the sparse groves that studded the plateau. The most dangerous of all had been the genie that had made its home on the cliff where Oumarou's father was buried. The Fulani said the cows had scared the genie away, that the genie had gone the way of hyenas and lions, but how could one know for sure? At this hour there were no cattle nearby. From time to time the girls called out each other's names, just to make sure.

"Hairatou?"

"What?"

"Nothing!"

They walked on east. Deeper into the brambles and out into the open again, then into another low forest. They carried no knives and broke no branches. They gathered only deadfall. Some bits of wood Hairatou would not touch. "These are someone else's," she said.

Whose? How could she tell? Invisible borders crisscrossed the bush.

After they could barely close their arms around their bundles the girls tied them one last time and lifted them onto their heads and turned back toward the river, toward camp. Djamba sang again. She had packed her firewood smartly, her sticks almost uniformly straight. Hairatou's bundle slightly more haphazard, lopsided on her head.

"Eh, girl! You pick crooked firewood, you'll have a husband with a crooked thing!"

Hairatou did not respond. Her load was heavy and uncomfortable, and there was yet water to fetch from the river, for cooking. And she did not want to think about the thing of her future husband, a boy named al Hajj Oumarou Kuna, who was camping with his parents on the west bank of the river. On the very rare occasions she talked about him she covered her face with a scarf in modesty and a kind of awe. She never had spoken to him. That she even knew his name was an accident, something a careless girlfriend had let slip without thinking, because Hairatou's father believed that it was better for the betrothed not to know the spouses their parents intended for them until the wedding day. Ideally, that also was the day they found out they had been betrothed in the first place. Such was the tradition, though in Oumarou's view it applied particularly to boys.

As for Djamba's own husband, Gouro, a son of Kumba and Saadou, she had not seen him for nearly two years. He and Djamba had been married only a few months when he asked his mother for a needle and thread to hem his best pants, ate a hearty breakfast, and jumped a bus first to Bamako, then to Côte d'Ivoire. Djamba had been in Djenné that morning, selling milk. He had been gone since. Whenever others discussed him in her presence Djamba would turn her head and look away. She never spoke of him, kindly or poorly. She was a proper Fulani woman, stoic and loyal. Gouro's father had married him well.

A father had three obligations before his sons. The first was to give them names when they were born and pay for the naming ceremonies. The second was to decide where to have them circumcised and pay for the circumcisions. The third was to find them good wives and pay the bride price. Once a son was married he became an adult, responsible for his own family, for his own children.

The bride could not be Songhai, or Bambara, or Dogon, or rimaibe, or Bozo. She especially could not be Bwa, like the people who lived in Hayré, because the Bwa were pagans. She had to be a Fulani.

The bride had to be younger than the groom by at least three or four years. She had to come from a good, dignified, big family, and she had to be beautiful. She had to have grown up in the bush because that was where she would spend her life with her cowboy husband.

She could not be someone the boy already knew, someone about whom he had already had an opportunity to form an opinion. There had to be about a man's future wife a mystery that he would discover gradually, in the course of his marriage.

The bride's very existence had to be a mystery. "Until I find a bride I like and bring her here for my son I'll tell him nothing," Oumarou said. "When I bring her here I will tell him that he is getting married to this girl I picked for him."

A boy who found out ahead of time which girl his father had selected for him might reject her. Other people could hear that and tell their friends, and through the rumor mill the girl and her parents inevitably would find out. That would upset the girl and embarrass both families.

Ousman met his bride Bobo on his wedding day. Neither had known that they had been engaged for three years. It was the same for Ousman's older brother, Boucary, and it would be the same for Allaye and Hassan.

These were Oumarou's rules, though he allowed for exceptions. Bomel, for example, married Adama, the son of Oumarou's youngest brother, Allaye, who, like some fathers, preferred that his sons married relatives. Oumarou had agreed to the marriage, though he personally thought such a preference a little silly. "When your son marries a woman who is a stranger, she's still a Fulani," he said. "When they have children, the children will travel to their mother's camp and so through them the two families will become one."

Oumarou himself had married Fanta, who grew up in a village, not in the bush. But that was an exception, too, because he had been the widowed father of two small children, not in a position to wait for a wife who fit all his criteria. Also, Fanta did know the bush well. And she and Oumarou did love each other. In a good marriage, love mattered a lot.

Now Oumarou was making inquiries about a bride for Hassan. Discreetly he asked the Fulani men on transhumance about girls who met his requirements. Hassan's mind, meanwhile, was on the cattle. Each night and each afternoon he drove his father's cows to pasture and each morning and each evening he returned with a herd that looked thinner than before. Although Oumarou had said nothing to him about it, Hassan was holding himself responsible for taking the animals from the dwindling grasslands of the bourgou and bringing them too early to this vicious, arid plateau. He should have listened to his father and waited until it had rained more. He watched nearly in tears the clouds that gathered and dispersed overhead. If he could have jumped up there and wrung water out of the sky with his hands he would have.

That evening Hassan drove the cows to camp in a cloud of dust. The animals walked right past the hitching rope at a hungry trot.

"Hairatou!" Ousman yelled. "Stop the cows!"

"Hairatou!" counterordered Oumarou. "Do your own work! Plenty of boys here."

Allaye, who had been listening to music on his cellphone, reluctantly rose from his mat. Oumarou rose as well. Frustrated with the dust, the rainless sky, his feckless sons.

"Go away. You don't know how to do it. You'll never separate the cows from the calves." He moved among the herd. In less than a minute the eight calves stood tethered to the rope in a neat line, the adult animals a few paces away. "See? This is how we do it."

The sun was an angry eye in the cloud-blackened west. Then it was gone. Ousman set some manure and straw to smolder over the hearth where Hairatou was cooking millet and carried that slow fire in his bare hands and laid it among the herd, to keep away mosquitoes. He wrapped a plastic bag around his right hand and drenched it in pesticide that smelled like paint thinner and with that he set to wiping the calves' hind legs. Ticks had been bothering the cattle since they had arrived in Ballé. He hung the pesticide bottle on a rope from Oumarou's thorn tree and rinsed his hands with water from the Bani and returned to the cows to milk.

Later he brought Afo to the calf rope to watch the cows breathe. He sat on his haunches before the herd and Afo sat naked on the hot ground next to him. Against a sky aglitter with shooting stars. Afo leaned into his father and sucked his thumb.

Night streamed down. Hairatou sang. After dinner and prayer, an owl shrieked in flight over the camp, looking for a child's soul to steal.

The only man on the plateau who did not seem tormented by anxiety about rain was Allaye. He was too busy obsessing over the bewildering workings of the human heart. He was in love.

That week Allaye fancied a girl named Binta, whose family had made camp halfway between Ballé and Hayré. Every night since the Diakayatés had arrived in Ballé, Allaye would sneak out of his father's camp and hike to see Binta. He would return at dawn, sated, exhausted, smiling, and sleep all day long. He did not talk about his escapades in front of his father.

"The old man will never accept such foolishness—to travel so far because of a woman!" he said. There was another problem. He wanted to marry Binta, but her parents had promised her to someone else. Maybe he should seek advice from a marabout? Or get her pregnant? And what would happen to her if she got pregnant but ended up having to marry the other man anyway?

"Oh, that's simple," said Gano. "If a girl has sex before marriage she goes to a marabout. The marabout opens a kola nut, puts a gris-gris inside, spits, and closes the lobes. The girl eats the kola nut and becomes a virgin again." Gano has heard of many such incidents of restored maidenhood from women friends.

Allaye had no idea that his father already had found him a bride, a girl a few years his junior, who camped with her family on the Niger River upstream from Moura, near Diafarabé. He had been betrothed for a year, since before he had left for Côte d'Ivoire.

Oumarou was not sure about looking for a bride for Drissa, who yet had years of Islamic scholarship ahead of him. He did not know if it was the place of a cowboy father to find a bride for a mara-bout son.

I visited Drissa twice, once during the rainy season and once in late fall. A decade into his Islamic studies he squatted in a cinder-block shack without electricity in a grimy unpaved square on San's outskirts. This was his madrassa. There was a dug well from which he and other talibs pulled water hand over hand with a leather bucket to drink and wash and do laundry. There were inkwells made of Vaseline jars from which they copied the Koran in neat penman-ship. They wiped their styluses on their hair. The buildings were tagged with spraypaint in English: MEN STIR DELBY. EXTRA-MEN CLAN. MEN STAR. North of the square shredded black and blue plastic bags flew from a fence of dry thornbrush. From here the boys set out into the straight provincial streets of the town with plastic lunchpails and the old tuneless beggar ditty in Fulfulde:

> *A Talib is God's friend.*
> *Respected mother, respected father,*
> *God will reward you.*

Drissa talked little and studied his hands a lot. He picked his toenails. He looked away to ask about his parents and siblings and the cattle. Both times I saw him, he wore the same polyester t-shirt with a portrait of Barack Obama, the second time still more faded than the first. He lived by begging, by trading odd jobs for food and hand-me-down clothes. A Bambara matron whose garden of mangoes and figs he watered and weeded daily in exchange for lunch said he was an excellent worker, honest and kind, but *wallahi*, he didn't talk! His parents told me he never had, that he was very shy. His tutor, Marabout Kola's son, said Drissa studied hard and was on track to becoming a very good marabout.

The second time I saw Drissa he was on an assignment for a healer who had asked him to pick twelve lotus flowers for a potion. He did not know what the potion was for. He let me come with him. We walked on an elevated asphalt road, then took a path down to a marsh on the northern edge of San. The marsh was endless and hummocked with small soggy islands in waxy white bloom, and on

229

one such island very far from the mainland stood a lone bay horse. The boy rolled up his pants, black with prints of red and yellow dragons, and waded in. Soon he was waist-deep. He pulled at each flower thoughtfully, slowly. It took him a few minutes. Then he waded back out and stood. The long ropy stems, slack and deflated in his hands, dripped water. He held them in front of his chest and slightly apart as if not knowing what they were. Or what he was. There was a lostness about him.

An old cowboy in the bush had told me: "A person who asks questions will never be lost in the world." But in the savannah the world aligned with family and millennial trade, which often were one and the same. The Fulani herded. The Bozo fished. Everyone told stories around the hearth after dinner. For those of us who inadvertently or by design—whose?—found ourselves without such structure, alone, it was so easy to feel disoriented, disconnected, off course. I felt sad for Drissa and his limp, sopping flowers.

I felt sad for me.

"Anna Bâ," Gano said to me once, out of the blue. "In your head is a map. But it's a one-way map. It only knows how to get there, it doesn't know how to come back." Back where? I was walking around the Sahel, following someone else's cattle. And my lover—where in the world was he? I didn't know. I had been cast off, cast adrift. I used to carry his gift of the pocket compass in my shoulder bag. I would smell its sour brass, finger it smooth. But during the Hoping I had to put it away: it was heavy. And the bearings it set were obsolete.

♦ ♦ ♦

The next day I woke before my hosts, blue and unbalanced after a recurring dream sequence of my beloved's returns and leave-takings. The merry-go-round of yearning and abandonment had become my companion on so many nights, permitting no rest. I was dispirited and bitter and scorned myself for it. I put on my sandals and walked to the river alone.

I walked past the waking camps: here and there, the glow of a cooking fire, the pale shaft of smoke dissolving into grayblue twilight. Past the cliff where sheer manmade nests of brambles tacked to the earth the graves of Oumarou's father, son, and daughter, and a dozen graves of the parents and children of other nomads. Past a small Bozo outpost: three banco huts on the lip of a naked bluff where the Fulani bought sugar and tea and charcoal and cigarettes and seasonal peanuts. Past a single tall doum palm growing out of a mound of rotting yellow fruit. The sky paled to smoky blue patches where it was clear and the clouds still held the night, and to the distant west lightning reddened the clouds, hinting at rain elsewhere. I pictured Oumarou waking inside his hut, pacing around the plateau, watching the clouds, wishing them close.

Walking was ever a treasure hunt. Its clues were ephemeral: clouds and dreams; its prizes temporary: rain and a healthy herd and a full stomach for a season—or altogether unreachable: release from heartache. If there was a solution it wasn't in walking. It may have been in walking on and on and on, forevermore from weather to river to graveyard to pasture.

Beyond the doum palm the river bent and I skidded down a

cutbank to the narrow strip of cropped grass. The air was the color of titanium. The river glowed with a prescient glow, the reflection of a day not yet dawned. "If there is magic on this planet," wrote the anthropologist Loren Eiseley, "it is contained in water." One way or another, everyone in the Sahel was looking for magic.

I checked up and down the current. There was no one in sight. I took off my headscarf and clothes and waded in and swam.

The day before, downstream from here, Hairatou, Djamba, and Kajita Pain-in-the-Ass had forded the Bani to go to Ballé because Hairatou needed to buy twenty cents' worth of peanut oil and wanted company. Gano and I tagged along. The girls took off their thin headscarves and discreetly wound them around their hips under their skirts. Then they took off their skirts and tied them on their heads to keep the fabric dry. Then they ordered Gano to go ahead and cross first.

"And don't look back!" they hollered after him. They sat down on the grass and watched him take off his shirt and canvas pants and they giggled and whispered indecencies to one another and fell back on the grass laughing. When he was halfway across they took off their shirts and plunged in. Hairatou had wrapped her sequined red and green and silver scarf around her narrow hips. The sequins shone in the water like fish scales, the skin on her small hard breasts shone, her wet hair. Upon Djamba's belly shone an exploded chrysanthemum of razor scars where a traditional healer had cut her to treat a persistent and powerful stomachache she'd had as a small child. The girls waded and paddled and joked their way across. Kajita moaned with delight. They reminded me of my sister and her girlfriends—when they were younger, when I still spent time with them. They were the same age as my son. They reached the other bank just in time for a cowherd to drive a thin and thirsty herd into the river. Hairatou plopped down in the water in her sparkling loincloth and cracked up with embarrassment and the plain joy of being wet.

Now, in the dawn river by myself, I remembered swimming with the girls and laughed. Then I laughed again, happy that I was laughing. Happiness, like magic, was both elusive and very simple.

When I returned to camp the Diakayatés were awake and Gano had set aside for me a cup of lukewarm Lipton.

"Where did you go? We woke up and you weren't here. We were all worried."

"I'm sorry. I only went for a swim."

"Then why are your clothes dry?"

"I took them off."

"Didn't people see you?"

"It was dark."

"What about the Bozo on the river?"

"They were far and it was dark."

"*Wallahi*, Anna Bâ. African eyes, they see far away."

That afternoon in pursuit of eggs, Gano and I crossed the Bani in a borrowed pirogue to visit Kotimi Genepo. A pair of Egyptian geese grazed by the water. A bearded man sat crosslegged on the ground and stitched a rip in his fishing net. A toddler with a distended stomach and a grotesque navel hernia fed mango peels to a billy goat. Skinny white kittens chased one another under palm trees.

For two dollars Kotimi loaded guinea eggs into the pockets of the khakis Gano had bought in Djenné from a pile of secondhand American donations and filled a ten-liter plastic bucket with mangoes. She handed the bucket to me.

"You'll bring the bucket back some other time," she said. And then: "So, there must be a river in the country from which you came?"

"Yes, many. Why do you ask?"

"Oh, we were watching you swim this morning. You swim pretty well. We figured you'd done it before."

Gano had worried also because of waterfolk. Waterfolk lived in the river. They dragged people underwater by their hair and gouged out their navels and eyes. Human eyes and bellybuttons were delicacies; waterfolk served them at their riverine weddings. They preferred their victims to be lightskinned. On slave ships they had hitched rides to the Caribbean; there, they stole men's shadows. They plucked people's limbs from their bodies. Some of them had one human foot and one cloven hoof. Some of them had feet that faced backward.

In the bourgou they kept their appearances secret. Often people would see an arm, the slippery curve of a hip, a glistening foot disappearing in the river with a splash. The other day Boucary's wife Abba saw the outline of a leg when she was washing the dishes in the river; now she would not let her children follow her to the water. The Diakayatés knew of no one who had sighted a water person head to toe and survived.

To protect yourself from waterfolk you took cattle to the river with you. You let the cows enter first, then you quickly dove in, washed, drank, and got out while the cows were still in the river. It was a good way to fool waterfolk, and crocodiles, too. I had been unwise to go swimming without any cows.

At least, Fanta said, I'd had enough sense to go in the dark. A person who washed in the daytime was always sick, poor, and mentally disturbed.

Late that night Sita strode into the camp to warn Oumarou to keep a close eye on his cows. A cattle thief was prowling the plateau, he said. He had heard a commotion by the river, in the Sankari camp.

"Oh, that's just Njobo Sankari," said Oumarou. "Nothing for us to worry about. He is after his own father's cattle."

Njobo had been stealing cows from his father's herd year after year, for several years in a row. He would sell the cows and buy jewelry, a cellphone, a motorcycle. Oumarou said that if he had been the boy's father he would have locked him up in a hut and given him only water and uncooked millet. "That'll teach him."

"How do you lock up anyone in a hut?" I asked. "A hut is made of grass and reeds, and there is no lock on the door."

"You tell your son: 'Stay here and do not leave.' A son must do what his father tells him."

"But why doesn't he obey his father's orders not to steal cattle in the first place?"

Oumarou thought about it.

"Maybe he is not a good son."

His own sons listened, dispassionate, respectful. Commonly a Fulani man will have stolen an animal from his father's herd by the time he reached adulthood. The stunt was meant to be a one-time thing, a rite of passage, a determinant of gender identity—a tame rendition of the cattle raids of yore in which pastoralist adolescents raided the cows of other tribes and took entire herds of animals as swag. In the mechanized Global North, some teenage boys stole cars this way. Because the boys usually took animals that belonged to their fathers or uncles the ritual raiding was not considered theft, and was not punished.

By custom unmarried Fulani boys passed the night not with their elders but with boys of their own age. Together they would take their fathers' cattle on nightherd. Together they would doze off

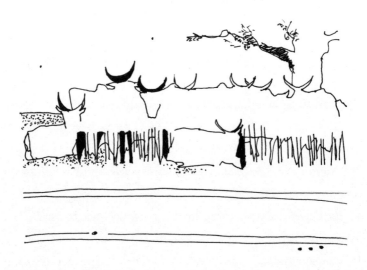

cocooned in thin cotton blankets among the sleeping cows. Together they would water them. Together, too, once in a while they would conspire to steal an animal and eat it. Most commonly, they stole goats.

It happened like this: The young men would be sitting together in a field, surrounded by the night breath of cows, and one of them would say, "Shares!" It meant, "Let's go get some fresh meat." Then the boys would stand up and go to the bush to find some goats, though one of the boys would stay behind to mind everyone's cattle. They would form a semicircle and separate one goat out of the herd and drive it toward water, because a goat would never try to swim away. After God had created the land and the water and the sky and put animals on the ground, He told all the animals to close their eyes so He could bring celestial creatures into the water unseen. All the animals closed their eyes but the goat, an animal of a cunning and deceitful nature. In response to God's order it cheated and only squinted, and it saw all the things that entered the river from the sky. That's why a goat is afraid of going in the water: it knows exactly what's in it.

Once the boys caught the goat they would slit its throat in a way prescribed by Islamic law, uttering the name of God and quickly severing the jugular veins and carotid arteries on both sides of the neck with a sharp blade the animal could not see, but leaving intact the spinal cord. They would skin and dress it and bury the head and the intestines and cut up the meat and hang it on a tree to dry. The next night they would collect the meat and divide it so that each of them, including the boy who had minded their cattle, got his share.

Sometimes, the boys would steal a bull instead and sell it and spend the money on a weeks-long binge of meat, tea, and girls. Four years earlier, Allaye and some friends stole a bull from Oumarou's herd, drove it to Djenné, sold it to a butcher there, and spent an entire month womanizing and feasting in Ballé. Then the money ran out and the boys came back. Oumarou had said nothing to reproach his son. Most cowboys had done the same thing, and most people disparaged a boy who had not stolen an animal by the time he turned twenty: such a boy, they said, was not a real Fulani. Boucary had done it. Ousman had done it. Gano had done it. Even Bamoussa Cissé, the lame and thin old muezzin who barely made his nightly way up the rampart of Djenné's Grande Mosquée to sing the evening azan, most likely had done it.

But times were changing. Dwindling pastures and sporadic rainy seasons put the herds in jeopardy and cattlemen became more fretful over the animals that remained. At the same time, an unprecedented amount of manufactured knickknacks flooded town markets. Cellphones, Chinese sneakers, knockoff Swiss army knives, handsome shoulder bags donated by charitable citizens of the Global North that tinkers sold from tall and multicolored mounds sorted by value and price—all stimulated greed for ownership, for cash. Young men were stealing goats and cows not for pleasure but for money. "They eat money," the Fulani said of such boys.

Of course, avarice and prodigality always had existed in the bush.

"Listen," Oumarou continued. "I once knew a man named Djanji Sankari. When he was young his father died and left him a lot of cows. A very big herd. This Djanji sold the cows and spent all the money on griots and parties. One time he hired griots for a night and spent a million francs! Then after a while he had no money and he had no more cows, and had to hire himself out as a cowherd to people in Côte d'Ivoire. The griots who once sang his praises now curse his name. And whenever he sees someone he knew back when he was rich he runs away in embarrassment. He is ashamed."

A Fulani without cows was like a woman without jewelry.

"Some sons steal all of their family cows one by one," said Ousman. "After that the family is poor forever."

Oumarou himself said he had never stolen anything in his life, not even when he was a teenage boy. "Whenever I needed money I asked my father. If my father didn't have money I asked him for a cow to sell. He would offer me two cows to choose from and sell at the market. I would use the money to buy meat, to flirt with girls, whatever I needed."

Ousman and Allaye said nothing. Their father's and grandfather's bygone wealth was the stuff of legend, still recounted around campfires in the bourgou. But now, through no fault of his own, Oumarou had no cows to spare.

Hassan said: "Sometimes at night I steal cows. Sometimes they are our cows, but often they are other people's cows. All I know is that they are in milk. I milk them and drink the milk. Then I let the cows go."

I pictured the gangling boy folding his praying mantis limbs to suck stolen milk like the two prehistoric children from the painted scarps of Jebel Ouenat. The image made me smile. But the men just nodded. Perhaps they envied him. They had not had enough milk since the cattle left the bourgou for Ballé.

Fanta strode into the camp eight days after she had gone to see her ailing brother. In a calabash on her head she carried smoked fish, a bag of hard Moroccan dates, and a plastic bag of ginger to spice up *boiri*, a viscous kissel of millet flour and tamarind juice, the traditional thirst-quencher for Ramadan meals. Ramadan, the month of fasting, would begin at nightfall.

Oumarou rose to greet his wife.

"How was your road?"

"Exhausting. How are the cows?"

"Hungry, Fanta. How is your brother?"

"He's still in this life. He has a fever and a cold. Has it rained here?"

"No. Has it rained where you were?"

"No. It has not rained anywhere. Everyone, everyone is worried, everyone."

Fanta's arrival gave the camp an impression of busyness. She wove a mat. She peeled all the ginger. She ordered Hairatou to pound five kilos of millet: "Ramadan is coming." She ordered Kajita and Amadou to stop clinging to her and put on some undergarments: "People are watching." She cleaned the fish she had brought, laying it out under a tree upon a gunnysack in three separate piles, each requiring its own processing method. Nile perch: keep the head, toss the guts. Killifish: tweeze out the bones, toss the heads. Catfish: check the belly for worms, otherwise keep whole.

She picked a spine out of Kajita's foot with a sewing needle longer than her forefinger. The little girl cried while Hairatou held her down and Adama, Saadou's teenage son, incanted stories about the many times he had the same procedure performed on his own feet. Finally the spine was out. It was almost an inch long. Fanta held it out for Kajita to see, the way a medic shows a wounded warrior the bullet extracted from his flesh. The child was so stunned by the size of the thorn that she stopped crying.

"*La ilaha il Allah!*" she whispered, wide-eyed, and everybody laughed.

Fanta tweezed dirt and thorns out of the soles of her own feet, looked around for something else to do, saw her grandson Hashem, and grabbed him by the penis.

"What do you think?" she called to Bobo. She pinched the toddler's foreskin and wielded the needle over it like a sword. "Should we circumcise him now?"

Bobo laughed. Hashem was disobedient and a menace even to his older cousins: quick to grab a stick or an unsheathed broadsword and swing it around, quick to bash Amadou's head with a fist-size rock. But he was untouchable—to Bobo because he was her firstborn, to Fanta because he was her grandson, to Oumarou because the boy was named after his late father. "He is stubborn and aggressive, and I know he's not a good child," Oumarou said of him. "But I cannot accept anyone messing with a child who bears my father's name." Hashem wriggled out of Fanta's grasp, hit her hard on the wrist, and took flight across the plateau. A tiny naked figure, a black fleck waterbrushed against an infinity of gold. In the sky above him hundreds of identical meringue clouds drifted, spotted the savannah. Somewhere to the northwest a storm gathered and dispersed.

Afo, on his newfound legs, roved around Fanta in wobbly circles. He was reaching for the fish she had left in the sun to dry. She kept slapping his hand gently, clicking her tongue: "Don't do that. Don't do that." Flies landed on the fish, explored. Amadou picked the discarded heads off the ground, scooped out whatever was edible with his pinkie, ate. On a mat a few paces apart Allaye lay on his back, legs bent and crossed at the knee, and studied himself in a tiny handheld mirror. The mirror's pink plastic frame held a faded color photograph of wind-bent palms on a turquoise seashore. Oumarou watched with pleasure his son preen. "The mirror is a person's second mother," he said. "When you're headed somewhere, to a wedding or a party, your mother says: 'Wait, you have some food stuck to the corner of your mouth,' or 'Wait, you have some dirt here.' When your mother is not around, you use a mirror."

The old man had been stooped with worry about the weather for days. Also, the family was running out of grain and the prospect of having to travel to Djenné to restock had made Oumarou very nervous. He had never bought rice on his own, only fabric and animals. But fabric and animals were sold by men. Rice was sold by women. "I don't know," Oumarou told his brother Saadou, "how to bargain with women." Fanta's return brought some relief. No longer did he have to fret by himself, or sleep alone in his new hut. And Fanta could go to the market and buy foodstuffs for the camp.

But Fanta's return delivered no rain. Angled sunrays lit a hard clay pan the color of eggshell and just as cracked. The nomads wandered between the camps aimlessly, cut for sign the dust that dragged behind the scraggly afternoon herds, clicked their tongues. The talismanic presence of cattle, the animals' smelly bulk, seemed reduced by the drought. Before sunset, the northwest darkened under heavy cloud and in the distance broad shafts of rain moved slowly south, parallel to the Bani, out of reach. The wind was from the east, from where the sickle moon would rise into a starry sky and Ramadan would bring thirst for all, not just the dead grass on the dry plateau.

Every Ramadan morning at two o'clock the muezzins and marabouts of Djenné stood upon the city's adobe crenellations and at the corners of the Grande Mosquée and walked the narrow streets in blue moonlight and sang awake the town's cooks. They sang awake Pygmée's servant girl and Gano's beautiful half-deaf mother. They sang awake Afo Bocoum's quiet wife and the women in the house of Ali the Griot. They sang awake the Songhai women who grilled spongy rice pancakes and the Bozo riverwomen who smoked catfish and perch. The calls of the clerics did not reach all the homes in the town's clay warrens, and some women woke to alarm clocks they set the night before. The holy Muslim month was the period of pious subjugation of man's needs and habits, and that included the Sahelian habit of dominating time, which was usually malleable and irrelevant. It was the month to abide by the very specific temporal restraints prescribed by the Koran: that no food or drink pass the lips of believers between the first and last light of day. In July, the sun in Mali rose just before six in the morning, and set approximately at seven at night.

On the camping ground outside Ballé there were no muezzins to wake the women to their cooking fires, no alarm clocks, no clocks at all. No numerical understanding of a twenty-four-hour day, which dated back to ancient Egypt circa third millennium BC. The Fulani women on the plateau used the circadian chronometer that people the world over have used for thousands of years: they roused themselves at first cockcrow, which came two or three hours before dawn. Maybe they also stirred themselves awake by memory of Ramadans past, by their own inconspicuous and steady devotion. Within a few minutes in the deep dark of the hour in all the camps on the plateau small cooking fires burned in expert synchronicity.

Fanta and Bobo cooked rice. They cooked fish sauce with fresh onions, and Lipton. They cooked a fresh batch of *boiri*. They washed a handful of mangoes in water Hairatou had hauled from the river the day before and doled out hard maggoty dates. Bobo had tied baby Afo to her back. They squatted in their lowcut boubous around the fire's glow, and in that occult red light they looked sacred, holy, sublime.

"Hurry-hurry, dive in, dive in," said Oumarou when Fanta served the meal almost two hours later. No one was hungry. Everybody wanted to crawl back under their blankets and sleep. "Eat a lot. It's better to finish quickly. We don't know when the east will begin to grow light. I don't want time to come and grab us by the wrist!"

After breakfast the nomads returned to their mats, for their second sleep. When they woke again the sun was a palm's width above the eastern trees and it was very hot. Hassan and the cattle were still gone. There were dishes to clean, laundry to wash, firewood to fetch. There was a long day ahead to lie in the speckled shade of a thorn tree, suffer the thirst, and watch the land shrivel in the sun.

Blackbirds and weavers pecked at the rice grains spilled around the hearth. By the river, spotted kingfishers fluttered in dizzying black-and-white drizzle, and four pied crows fought over a dried piece of carrion. An African fish-eagle flashed its fleecy throat in circles round the sun, which rose another palm, inched southward. Oumarou and Fanta stood up and moved their mats to keep them in the shade.

A Fulani family trundled toward Hayré in a cart drawn by a lovely dapple horse. Oumarou followed the cart with his eyes. Thirsty, tired people to match the thirsty landscape and spent live-stock.

"Where are they going, idiots? There's no water in Hayré now. They'll have nothing to drink there." But Fanta rose from her mat and wandered over to the campsite of the departed family to salvage a perfectly fine clay waterjug they had left behind. She hoisted it upon her head. On the walk back she paused over something on the ground. A large dead Nile perch. She bent her knees, picked up the fish by the tail, and returned to camp with her two finds. She set the jug inside the hut, dropped the fish on the ground by the hearth, palmed some dry clay over it. "It will be delicious with rice later on," she said. Then she lay back down, exhausted and in pain.

Sita Dangéré walked up, leaned on his clubbed staff, foot on knee. He greeted his uncle and aunt.

"May we see another Ramadan."

"Amen, amen, amen. How are the animals?"

"They are eating very little. If we have one big rain—just one big rain—there will be enough for them to eat. How are your animals?"

"The same. Hungry. Everyone is waiting for rain."

"Indeed. God willing, it will rain soon."

The sun stood at its apex. Oumarou and Fanta moved their mats to keep them in the shade. Except for the buzzing of flies it was absolutely quiet.

It was true that the year was uncommonly dry, that the rain was unusually late. Yet the echoed laments and the underlying worry were as practiced as the journey itself: well-worn implements from the toolkit of transhumance that the Fulani deployed with familiarity in response to trials that were as old as nomadism itself. There had been dry spells before and there would be again. To an outside eye the Fulani on the plateau looked like a flock of evacuees, skinny refugees fleeing with emaciated herds some unspeakable calamity. Up close, each hour of their hardship seemed dreadful, draining. But they were not refugees at all. They belonged exactly where they were at any given moment: they were here now. Every movement and pause had been choreographed over centuries, and this excruciating waiting was an inherent and ritual part of life in motion, just as the difficult Ramadan fast was an inherent and ritual part of belief. In some way, the waiting also was relief—a stop along the journey like a breath drawn, a caesura. Inevitably, after every break came the next step, and within each footfall there lay a wonderment, a precious not-knowing of what came after.

Time passed. It was hot and humid. Fanta wove for a bit, then napped. In the afternoon came distant thunder, and a single raindrop fell from a furrowed sky. Then the sun came out again. Oumarou and Fanta moved their mats to keep them in the shade. I lay on my back with a copy of Hampâté Bâ's rendition of *Kaïdara*, the Fulani initiatory epic that predated Islam. The English translation read:

> *It was only a few years after the mountains had hardened,*
> *when the world-forces were just finishing carving out the river*
> *beds . . .*

"*Kaïdara?*"

"What's it about, Anna Bâ?"

"It's about the beginning of everything, and the search for the meaning of life."

"Eh? Never heard of it."

"But it's part of your own tradition, Fulani tradition."

"No, Anna Bâ. We only know what we heard from the Koran."

From the faraway hills of Bandiagara, where Hampâté Bâ was born in 1901, dark medusas of rain dragged toward the plateau. Dust blew strong and hard and Fanta and Oumarou rose and rolled up their mats and dragged them into their hut. "Life in the bush is hard," said Fanta. "No it's not," Oumarou replied. "Not if you are used to it."

The wind died down. Late afternoon sky pressed to the ground the hot air. A faint stink of rot escaped from the dead fish mound. Oumarou and Fanta took the mats out of the hut again and laid them in the shade. They napped some more.

The first day of Ramadan ended in a celestial lightshow. Stormcells rimmed the earth, lightning crackled on the horizon, pressed closer from all sides. Immediately overhead, in the infinite space between galaxies that could accommodate the secrets and pains of the heart, stars shot in every direction with an almost audible whoosh. Some said it was Satan throwing rocks. Some said it was the souls of men of consequence. If you swallowed as a shooting star peeled off the Milky Way you were protected from all curses.

We broke fast with *boiri* and dates and millet *toh*, our first meal in seventeen hours. We drank tea and river water and more tea. Cicadas drowned out thunder. After dinner Hassan took the cattle out to pasture.

The storm crashed into the camp all at once. The air filled suddenly with thick dust and after a few beats a tremendous squall spun into the plateau. It flogged the land with heavy rain, stabbed it with lightning, whipped it with mud. Walls of water collapsed one onto another. Nine sodden disoriented sleepers squeezed into Oumarou's hut. It leaked near the entrance, at the edge of the blue tarp. Fanta tried to catch the stream in a plastic bucket and the water splashed upward, sprayed people and blankets and mats. Inside and outside it rained and rained all night.

> *The sky met the earth*
> *and weighed down on it with rain and wind.*
> *Columns of water could be heard falling*
> *and thunder sounded like gunpowder. . . .*

Caught between these vast spaces,
men and animals were mere buds bursting
amid the tumult of that foaming, unleashed sea.

—AMADOU HAMPÂTÉ BÂ, *Kaïdara*

The storm was so loud that the women slept through cockcrow. The Diakayatés would fast that day dehydrated from the start. But when they woke, sore and chilled in damp clothes, a striped scarlet and purple dawn lay reflected in enormous pools of rainwater and frogs were singing everywhere.

The plateau was inundated. New short grass had sprouted overnight and bristled in drowned fields. Between its blades an inverted sky blued. The air was still and clear like glass, and everything shone. More termites had corkscrewed out of the flooded earth and the crystal shards of their discarded wings twinkled in puddles. In the sparkling wadis frogs in necklaces of brilliant bubbles croaked laconic mating chants: pick me, pick me, pick me, pick me. Women with waterjugs slid across the clay, squinting at all the light, laughing despite their Ramadan privations. Mud clung to bare feet, to rubber shoes, weighed down walkers. Red soil lipped pale spills of rainwater. The sun was bright like a song.

Oumarou walked a fastpaced lap around the plateau, greeting the neighbors, looking for something. He returned to his campsite and stopped by the hearth.

"Where is Allaye?"

In all directions, an unpeopled pink and bluegreen expanse of water and sky.

"He was wandering around the camp last night, with his music on."

"He was strangely quiet yesterday. And he asked about his ID."

"Look!" said Fanta. She pointed to a wet length of blue and purple cotton cloth. "He left his blanket here. He never leaves his blanket. Maybe he left."

"And his bag, too," said Hairatou. She picked up her brother's small polyurethane bag with broken zippers, went through it. Some extra cellphone batteries. A small jar of petroleum jelly. A ballpoint pen. Nothing else. He had taken his cologne and his rings.

"I know him," Isiaka had said soon after Allaye had returned from Côte d'Ivoire. "He'll go off again. He's ready. He's been to a big city and he's changed. He'll never want to stay in the bush now."

Oumarou stood in the middle of the camp. All of a sudden he seemed terribly small. A stick figure in a green boubou that was beating hard in the morning wind, in a turban that left only his eyes uncovered. All around him the glorious, radiant, indifferent vastness of his choosing, the vastness Allaye so consistently spurned.

From the folds of his turban Oumarou's voice sounded flat and old.

"That morning at the end of the last rainy season, in Hayré, I woke up and Allaye took two, three cups of tea. Then he walked away. I thought he was just going to greet the neighbors. It was the day he was supposed to herd cows, so I thought he'd gone to find them where they were grazing. Then he didn't return and the next afternoon he called and said—and not even to me directly—'Hello, I'm in Bamako.' I couldn't accept that. He should have said, 'Father, I'm going to travel.' Why run away like that?"

Fanta clutched a handful of rainsoaked blankets to her chest. "If he's gone," she said, "who knows if we will see each other again in this life? I am old."

And then Hairatou pointed at the sparkling wet eastern horizon. "Look, Papa! That's Allaye!"

Trim and smiling, the boy approached through the puddles. He greeted his parents, his sister, his sister-in-law, his nephews and niece. He said he had spent the night with Hassan and the cows, and that the cows were very happy with the rain.

When his parents were out of earshot, Allaye told me that before he joined Hassan he had spent a few hours with his new sweetheart. Her name was Hajja, and she was very beautiful. Her parents' camp was between Oumarou's hut and the Bani. Hajja was engaged but she had agreed to run away with Allaye to Senegal.

"What about Binta?"

"I don't love her anymore. I love Hajja now." Allaye smiled. He had discovered passion and he loved being in love, the regenerating aliveness of it.

I saw Hajja later that day, at noon. It was time to water the cows and Allaye and Saadou's son Hassan took their fathers' herds to the river. The animals moved slowly and stopped to piss. Their humps hung to the side. Allaye teased his cousin.

"Hassan has a wife, Kajata. He wanted to take a second wife. To

251

pay for that wife he was going to sell a bull—that brown one over there, the big one, see it? But the bull refused to go. It just wouldn't go to the market. No one could make it go! It's because Kajata had gone to a marabout and the marabout cast a protective spell so Hassan doesn't marry again."

"All lies," Hassan said, and laughed.

Everyone knew that you could charm an animal any way you wanted. When a bull refused to go to market, you whispered a special sentence from the Koran upon a stick, you spat on it, and when you whipped the disobedient animal with that stick the animal was no longer defiant. In Gagna, the village where Bomel and her skinny daughter lived in a mudbrick house that tilted toward sunset like an open palm asking for rain, there was an old cowboy named Boucary Sankare. He was blind and his arthritic hands no longer could clutch a staff or milk a cow. But he was a very pious man, a man initiated into the mysteries of the Koran, and he was famous for knowing just the right incantation. Many old people in Gagna were famous for spells that broke disobedient cattle.

We reached the river. It was silty, swollen with rainfall. Next to it, on a low cliff gashed by runoff, beneath a swift marbling of cloud, Hajja stood with her family's laundry. She spread the clean, wrung clothes on wilting couchgrass, arranged the bright rectangles of pagnes and blankets at deliberate right angles. It was Sunday, laundry day in the bourgou, in Mali, perhaps in all of West Africa. Imagine: an expanse as large as the United States slapping wet pagnes against washboards. A half a continent of suds.

Hajja kept her back to Allaye. She looked at him longingly under her arm each time she bent down, then turned away again.

Gold coins weighed down her thick long cornrows, and her skin was creamy and smooth.

Allaye pretended he was not looking.

"Women in the bush are so shy," he said. "They don't let the men touch them anywhere, or even look at their bodies. When they have sex they only want to be penetrated, but not touched. Not even their breasts."

Now he was walking away from Hajja, strolling upstream with Hassan. The men walked arm in arm. The river was a sluggish green mire at their feet. The cows waded in knee-deep and stood drinking.

"In Côte d'Ivoire city women let you touch them. If you touch them you get hard. And those women touch you back, too. I think if a girl likes you she shouldn't be afraid to touch you. But not with her mouth. I saw in a film once women touching men with their mouths. It was pretty disgusting."

At that point Hassan said that if he kept listening to any more sex talk he would end up breaking his fast. And that was that.

By the time the cows finished drinking, the plateau had hardened into a rock-smooth sheet. At Oumarou's camp night blankets and mats hung from the thorn tree to dry: ensigns of a happily waterlogged nation, releasing clammy smells of sour milk and baby pee. Fanta disinterred the dead perch and hung it up to dry as well, in a scavenged fishtrap. It stank like death, and the soft wind bathed the camp in its heavy odor. For many nights everyone would sleep in licks of putrefaction. Eventually, Fanta would deem the fish too rotten to eat.

Afternoon shadows were long and the light golden. Toward evening stormcells once more trailed rain toward Ballé.

At last, days of drizzle began—but not enough, the Fulani said, not enough. Fine rain sieved from the sky, but by now it should have been a deluge. It should have been sweeping away entire hamlets in flash floods. A marabout in Senossa ordered the villagers to walk in circles around the village, asking God to send rain to the bush. A marabout in Gagna ordered the villagers to recite under their breath a secret word in Arabic three hundred and thirty times. Of course, each marabout possessed a knowledge the others did not. Each had his own way to ask for rain.

Still, what rain did fall brought some comfort. The bush swelled with frogsong and the sated lowing of cattle. The cows began to eat enough and to lie down at pasture, signaling full stomachs. By the end of July the herds returned to camp each afternoon fatter than the day before. No longer did dust trail their unhurried step. For the first time in weeks the women in Oumarou's family had some extra milk to take to Djenné to trade.

The fast had rendered Djenné catatonic. Few adults were out of doors. Petrol dealers dozed in front of greasy rows of Bordeaux and J&B bottles. Housewives dozed in front of flickering television screens, the volume turned low. Men of piety prayed and listened to sura recordings on their cellphones. Men of means sat on bamboo

chairs in the shade and measured out half-kilo bags of Ramadan sugar to distribute among needier neighbors. Pygmée's bar turned off the disco lights, turned down the volume of its television. Schools were not in session but foosball tables stood on street corners unused, rainwarped. Cricket songs and frog croak replaced the usual nighttime revelry of laughter and cassette music, and after iftar men and women prostrated themselves in the last prayer of the night in streets filled with steam rising from seasonal marshes. Even the town smells were subdued, as if the month's inertia extended somehow to motorcycle exhaust, to the petrol-oil mix on which small corner grain mills ran, to sewage rotting in the streets and sewers clogged with plastic bags, to laundry soap and grilled meat and smoked fish. Here on display was the luxury of city life that Allaye craved: the luxury of winding down work for a full month—of ascetic devotion, or simply of sanctioned idleness. In the bush, work never stopped.

Fanta, Kumba, Kajita Pain-in-the-Ass, Djamba, and Allaye's sweetheart Hajja had hiked four hours to reach Djenné and moved slowly through the empty streets, pausing in sleepy doorways, calling out their wares into the quiet clay semidarkness of courtyards. They stopped by the house of Gano's mother. Outside the narrow anteroom of the parents of Amfala Koïta. In the middle of the square where René Caillié had lodged almost two centuries earlier in a second-floor room he described as "exceedingly wretched and dirty." They walked slowly and with purpose through the woven alleys of the town mostly emptied of other walkers, a town trying to survive the month of ceremonial thirst. They marveled at the presidential election posters that plastered every house, every gate. They could not read the posters, did not recognize the candidates. They would miss the vote, which would take place at the end of July with a huge turnout and largely without incident, although at the polling station established inside the Sory Ibrahim Thiocary School someone would shoot out the eye of a sixteen-year-old girl with an arrow.

In the deserted square by the Grande Mosquée a friend beckoned me, the young man who in spring had shared with his friends the lynching video from Gao. It had turned out, he said, that the man who in the video had appeared hacked in half had not been an al Qaeda executioner. That the man in the video never had performed any floggings and amputations. He had been some other man altogether, not a criminal at all. My friend was dispirited. "I think," he said, "that war is not good. It makes people crazy."

Elizabeth Costello, the title character of a Coetzee novel,

proposes that broadcast violence is obscene "because such things ought not to take place, and then obscene again because having taken place they ought not to be brought into the light but covered up and hidden for ever in the bowels of the earth, like what goes on in the slaughterhouses of the world, if one wishes to save one's sanity." I have written about violence up close because I believed its obscenity had to be exposed and examined so we could take collective responsibility, both for it and for our inherent and ruinous capacity to perpetrate or condone or even ignore it. I wrote: Behold the charred remnants of a suicide bomber flung into a housewife's cooking. Behold the children killed by a mine that had been lying in wait since before they were born. Behold a soldier shoving condolence cash into the limp hands of a widower deranged by grief. I hoped my work somehow could stem the obscenity of war. But there was a risk that instead I, like the videographer from Gao, was helping it flourish.

The double-edged power of a narrative to devastate or strengthen extended beyond accounts of ignominy. All storytelling was magic. It could cast spells. It affected lives in profound and unpredictable ways. Maybe it even begot lives—maybe it was the *poïesis* that mapped the existence of things and determined their being. Its faculty underlay the authority of griots, the pervasive public fear of their transcendent skill.

But how much storytelling was too much? There was no blueprint. No matter the deference, no matter the elusive sense of entitlement, the loftily so-called poetic license to represent before my readers the iniquities I witnessed, there existed an inherent contradiction in the purpose of my writing—to bring the world closer, to make it accountable—and my keen awareness that I was intruding upon and exposing something exceedingly private. It baffled me. Maybe a true writer of conscience was one who never put down a single word.

In the early nights of the Hoping I had a dream in which I needed to transport a snow leopard to the United States by plane. In my dream my task seemed unfair: Who gave me the right to package something so magical, and why? What if all life could only be truly beheld on its home ground? Awake, I wondered about the straightforward covenant between my hosts and me: that I would absorb their caring instruction and recount their story to the world. "Mother?" little Kajita reported to Fanta once, jubilant. "Amadou was running and Anna Bâ was writing him run!" They trusted me with all their intimacies without hesitation, and their absolute and instantaneous acceptance humbled me. But I was flailing. I was full of doubt.

My friend and I sat on a bench in front of the Grande Mosquée, thirsty and silent. A goat tethered to our bench ate pineapple bark, and a small boy turned and turned the wheel of an upended cart like a Tibetan prayer wheel. Swallows flew from steeples. I thought of the mosque floor. It was made of sand. Like the floor of the ocean, the oldest sanctuary of all life on Earth. As in the ocean the sand in the mosque rippled in asymmetrical tongueshaped waves, ordered and reordered ad infinitum by the ebb and flow of thousands of feet. Most parishioners came in for one or two of the five daily prayers. But some men knelt on that ersatz seabed for hours, meditating in the light that sifted calm and lean through vent openings in the startlingly high roof thatch that rested on ninety-nine oblique and unembellished clay pillars. What did they learn there, these seekers in the deep of spirit? Could they have been learning that there was no absolute knowledge, no absolute right? Could they have been learning to put their faith in doubt?

A Fulani woman in Somena told me once that the Grande Mosquée never could appear in a photograph. That if you photographed it the picture would show only a blank spot, or a blur. It was not so, of course. But like Elizabeth Costello, she wished for a world in which some zone of sanctity lay beyond the manipulations of storytelling—a world in which something holy in the soul could remain unmarred.

All trade was finished by midday. Fanta and her companions took turns napping in the shade of the meat aisle inside the empty market, watching over one another's purchases: a new pair of flipflops, a calabash of mangoes, some spices, millet, salt. They spread extra pagnes on the ground and prayed, folding their feet to the side neatly. At last they covered their calabashes with lids woven of straw and gunnysack string, stacked them into pyramids, hoisted them onto their heads, and set off for Ballé.

They walked out of the town's east gate single file. They crossed a paved bridge to where a new pirogue sat in the wharf, freshly painted at the bow and stern with the maker's signature of geometric shapes in bright colors; passed the point bar where old boats sat sunken to the gunwales and the slipoff slope where city artisans fired clay vessels and braziers by day and where by night lovers met to make out in the dark; crossed a gully that in two months would rush with neck-deep water; and leveled out onto a long walk through the bush.

Gone was the bourgou's dry idle pasture. In its place was a rolling pastiche of farmland, uneven tesserae primed for crops. Everywhere rimaibe and Bambara farmers, men and women in broad straw hats, tilled and planted, their handheld ploughs so sun-bleached that the farmers looked as if they were picking at the dirt with wishbones. Lines of young millet—some shoots only a few fingers tall, some a foot—undulated like the braids on the head of a Fulani girl. The roads were soaked and motorcycles wove dangerously in and out of the red mud, spraying it as they swerved. The Bani had begun to rise, and nearer Djenné the slopes of the wadis were completely green with low thick grass that glistened in the wind. Steam rose from the ground. The air smelled of manure. Tattered pale mushrooms flared along the roads.

Fanta walked first with a load of millet and mangoes on her head. Now and then, with a slight motion of her fingers, she pointed out dangerous thorns, slippery patches of mud, the tail of a lethal saw-scaled viper. When her path ran into a young bull she slipped her right foot out of her flipflop, picked up a stick with her toes, grabbed it with her right hand, and tossed it underhand at the bull, in one fluid and casual movement and without bending her head. The bull shied away. The women passed.

They talked, of course. About fasting, about being tired, about the people they had met in Djenné, about how the cattle were filling out at last. They pointed out bush rats, green bee-eaters, hoopoes, jackalberry bushes, dwarf persimmons, mimosas in bloom, things they already knew by heart. As though simply to fill the savannah with voice. Their jabber was as wasteful—of breath, of words, of precious biofluids on a hot day of thirsty Ramadan—as it was ancient. In the seventh century, Abdullah Ibn Mas'ud, the companion of the Prophet Mohammed, praised a pious man's silence over the indulgent prattle of nonbelievers. In the nineteen fifties, a French abbot told the travel writer Patrick Leigh Fermor: "In the outside world, speech is gravely abused." But chatter was a prerequisite to human dispersal across the planet. The command of complex language enabled our ancestors to share plans; without it, we might never have had the cohesion to strike out from the mother continent. Sixty thousand years ago, as they walked single file out of Africa, did our foremothers also list the familiar shrubs as they passed, did they sing out the names of wildlife?

To be sure, the Sahel sang back. With the whistle of rose-ringed parakeets, the gurgle of turtledoves. With the high twitter of redheaded lovebirds, the squeal of Senegal parrots whose apple chests swelled like externalized hearts. With the moaning of cattle and the hollow flutter of a bright blue moth wrestling out of a cage of brambles. With the ultrasonic clicking of insects and fish, pitched too high for the walkers to hear. The bush was full of such old sounds— as old as Abel, older still. They measured the heartbeat of the world, and the world was clamorous.

> the calf its bleat
> the crow its caw
> the tongue the tremor

> —HASSEN SAKER

The women quieted when a donkey cart overtook them; the driver, legs dangling from the singletree, was talking on his cellphone. They stepped off the road for men on motorscooters to pass. They paused to rest, to douse their necks with water from a bottle, to take off their flipflops and loads for a minute and squat, then hoist them up again. They greeted rimaibe women who lugged on their heads firewood, gunnysacks of grain, doum palm fruit. They tossed no coins at the group of preteen boys in blue homespun who announced their recent circumcision with the jangle of wooden rattles and begged passersby for celebration money. They walked for hours and the sun swung down from above and began to soften slowly into the bush behind them.

And the land unscrolled, unscrolled, as if the Earth spun underfoot like a circus ball and the women on it walked in place, fixed against a fixed blue sky.

That day in Djenné by a water pump near Pygmée's house, next to the severed head of a black bull, two boys stood holding a pied crow chick by its wings.

Gano called out to the boys. "Hey, wait, stop, stop! Show me that bird!"

The bird was maybe a few weeks old, still downy around the neck. Sticky droplets of blood were drying on the upperwing coverts. Gano told the boys to hold it still and pulled back its eyelids. First the left eye. No Koranic calligraphy there, just worried and moist darkness. Then the right. Nothing there, either. Gano walked away, disappointed. "Probably because it's still young. It hasn't had the time to grow wise. The writing hasn't yet developed."

The rain brought scorpions, fever, dysentery. It filled the fens with diseased water. It ushered forth mosquitoes. In Djenné my Fulfulde teacher, Monsieur Koulibaly, fell ill with malaria. I battled the abdominal pain and headaches of typhoid. On the plateau outside Ballé, Saadou's daughter-in-law Kajata, who may or may not have put a spell on her husband's bull to stop him from marrying a second time, had developed an abscess around one of her black misshapen teeth. She responded with hesitation to my advice to gargle with salt to bring down the abscess: to let even saltwater pass her lips meant to break Ramadan fast. Her daughter Hiretou ran a mysterious fever. One of Oumarou's cows, a yellow roan yearling, began to have loose and bloody stools.

For a few days Oumarou watched the cow closely. When the animal began to shiver he knew it would die. But no Fulani liked a cow to die in vain, and the old man decided to slaughter and jerk it. He shared cuts of beef with everyone on the plateau, even the Bozo who sold tea and sugar at their homestead by the river. Such is the tradition in cultures of scarcity. I remembered it from my own childhood, when a rare treat—a jar of olives, a cheese—was shared with friends, family, anyone who stepped into the kitchen. I remembered slicing to lace-thin wafers a stick of salami that came in a box of German humanitarian aid, and not drinking for hours to retain the aftertaste of the single slice I got to have myself.

Even so, it took a full day to cook what Oumarou's family had kept of the beef. Hairatou and Allaye took turns tending the fire. When Hairatou was not turning the meat over the coals, she cut with a broadsword bite-size pieces from a femur and chewed. Allaye nibbled on a rib. Hairatou, Allaye, and Hassan were not observing the Ramadan fast. Hairatou, because she was still young, and because someone had to reheat the rice or millet and feed the young children in the camp, and it would have been cruel to request that of a fasting woman, though married women all across the bourgou did it. Hassan was not fasting because he was herding cattle, a job too exhausting to do on an empty stomach and with a mouth sandpapered with thirst. Allaye was old enough and was performing no hard work, but perhaps, Oumarou suggested, he didn't fast because in his mind he was still a child. And Fanta explained: "Everyone does what God tells him." When his parents weren't there to listen, Allaye explained that it was no use fasting because every night he broke the laws of chastity with Hajja.

The siblings grilled the meat unevenly. Some of it was smoked, some charred, some bloody. They ate the liver raw. Even the most thoroughly cooked bits gave off a slight tang of rot.

Oumarou did not know what had caused the cow to bleed and shiver. "Illness," he said. Eating the meat of a sick cow was not taboo, though it was wise to avoid beef under two circumstances: if the butcher had placed his foot on the head of the cow while he was skinning it, even if that cow had been perfectly healthy; and if the cow had died of blackleg, an acute bacterial infection that caused necrosis. Blackleg meat smelled sour and looked unusually dark. Still, such meat could be made edible if you studded it with thorns before cooking it. There was no cure for the meat of an improperly skinned cow.

The Diakayatés' iftar meal after the slaughter was a feast of rice with meat stew. That night Hairatou and Fanta suffered from cramps and diarrhea. The following morning Oumarou became violently sick. All day he staggered miserably between his hut and the nearest jackalberry thicket. There, out of everyone's sight—because a Fulani adult could not publicly display discomfort or need or perform any function of the body—he retched and retched. Finally, he just stayed in the thicket. He was too weak to walk. He was too sick to be among family. The day was gray and the low sky pressed warm moisture into the plateau, pressed the wind westward, suffocated the land. Golden weavers streamed in scarves in and out of Oumarou's unattended hut.

Allaye paced around his father in broad and worried circles. He brewed strong sweet tea and infused it with drops of Chinese-made potion of camphoric oil and menthol, panacea of the globalized Sahel. He covered the old man with a thin cotton blanket and took it off again. He cycled back to camp to fetch more tea and sugar. There Hairatou squatted by the hearth, near tears.

"Every year!" she whispered. "Every year when we come here he gets sick. Every year. Always his stomach. And every year we cry because we think he's dying."

Her eyes were on the shrubs behind which Oumarou was convalescing. Whenever she would see Allaye walk toward camp she would spring up, attentive, squinting, trying to discern from her brother's walk: what news?

"It's the meat," said her mother, and set to steep in hot water a handful of kinkéliba leaves, *Combretum micranthum*, West African superfood, a mild antibiotic, painkiller, and antipyretic that tasted like loam. "Sit, Hairatou. You are making me nervous."

By nightfall Oumarou felt well enough to return to camp. He sneaked extra iftar dates to Hashem, his favorite grandson. He urged his family toward another dinner of blighted meat sauce and *toh*— "Dive in, dive in"—but he himself did not eat. Gano offered to drive him to the hospital in Djenné.

"Djenné?" the old man said. "Forget it. My hospital is my cows. When I'm sick, all I need is a fat, healthy cow that has eaten a lot of grass. If I drink her milk, that's my medicine."

A fat cow gave so much milk two people could not drink it all in one sitting. Her milk tasted differently. You could taste the fresh grass in it.

Another good medicine was cow urine. You caught it with the cupped palm of your hand straight out of the cow's urethral sphincter and drank it warm and foaming. Cow urine was good for stomachache, worms, small abrasions, and minor burns, and it increased your appetite. It was very potent and extremely salty. But if you drank a lot of it you could die, and small children were not allowed to drink it at all. For small children, the best medicine was goat milk drawn from the teat directly into the sick child's mouth.

Oumarou incanted the ancient list of cowboy remedies on one of the reed mats Fanta had woven, with his feet tucked in. Ashy and thin, a shadow of a man. Bats zigzagged overhead. Mosquitoes whined. The empty bottle of pesticide beat against the thorn tree, keeping hollow, sepulchral time. He pulled up the bottom loop of his turban over the stubbly chin, covered his mouth. Only his bloodshot eyes showed.

"Tomorrow I'm going to herd my cows. That's where I'm going. No hospitals."

Kajata's abscess by now had swelled her left cheek and all of her neck, but when Gano proposed to take her to the hospital, her in-laws refused to let her go.

"I don't think it's really necessary," said Saadou.

"If they take her to a doctor the doctor will want to do surgery, and I heard that last year two women died after such surgeries," said Kumba.

"A bush doctor won't do surgery," said Fanta. "If we hear about a good bush doctor nearby, we'll take her there."

Kajata's only son, a two-year-old, had died on the plateau that spring. It was then that Fanta had walked from Doundéré to pay condolences to the young woman. An owl had taken the child, the elders had said. Hassan and Saadou had buried him on the bluff near the graves of Oumarou's father and children.

Some people said that many years ago that bluff had been the site of a small hamlet, maybe a village. That the bones of many others lay in its eroding sandstone. Each with a story of staying and going.

Heat lightning in the west. After dinner the cows woke and walked through camp, defecating and pissing and clattering dishes and eating leftover *toh* out of the pot and butting one another above my mat. Allaye ambled around with his music on, also restless. Then the wind grew stiff and cold, the cows left, and night quieted into dawn.

At some point late that night, in salmon moonrise, a chestnut cow calved out on pasture. Oumarou named the calf Mallé: Piebald.

A loud and fierce sunup. Frogs orchestral. From the indigo west white egrets flew toward the plateau in tattered skeins on their daily migration. From his mat under the thorn tree, Oumarou sent Allaye to the bush near Gagna, where his eldest son, Boucary, camped with his wife and livestock. Boucary, the luckless shepherd, had lost a goat. Oumarou wanted Allaye to help him find it.

Allaye had been plucking his eyebrows in his handheld mirror. He let go of the mirror, stood up, picked up a staff, donned his hat of canvas and cowhide, raised both his palms in a simple and general farewell, turned up the love song screeching on his cellphone, and headed toward the Bani. Because he herded only goats, not cows, Boucary did not migrate from the bourgou. His wife, Hawa, kept impeccably neat their spacious wainscoted year-round hut with an indoor hearth. Allaye would reach his brother's camp by the midafternoon prayer. If he indeed went there. If he didn't hop on a westbound bus to Bamako instead.

When Allaye was a toddler, Boucary, then in his late teens, left his father's camp and his newlywed bride one morning and was gone for two years. It was before anyone had cellphones. Through some relatives Oumarou learned that Boucary was in Koutiala, a hundred and fifty miles south of the bourgou. That was all Oumarou ever had learned about Boucary's absence. "When he returned he told me nothing and I told him nothing," he said. "We never spoke about it." He seemed proud of this not-knowing: to pry would have been to lose his composure, to betray concern.

Never display sorrow. Never show grief. For Oumarou and Fanta to express anguish would have meant to stop being Fulani, and to stop being Fulani was impossible. Neither of them had told Allaye how their hearts had sunk that morning the year before when they had found him gone. Nor had they ever told him how crushed they had been by his seven-month absence.

Now they squinted to watch his raggedy and angled silhouette become smaller in the strange light of an early sky. For a while no one said anything. When they no longer could hear his cellphone song Hairatou said:

"He is a very caring person, Allaye. He would not leave for good knowing that Papa is sick."

That night after iftar we sat watching the Earth's passage through the night. Scorpio hooked its tail around the hearth and dragged it higher and higher into the turning sky. The air was deep and spongy. Oumarou, who was feeling better, *al ham du lillah*, though still too weak to rise from his mat and very nauseated, told me he could not fathom the wanderlust of his sons.

"Kids these days. They always need to be on the move."

"They are Fulani," I said.

"No. There's movement and then there's movement. If you are a

Fulani you travel with your cows, with your family. Not all by yourself. The Fulani are always moving. But the movement is never arbitrary."

When Allaye returned from his brother's camp the next day he explained that the goat had not gotten lost at all. A hunter had killed it. The hunter had been stalking the bush around Gagna for several weeks. He had killed three goats that belonged to a Fulani who camped close to Boucary. Twice, the men saw him stuff the animals into his hunting bag and take off on his motorcycle. Once, the hunter dropped the goat he'd shot and split; the Fulani were unsure whether a shot goat was halal to eat and left it there to rot. Finally, three days earlier, the men heard a shot and when they ran toward it they saw bloodsmeared grass and a motorcycle crashing away through the bush, with Boucary's goat slack and draped over the passenger seat.

"Before it was just kids without guns, and they'd take only one goat. But now it's the hunters, with guns. If you confront them they might kill you," said al Hajj Saadou when he heard the story.

"They've hunted out all the wildlife, now they come after people's private animals," said Oumarou.

Gano said he knew of a hunter in Djenné who hunted people's livestock and sold it to butchers in the market. No one but the butchers knew who the hunter was, and the butchers weren't telling.

"But the moment they catch him they will kill him, *wallahi!*"

Allaye said, too, that Sita Louchéré and Isiaka were still in Doundéré, waiting to travel west, and that in the bourgou it had rained plenty. He said he had seen many Fulani carts travel to Hayré. He had seen the wind flap the girls' skirts as they walked alongside the carts.

All over the bourgou rivers of cattle were moving, too, slow and heavy and grounded against the roiling sky of late July, and cowboys ululated and called *jot jot jot jot* to urge the animals onward, and the rainy-season cattle drive crescendoed through the Sahel.

Oumarou said the family would move to Hayré in a week, after the last day of Ramadan. The families of Sita and Saadou would be coming as well.

THE
CROSSING

◇ ◇ ◇

We travel like other people, but we return to nowhere.
   As if traveling
is the way of the clouds. We have buried our loved ones in the
   darkness of the clouds, between the roots of the trees.

—Mahmoud Darwish

The tablelands of Hayré reached toward the sun in tremendous emptiness. Feldspar shone like shattered meteorites through open swells of untamed grass. Wispy groves of jackalberry and gigilé and dwarf persimmons splotched gargantuan pale horizons. Here and there a baobab loomed. There were few farms. All surface water was seasonal. When it rained the plains turned a rolling nitric green. By the time the dry months began the sun bleached the grass to platinum lace, the igneous bedrock to scrimshaw.

The Fulani built their huts sparsely beneath the rare thickets of low brush, each camp invisible from the next. During the grazing season the highlands became a six-thousand-square-mile Mark Rothko multiform in motion. In the foreground floated columns of women with water buckets on their heads, with calabashes of millet and milk. Farther out, cows migrated to and from pasture and shallow stagnant pools and hand-dug wells. And above, the broad cyan brushstroke of sky beamed down hot daylight that shone equally on men and animals, caressed and punished them in equal measure.

Oral histories told little of Hayré, a shelterless plateau on the periphery of ancient kingdoms, a lesser province of scant interest to the Sahel's political elite, overrun by one West African empire after another not for its own sake but because it was on the way to somewhere more coveted. Of all the invaders only the Fulani, it seemed, had specific interest in Hayré.

The griots said the Fulani first arrived at the height of the Kingdom of Ségou. At the time, Hayré was a land of Dogon and Bwa farmers. The Dogon were born genderless into a world that had originated from an exploded grain of fonio and possessed the advanced astronomical knowledge of their serpentlike twin ancestors who had descended onto Earth from an egg hatched in space. They husbanded the northern part of the plateau from their cliff dwellings on the sandstone Bandiagara Escarpment. The Bwa farmed farther from the hills, forever trying to atone for upsetting the perfect symmetry between the domestic and the wild, man and nature—the symmetry in which God had created their world and which he then had upended because a woman pounding millet had hit and wounded him with her pestle.

Here the Fulani came with cows and horses and dogs. They fought the Dogon and the Bwa for water rights and land use and they fought Kel Tamashek raiders from the north for livestock. They took slaves from the farming villagers and set up chiefdoms and pastured their cows, and within a hundred years they came to dominate the plain. When Sekou Amadou's jihad reached Hayré in the early nineteenth century, and functionaries of the Massina Empire were drawing up schedules that explained how farmers and herders would take turns with the fertile riches of the bourgou, they formally included the elevated plains into the annual itinerary of nomadic pastoralists. The jihad found converts almost exclusively among the Fulani. The sedentary people converted later, or not at all.

By then the ancestors of Oumarou Diakayaté were already grazing cattle in Hayré.

The Diakayatés made rainy-season camp where they always had, at the edge of a meadow a mile or so south of the Bwa village of Konkorno. The villagers were friendly enough and every Thursday they hired out horsecarts to take the Fulani to the weekly market in Madiama. But they were heathen. They raised pigs. They kept millet in cylindrical elevated granaries with single windows and conical straw roofs, and they brewed millet beer and drank it, often during the day. They ate dog meat. They greeted guests with idolatrous curtsies and handclaps. They played strange music that did not move forward but bounced up and down. The Diakayatés could hear from the camp the pagan throb of their drumbeat.

Although the rainy season arrived late that year, the dry season came early. Green grass lasted a month. By September, instead of gently watering Hayré's pasturelands and farms, Rijl al Awwa—the Foot of the Barking Dog, Mu Virginis—spread the high blue skies of autumn. In October hundreds of cattle egrets stood stock-still in withered halfgrown millet, and in the evaporating sludge of the few rice paddies white lotuses bloomed. The air smelled like blossoms, like chewed hay. The forage in Hayré was exhausted and the animals were slatribbed once more. People and animals gathered around wells where Fulani girls hung laundry to dry from brittle golden stalks. Cows swished past kaleidoscopic prints flying in soft, honeyed wind, skidded on silent windchiseled rimrock. Their humps listed to the side.

In the bourgou the millet was halfgrown and the rice stood in barely two palms of water. Most grain husks hadn't had the time to germinate and were translucent, empty. Only hippo grass, the sweetest fodder, stood lush in the still fens, and fish jumped there. Even so, no cattle were allowed in or near the bourgou until the end of the meager harvest.

When Sekou Amadou established the Massina Empire he appointed a handful of loyal Fulani nobles as the ultimate landlords in the bourgou. Their ownership of the land was hereditary and irrevocable and extended to almost all of the Inner Delta. These landlords were called *dioro* and they singlehandedly decided how much to charge for passage and for pasture, how much to tax farmers and fishermen. Efforts by the French colonists and the bankrupt post-independence kleptocracies to reorganize this practice did not take. Two hundred years after Sekou Amadou's jihad, land use in his former empire still was governed by the preferential feudal system everyone called simply *dina*: Islamic faith.

At the end of each rainy season the *dioro* queried the farmers about their harvest deadlines and then determined the time and the price of transit and grazing for the nomads. Each *dioro* set his price; every year Oumarou paid two *dioro* for the right to pass through their land, and one for dry-season pasturage. Each also established the fines for violators. The fines were steep and escalated swiftly: the price of three goats, of a heifer, of a fullgrown bull—and those did not include the penalties farmers in the bourgou independently charged the Fulani whose cows damaged unharvested fields. At best, the Fulani who failed to pay for passage or trespass ended up in jail for contempt of *dina*. Often, frustrated farmers took matters into their own hands, arming themselves with clubs and broadswords, with handmade muzzle-loaders, with .20-caliber pistols welded out of car parts. Each year upon the ancient earth Cain murdered Abel anew.

This year the *dioro* were telling the herders: not yet. Marooned in the dry highlands the cows and the cowboys ambulated in fatigued twice-daily loops. Hour after hour, still as breath, Oumarou sat in practiced forbearance by the door of the low rainy-season hut Allaye and Ousman had built for him and Fanta. The pulse of Konkorno's drums counted out the time of thirst and hunger, the time of life and sorrow, the time of waiting until it became time to walk again.

In early October Ousman and Bobo and their sons, Hashem and Afo, traveled through the arid wilderness to the border with Burkina Faso to pay a condolence visit: a distant relative had died, an old man, and the couple went to sit with his family in mourning and pray for his soul. The relative's family lived about a day's walk away. On the border Afo became ill with fever. Ousman took him to the doctor in the nearest town. The doctor prescribed some pills. After five days, in the night, Afo died. He was one year old.

Bobo returned to her in-laws' camp hollow-eyed and mute, as if her heart were squeezed in ways no words could describe. She barely touched her food. She barely touched her surviving son, Hashem. She shrank into the shade of a jackalberry bush and wove calabash lids out of dead grass. Ousman ranged alone around the highlands all day and returned only at sunset, to milk. To show grief was to trespass against God. To withhold it was to trespass against love. The Fulani had been honing the equilibrium for centuries but it remained ever out of reach.

It became Bobo's turn to receive the relatives who came to sit with her in mourning, to express to her their wish that God protect Afo's soul. After a few days, no one came. And after that, the Diakayatés rarely spoke of Afo. "When God takes a child who is too young to know anything it means it was time for that child to go," explained Oumarou. A snap of heavenly fingers, a racking flash, and poof. As if a child's life was weightless. It was not. But nor did grief build up into some residue of loss until the heart cracked under its weight or turned wooden with lesions. Each loss stood distinct in its unique and awful wretchedness. Each new love and separation had to be lived alone and from scratch. Every time Oumarou walked to Konkorno he said a prayer for his daughter Salimata, who had died an infant right here at this campsite more than thirty years before.

And still the cattle streamed on the speckled horizon and milkmaids walked with their wares past the camp and past that grave and past all the graves of all the children who ever had died upon this tract of the Sahel, and each dawn still shone like porcelain, and egrets lifted into the October sky by the hundred as they always did.

◇ ◇ ◇

That month and the next I walked from the bush to Djenné and back every few days. In Djenné I transcribed my notes on the second floor of Gano's house, five narrow alley blocks from the Grande Mosquée. Lizards clicked above my sleeping mat and in the porous clay wall above my door a rock pigeon had built a nest. A rural bird, with her scarlet eyeliner; wherever she nested in town was rare and lucky and sacred. To leave or enter my room I had to step through a white stripe of holy shit.

I walked alone. Fastpaced four-hour walks on the unmarked paths through the pointillist savannah. In forenoon sun the land was ash. I spooked rabbits, and bands of vervets that dragged their long pale tails through the dust trawling odd tracks, like cyclists arriving and leaving. I foraged for unripe wild persimmons that drew my mouth. I walked under a ringing blue sky so low it seemed unctuous, ozone on the move. Warplanes bored slowly toward the Sahara. From the ground and from the air French and Malian troops were searching the desert for the murderers of two French radio journalists whose bodies had been found in its sands, throats slit.

I walked into rimaibe girls with firewood on their heads and memorized their soccer t-shirts: ALONSO 14. GÖTZE 10. DROGBA 11. FORLÁN 9. Wind flapped our pagnes to northward in synchrony. Preteen goatherds hit mimosa shrubs with their clubbed sticks to watch the responsive leaves fold and droop in retreat. *Mimosa pudica*: shy, bashful. "Woman," they sang to the shrinking herb, "close your

281

legs, your husband's coming." The adult Fulani I met on those walks stopped for chitchat:

"Anna Bâ! Where are you going?"

"Konkorno. And you?"

"Sin."

"Is there grass there?"

"Some."

"Well, go with God."

"Amen, amen, amen."

Elemental land. Its beveled horizons peeled me back until beauty and sorrow and a kind of long, gut-pulling love all came in waves along with the saccharine fragrance of lotuses and the stench of decomposing livestock. Walking through the bush offered not a solution but a reclamation of sorts: it sang back to me my dream-map, a songline of my own. A croak perhaps, a stutter even, but mine.

My hosts disapproved of my goings. "When you leave for Djenné," Fanta told me one time, "it's like a tree has been cut." Because neither rigid codes of conduct nor a long life on the road conditioned us to constantly saying goodbye, and the beauty of movement was forever laced with longing.

Several weeks later, at the end of November, I left the Sahel. I shook left hands with my hosts so that we would see one another again and begged their forgiveness so that our long time apart would not rankle with resentment. When the turn came for me to say goodbye to Hairatou she spun away from me and wept. I stood at her back and embraced her and closed my eyes. I was very sad but I didn't cry. For a frightening instant I imagined that each time I farewelled the people I loved my heart slivered thinner and thinner—except just then I felt so alive in my sorrow that it almost felt like joy.

"It's very hard," Fanta had said. "Very hard, Anna Bâ. Some don't cry, some cry—that depends on the heart. But all of us miss one another." When I had last said goodbye to my lover I had been so delirious with shock, with disbelief, my soul so riven, that when I walked away from him into the cold Philadelphia night I was laughing. A year had passed since, and I still missed him fiercely, every day anew.

We walk into one another's lives, we change them and are changed deeply and forever, we part ways. Each time a part of our hearts seems to shrivel and die, it doesn't. Simply, our hearts learn to beat a different way. We mourn, we break down, then we stand up, and we keep going. Two thousand footsteps per mile. Twenty to forty thousand footsteps per day. Every footfall brings the walkers closer to a reunion. Every footfall begets a separation. Our forward movement, erratic, fragile, relentless, is a quest: for comfort, for deliverance, for squaring the ideal of endurance with the practice of love.

In the last days of Ash Shaulah, the Raised Tail of the Scorpion, the nomads who had summered in Hayré began the journey to the Inner Niger Delta. Boys drove their fathers' cattle to the periphery of the forbidden grasslands, and families loaded onto carts and rattled closer to the bourgou. With his father's blessing Hassan slung over his shoulder the black milking calabash, a stoppered gourd with millet couscous his mother had prepared, a blue tarp wrapped with lengths of rope that could double as lassoes, and took the cows west.

The cows set out with an incredible lowing. Hooves clinked on plutonic rock like hail. Hooves sucked into sand. Flanks swished against dry reeds, against the hot and dusty hides of other cows. They walked slowly, jerkily, stopped to eat, to rest. Hassan flowed among them, ululating, sucking his teeth, grunting in warning, throwing his clubbed stick and fetching it and throwing it again.

Jot jot jot! Hassan drove the herd past an abandoned millet field, the stalks knee-high and broken, aborted. Across a shallow dip where stale green water plumed in a bed of chalk, skeletons of sea creatures that lived here two billion years ago when the planet was still wet. He passed a cornfield where a white horse stood like a ghost, and he passed thornbrush cattle pens in which villagers impounded the cows that trespassed on their unharvested farmland.

At the first paved road on his route he stopped the cows to let

a silver SUV whiz southwest toward Bamako. It had a bullet hole in the trunk door. The air quivered in the car's wake, the scent of hot tar billowed, stilled once more. The cows lowered their heads as they crossed. Hooves clacked unfamiliarly on asphalt, like so many beans spilling. Dragonflies zipped between shanks.

He walked. He let the animals fall in with other herds that belonged to the Sankaris, the Sidibés, the Sows, the Barris, herds he recognized by their shape from a mile away, and he walked stretches of the savannah with boys his age who told him jokes and told him also about the meager rain in other parts of Hayre. Then he walked alone again, seeking out the highest routes where no rice grew and little forage, taking no shortcuts and instead choosing detours many hours long under the pewter sun. Not merely protecting the cattle from village cow jails but also protecting his own stature as a cowboy skilled and wise enough to keep the animals out of trouble, because he accepted as an indisputable and only truth what his father had taught him: that the cows in his care were not his cows nor were they Oumarou's or Oumarou's father's cows but that they were the very first cows of his very first ancestors who drove them from Ethiopia, and that the integrity of such a herd and his integrity as its herder were one. His integrity as a herder and his identity as a Fulani were one.

Already the odds were against him. In the nomad tradition a cowboy's proficiency hinged on how fat and erect were the humps of his cows after the rainy season, on how many new additions there were to his herd. But this had been a lean and thirsty year. True, one new calf had been born during the rainy season, but in addition to the sick cow that had to be slaughtered and nearly killed Oumarou during Ramadan, a yearling bull, Swayback, had disappeared on Hassan's watch in Hayré. Ousman would find its carcass on his solitary wanderings days later, after Hassan had left. It had been born with a deformity and in its hungry exhaustion it fell and couldn't get up. It died of hunger, or thirst, or pain. A horsecart full of Bwa would fetch it from the bush and butcher it and eat it, because Bwa ate anything, even carrion.

"Some of them will even eat a human," said Ousman.

Hassan drove the cows on gravel and on the crazed webbing of dry dirt and on sand that accommodated the shape of the feet that last trod on it. By nightfall he and the herd arrived at a drowned swale outside Sin, an hour from Ballé. Here he would wait for the *dioro*'s permission to approach the river. Some boys he knew took their herds closer to the bourgou. "All the rice fields are ruined this year anyway," they said. "If the farms don't have a harvest, why not just allow cows to go in and eat?" A foolhardy relative ended up having to pay the price of two bulls in fines after trying to sneak his father's cows through an unharvested rice field. Hassan was taking no risks. He was learning the hardest and most crucial art of cowboying in the Sahel, of life: the art of patience. Perhaps he could reclaim his standing as a great cowherd in a week, when it was his turn to swim at the head of the herd across the fast and rain-swollen Bani River.

Back at the camp the Diakayatés prepared for their own return journey. Hairatou pounded millet and shined castiron pots with her feet. Kajita Pain-in-the-Ass and Bobo took a daylong roundtrip hike to harvest chunks of chalk with which to whiten the calabashes they used to carry buttermilk for sale. They softened the chalk with precious well water and shaped that pliable goo into cylinders and laid them on three gunnysacks to dry.

The day before departure Fanta went to Konkorno to bargain with horsecart drivers about the price of a ride to Ballé. It was high noon. Harsh light rendered granaries in sharp contrast of ivory and indigo. Dogs lay in the pooled circular shadows under the granaries' raised walls, lolling tongues crusted with sand. Women curtsied and called out asking Fanta for milk and men who weren't harvesting the drought-stricken millet invited her to drink homemade beer in mango-shaded yards. Already they were slightly drunk and merry. Fanta walked tall and straight past such men and pursed her lips and pursed her lips again at the sight of their neatly fenced pigsties. She ended up agreeing with a bald and toothless old man who slurred his speech from drink or heat or simply exhaustion with so many years of hardship that he would send his son to fetch the Diakayatés the next morning. On the walk back to camp she said:

"I'm afraid of these people, Anna Bâ."

That night a young man from Konkorno stopped by the camp. His name was Seri Koulibali and he spoke fluent Fulfulde. He told the Diakayatés where to find wild dogs and rabbits to hunt. He told them where to find wild honey to sweeten the evening meal. He told stories of his misfortunes—millet fields scorched by drought one year, drowned and washed away by heavy rains the next. Four children, two wives, two months in a debtors' jail. Next year, he said, he would hire himself out to a gold mine in Côte d'Ivoire.

"I have a friend in Côte d'Ivoire," said Allaye. "We should call him and go together."

"Next time you speak to your friend in Côte d'Ivoire," said Oumarou, "pass me the phone. I'll tell him what's what."

He changed the subject.

"Seri's father and I were good friends. We helped each other out. I know Seri since he was a little child, like Amadou."

"True," Seri said. "My family has always had a good relationship with Fulani in the bush. I can't speak for the rest of the village. But for me, I trust them. They come to take tea, to charge their phones in my house, even though we are not the same religion."

"What's your religion?" I asked.

"Oh, the whole village is Christian."

"Christian?" Fanta was stunned. "Christian?"

"Of course. You hear that drumming? Tomorrow is Sunday and the people of the village are celebrating Mass."

The nomads fell quiet. Seri's revelation challenged their understanding of the world's order more acutely than my rendition of the Big Bang theory or the history of early human migration over the Levantine Corridor, or the French airplanes fighting a mechanized war in the Sahara. The villagers of Konkorno did not worship idols, did not make human sacrifices, did not summon malevolent spirits to harm Fulani in the night. They believed in the oneness of God, the Merciful, the Compassionate, and it was that God they celebrated with their lush drum pattern that now blossomed on the wind, the rhythm of hoes striking dirt, of emerald cuckoos somersaulting from baobab branches, of mango harvest, a rhythm that did not exhort a searching but asserted an ebullient sense of place, a rhythm that seemed more fitted to a jungle than to this austere arid land.

"*La ilaha il Allah!*" Fanta said at last.

Gano lit a cigarette and offered one to Seri. Oumarou, forever on a quest for health formulas, said:

"Smoking isn't good for you. But if you smoke cigarettes but drink a lot of milk, it's good for you."

This was familiar territory. He went on:

"Here we are not supposed to drink alcohol. But in heaven there are four rivers. A river of milk, a river of honey, a river of water, and a river of alcohol. I'll drink from all the rivers and all of them will taste very good. Milk in heaven tastes exactly like milk here in life.

"Also in heaven I will get a hundred women and all of them will like me, and I will have sex with all of them. You can spend time with all of them and they don't become jealous. It's different from here. Here if you have sex with everybody you'll get sick. If you have sex with everybody you'll spend all your money. If you have sex with everybody, even if you pray, when you die you'll go to hell. But in heaven everyone is very clean and no one gets ill. Everyone is the same age: young. In heaven, I will be as young as Allaye, and Fanta here, she will be as young as Hairatou or Djamba. May God bring us all to heaven."

"Amen, amen, amen."

Darkness fell abruptly. Across the sky the Milky Way snaked so thick it seemed to bulge. Shooting stars tore off, flamed down. The cooking fire died. In the dust near the adults little Amadou drew cows with his right forefinger. First the vertical lines of their bodies. The horns from the top of each line like the cross-stroke of a capital T. In the middle of each line a fat wishful circle of a hump.

When he had populated with cows all the dust within his reach he held his fists above each drawing in turn and milked, and milked.

All along the way from Hayré stretched herds of cattle and goats and sheep. Families camped under roadside thorn trees on bags of belongings with their carts still hitched, waiting to be permitted into the pastures of Ballé. And more nomads were coming, from Sin, from Madiama, from Tombonka, from Won, from Tominian. Acolytes who walked on foot among their herds and rode in carts with chickens and baby goats and infants and guineafowl in their laps and sat astride donkeys and called to one another: "How was your journey?" "Are your cows healthy?" "Was there grass where you were?" and the music they played on their cassette players and cellphones blurred into a dissonant signifier of constant motion. Go on, go on, past cucumber stands and past freshly caught minnows Bozo fishermen dumped in tall shimmering drifts on the ground and past long-stemmed lotuses and long-legged cattle egrets. Herders young and old and most of them male, though Yerourou Sankari, who rainy-seasoned near Madiama, had dispatched his two teenage daughters with his cows because his sons were still too young to cowboy. And the closer these vagrants drew to the Bani the greener became the land, the taller the grass around the irregular rectangles of the year's poor millet.

The cart ride from Konkorno to the riverside plateau took half a day. The land was luminescent green and absolutely empty of animals. Sita and Saadou made camp in the same spots as before. Oumarou ordered the women to pile their bags much closer to the water. He was eager to leave, to continue on toward Doundéré, to move on, to move. To see again the reserved Sita Louchéré and the babbling Isiaka and to see his cows eat and jump, eat and jump in hippo grass fens. He watched Ousman stake the calf rope north of the thorn tree where the women had arranged their bundles and calabashes and watched the women build a hearth and then, just after the early afternoon prayer, he and Sita Dangéré and several elders from other Fulani families marched to the little Bozo outpost by the river to negotiate the price of transit with the *dioro* of Ballé.

He was gone less than an hour when the world changed color. Just the slightest paling of the light, the barest diffusion of shadows. The air turned titanium and the sky dimmed as if someone had wedged a lens of tinted glass between heaven and earth. The weavers in the thorn tree hushed. Only through a pinprick hole in a piece of paper could you see it: the moon's dark disk chipping off the bottom eighth of the sun. Just a nailclip. Just for a minute. The Fulani noticed it acutely.

"It's suddenly dark, what happened?" asked Bobo. And Saadou strolled into the camp very quickly and frowned and said: "Is it day or night? Why is it dark?"

"It's because someone important died today," Fanta said. "When my father died forty years ago the day became dark."

That year, on the thirtieth of June, the path of totality passed over the Sahel. Over Gao the sun disappeared completely for seven minutes and thirty-nine seconds, the third-longest observed solar eclipse in almost fifteen centuries. That was the last year of a five-year famine, one of the worst in living memory to strike the West

African savannah, though not as bad as the famine of the nineteen eighties, during which Oumarou lost most of his cattle. That later famine the Fulani called simply the Hunger.

Saadou nodded and sat down. It was probably Kumba's uncle, he said. He had died that morning a few hours' walk north of Ballé. He had been ninety-seven years old, blind for years, almost completely deaf. May God protect his soul, his children, and his animals. Already other women who had arrived on the plateau that day were assembling in their vibrant clothes beside Kumba's hearth, sitting on Kumba's mat in sympathy. In a few minutes they would rise and lift their hands palms-forward in farewell and walk over to see Bobo and mourn with her for baby Afo. Then they would rise again and continue their colorful and morbid rounds, saying hello and praying for all the dead who had gone since their last meeting.

Oumarou returned to the campsite past sundown. The negotiations had been difficult and the price disadvantageous but the *dioro* did invite the cattlemen to bring their animals to the plateau that same night and promised to allow the herds and the herders who wanted to continue to the bourgou to swim across the Bani in four days. The rest of the families would cross by pirogue a few days after that. The nomads would advance toward the bourgou's waterlogged green heart but they would move no farther than a mile inland until the *dioro* in Senossa gave his consent for cattle to pass through his land, and yet another *dioro*, in Ouro Ali, permitted Fulani cows on the dry hummock between Dakabalal and Doundéré.

It was very late when cattle began to reach the river. Scores, hundreds, thousands. They came unseen in the night. Only the horizon line in the west undulated where their moving contour rippled under the immense starry cosmos. Only the beams of the cowboys' flashlights, the ceaseless tramping of hooves, the potent smell of chewed grass, the authoritative sonorous bellowing. Hassan arrived with Oumarou's herd and the animals shuffled into a tired circle in this new and unfamiliar spot and urinated long and noisily into the short grass they had not yet trampled or eaten and afterward they lay down in it and sighed heavily and finally fell asleep. From my mat I could feel their body heat, and the steady and endless thrum of the hoof-falls of the multitudes of other cows still coming. I lay awake and felt that invisible herd swell. The last thing I saw that night, after everyone else in the camp had gone to sleep and only the distant campfires of newcome cowboys were still bleeding into the midnight fog, was Oumarou sitting on a goatskin mat alone, erect, transfixed, like some protective deity quarried out of ancient stone. He sat there long and long watching the animals walk onto the plateau through the chill and the dew.

The cows kept coming all night. At cold and damp predawn the camping ground was white with milling animals, and still more were flowing in past dry rice paddies in the east. They glutted the plateau. Like runnels of milk, pouring, pouring into one breathtaking primordial tide of cowness. Their moaning the grounding base note to all the other sounds of daybreak savannah: the parrots, the roosters, the red-eyed rock pigeons cooing in the brush, the lonesome cries of a kingfisher, the goats and the goatherds, the hammering into the ground of wooden spokes for calf ropes. The muffled chomping of broadswords into the limestone of the wooded cliff where the elders were digging a new grave. A small one, for an infant. He had come in the night by donkey cart, with his mother and two siblings. Just a tad feverish, though it may have been the sun on his skin. The family fell asleep under a large acacia tree to the victorious mooing of cattle, and in the morning the baby didn't wake up.

Fanta and Kumba helped wash him for burial. His father was still en route to the plateau and so other men prayed over his tiny body and put it in the ground on its side facing Mecca and threw thorn tree branches on top and weighed them down with bits of mudbrick to keep wild dogs from digging up the remains. Next to eight other graves recently so covered. Next to the graves of Oumarou's father, Hashem al Hajj, and children, Adama and Fanta. Next to one of Saadou's grandsons, the son of Hassan and Kajata.

Across the river, in Kotimi Genepo's heavenly orchard, there was another fresh grave. Kotimi's grandson Soumana, the toddler with the distended stomach and the navel hernia, had died during the rainy season. An owl killed him, maybe that owl I once had seen fly out of the palm fronds of Kotimi's oasis. It gave the child malaria and took his soul.

Allaye arrived in midmorning with Oumarou's goats. He tethered the nannies next to the hearth, inquired after his parents' health and the health of the cows, then turned around and walked back to Konkorno where he had made an appointment with a Bwa bush doctor. The bush doctor had promised him a special love potion that would make him irresistible to women. The plan was to sneak the potion into a girl's tea. After drinking the tea, should the girl touch Allaye's hand, she would fall in love with him immediately. Such a potion was well worth a daylong roundtrip to Hayré and back. Allaye's unremitting pursuit of love, the out-and-out force of it, made my heart leap and catch at once.

"How much did you pay that bush doctor?" Gano asked.

"Five thousand francs," said Allaye—about ten dollars.

"*Wallahi*, I don't believe in this potion."

"Why do you believe in kola nut magic that makes a woman a virgin again, but not in Allaye's love potion from Konkorno?" I asked.

"Because the kola nut magic is true!"

295

He thought about it.

"Even if this potion is real it's not as good as in the past. Because now everyone wants money, and they sell magic for cheap. You tell me, Anna Bâ: what can you get from cheap magic?"

That evening I carried the Diakayatés' wash from the river to camp and all of a sudden, so heaped with another family's clothes in which each faded fold trapped the intimacy and old surety of their love, I felt drenchingly lonely, bereft of an innermost knowledge of the other. For years my beloved and I had danced around that kind of closeness. "This almost feels like domesticity," he had said once, in a supermarket, and smiled—and right away we had recoiled, set off to separate aisles. Now, clutching my hosts' clothes a year after our parting, I realized that our love had never held any prospect of an old and lasting kinship because we had let it exist only in the moment: in this one gratifying phone call, this one idyllic rendezvous. It had allowed for no plans, no tomorrow—and so, for no history, nothing that ever could linger in a stack of laundry.

I lifted the clothes to my face and breathed.

In canted early sun the cows of Oumarou and Sita Dangéré swarmed in a single herd on the hardpan in the middle of the plateau. Before them stood al Hajj Saadou, Oumarou's younger brother, Sita's uncle. He cupped his palms and brought them together and looked into them, remembering. He prayed.

He prayed that the animals' journey across the river would be safe. That they would not drown or hurt the strong young men who would lead them through the water. That on the other bank they would stay out of harm's way and out of the unharvested fields of anxious, jumpy farmers. Already downstream in the village of Taga a dozen rimaibe villagers had attacked a group of returning nomads with clubs and hoes and one had to be taken to the hospital in Djenné. The previous year a daylong land war between herders and farmers near the Burkina border killed thirty men, mostly Fulani.

He prayed that there would be plenty of hippo grass in the bourgou when the cows finally arrived near Doundéré. That the dry season would be kind to the animals. That he, Saadou, who would spend the dry season on this plateau across the river from Ballé, would live to see these cows and their owners again.

He spat into his palms three times and dropped his hands and looked at Oumarou. The cows had been blessed. Oumarou raised his staff in the air.

Jot!

The herd moved downstream upon a white clay road chinked with thousands of crescent hoof tracks. After four days on the green plateau the animals were finally sated and their large erect humps swayed regally and slowly. Walking behind the herd Oumarou watched with pleasure their slight metronomic oscillation. Watched his sons and grandnephews drive the animals to the river crossing downstream, where the bloated Bani stretched muddy and rapid a mile wide between the two banks. The young men glamorous beyond imagination. Entitled, arrogant, handsome, fast and fluid like shadows. They told the cows they were switching pasturelands: *jet jet jet jet jet!* and to keep in line: *shht*, girl—die, die! *Shht*, bitch! and to keep moving: *jot jot jot jot!* They walked past nipple rows of harvested millet, dried-up rice paddies, briers, reeds. They let other cows join their herd until it grew to several hundred head. Each hoof-fall exploded in a plume of fine bleached dust. As they approached the crossing the cowboys set the animals to a trot and the herds and their herders disappeared in a tall and near-solid cloud of atomized sand and in that white pall they poured onto the open grassy slope man and beast, the cows febrile and lowing terribly and the young men whitefaced and sweating and stripping off their swords and their blue boubous as they drove the herds at a canter straight into the roiling muck of the Bani.

They plunged in. The men armed with clubs and naked except for cutoff tricot undershorts yelped and hissed and ululated the cows into the water, and swam with the cows and ahead of them, and whacked their hides with staves and open palms, and the cows whirled in tight crazed circles in the sucking silty mud near the shore at first and finally stretched out centrifugally into several frenzied and roaring wedges. Bozo fishers in pirogues that carried other Fulani men and sheep and goats and the clothes of the swimmers paddled their lopsided and bleating Noah's Arks with furious strokes behind the cows to cut them off from the east bank where more herders shook their clubs and hands at the river and yelled "Go! Go in God's name, go!" and the paddlers stabbed the water with oars wildly and the animals thrashed and pushed one another in the mudcolored churn of cows and men, and pushed one another under in a wet demented stampede, and climbed one another and their drivers, who kept on swimming across the relentless torrent because this very crossing, this ancient and phantasmagorical baptism, this manic race determined their masculinity and prowess: determined everything.

Once upon a time huge festivals accompanied annual river crossings. They celebrated the end of the rainy season and the return of the fattened herds to the Inner Niger Delta, and feted the biggest cow, the bravest cowherd. Girls hennaed their hands and feet in dark geometric patterns for the occasion and wore gold hoop earrings and stacks of gold bangles and wove silver and gold coins and heavy amber beads into their cornrows. To the young cattle drivers who caught their fancy they handed kola nut with its sensual analeptic lobes that held the power to tame hunger and restore peace and repair hymens and bless unions and bind friends and lovers. And the boys so honored announced in public the names of the girls who had lavished them with such provocative attention, and sang praise songs to their favorite cows. Elders picked the fattest cow among all the herds and declared the champion of the crossing among all the men and such champion received even more attention from the girls, more kola nut, and firewood for his evening fires, and a large blanket handwoven in primary colors for the comfort of his sleep during the impending cold months. In return he slaughtered a bull large enough to feed everyone. Along the shores at each crossing point fires burned through the night for many nights and people drank milk by the gourdful, and men bragged about their rainy-season feats real and invented, and griots recounted heroisms of crossings past and esteemed the cowherds whose families employed them and ridiculed the rest, and young unwed couples stole away into the dark bush to make love by starlight.

But that was a long time ago, when the whole world was covered in grass for the cows, when the Fulani drank only milk and never touched millet or rice, when rain came on schedule and plentiful, when griots came to every celebration poor and went away rich. Before the land had become scalpeled with farms and fast paved roads and before the sky had become scalpeled with warplanes, before electric beams of flashlights interfered with the night and greed for modern things seduced the hearts of Fulani youth. In Mali the only festival that in recent memory still celebrated the cattle's return was the Traversée des Animaux held at Diafarabé, on the Niger River. Since the war had begun in the country's north that festival, too, had been abandoned.

The cows flowed across the Bani in frenetic corkscrewed queues. A bull strayed from a herd in the middle of the river, swam downstream, fought his way back. A dead cow floated north, all four legs extended sideways. Then another. A fisherman's pirogue dragged it to shore. The Bozo believed it halal to eat drowned animals; they would butcher it later. On the shore, Oumarou and Sita and Saadou and other Fulani clicked their tongues at the lost animals and their unfortunate driver, a boy they did not know well.

"That fucking idiot!"

"He's supposed to be swimming among the cows, not next to them."

"Now he's swimming on his own and his cows are dying one by one!"

Allaye and Hassan swam with Oumarou's herd in neat, practiced strokes. They were head bulls. Competent and composed.

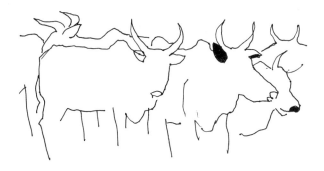

They swam before the cows and when some animals scrambled in
the water they took turns diving and doubling back and resurfacing
at the cows' dewlaps and grabbing them by the horns and humps
and urging them to keep swimming. A chestnut cow struggled, legs
up in the air for a beat, two, five, ten, too long, then recovered. The
brothers steered the herd to a small grassy island two hundred yards
offshore to give the animals some time to rest, to catch their breath.
Only when the boys and most of the animals had crossed the island
and plunged into the water once more on the other side did Saadou
realize that the chestnut had never made it upslope. Her legs had
buckled and she was falling on the grass, rasping, dying.

"A sword," he yelled, "a sword, quickly! Somebody kill it, kill it
with a sword!"

On the shore Oumarou teetered on his feet. He slumped down
on trampled muddy grass. He said absolutely nothing. He watched
a grandnephew draw his sword. He watched men drag the chestnut
out of the water. He watched Saadou verify that the cut had been
properly performed, severing the arteries on both sides but leaving

the spinal cord undamaged. He waited for someone else to tell him this really was his cow. Or that it wasn't. Now he had lost three cows since the beginning of the rainy season and he had only one new calf, Piebald. It stood on the other bank, an uncertain motley dot, waiting for its mother. In his shock Oumarou had forgotten to notice that the rest of the herd had crossed the river safely.

Now Saadou stood over his brother.

"Oumarou," he said. "The final destination of this cow is here. Go back to camp." And Oumarou stood up without a word and staggered away, weaving up the path, drunk with sadness.

The cow had died in the river, the domain of the Bozo. To show respect, as was the custom, Saadou asked the fisherpeople to skin and butcher it, in return for the neck and some stomach and a chunk of the liver. The hide and most of the rest of the meat he sold to them at a tenth the market price because they refused to pay more.

The money and the head and the remaining meat and the hump he carried back to Oumarou, because a Fulani elder never shared his cow's hump with anyone.

The hump of sorrow. "We eat the hump and it tastes so good and we cry: 'Oh, my beautiful cow died!'" said Saadou. "Really, we should feel lucky the boys are safe. Allaye and Hassan were right in the middle of the herd, swimming very well. Sometimes the cows crush the boys who swim with them. So we are lucky, *al ham du lillah*."

At sunset egrets streamed in from all cardinal points to skim the gilded river that took Oumarou's cow and landed on sundown-lit islands where they nested in night bushes like giant fruit. Hundreds upon hundreds of them, all the egrets in the world, beating their wings against the last hour of light, landing and landing forever. Around the islands the river moved northward. Oumarou sat on a sheet of black plastic with his back to the water and his turban tight over his mouth and watched the cow's head bleed out onto a goatskin next to him. Men stopped by to greet him and he raised his hands to return their salaams and gave away chunks of his share of meat one by one. In a daze he gave away, to a distant relative, the hump.

"It's not my luck today, it's his," he said after he had realized his mistake. "Anna Bâ? Being a cowherd is very hard."

The hump of regret.

When it grew dark Ousman doled out chunks of grilled cow liver and Fanta and Bobo served rice with fish sauce. "Dive in, dive in," said Oumarou.

"A lot of cows die during the crossing for nothing, they aren't even killed. This cow, at least we're eating it. Besides," he said a few minutes later, after giving it a thought, "the cow was a little sick."

After dinner Ousman, Gano, and Saadou's son Allaye whipped out their cellphones and vanished into the ghostly blue light of LED screens. On the western bank of the river Hassan and Allaye staked a calf rope to the south of Ballé's clay walls and talked the cows calm and submissive and milked them. Against the depthless night they built a fire by which to nurse their battered bodies. A cow had kicked Hassan in the jaw; for a day he could barely move it. Allaye spent the hours before dawn coughing up blood. Later elders would say it was because he'd had a full breakfast before driving the cows across the Bani. Everyone knew that if you ate before swimming you would bleed from your mouth.

The pirogue listed in the strong evening chop, taking the sunset waves broadside, the river white in the slant light. Seventeen terrified people gripped the gunwales. Seventeen sets of knuckles ashgray on the redwood porous from water rot. No one spoke. Oumarou's goatskin blew off in the water. Salimata hesitated, let go her grip, clawed out the goatskin, reclaimed her hold on the boat. A blue tarp luffed like a sail, dragged on the water, unleashed in its wake a hoop of drops like sparks. *"Ya Allah!"* someone whispered. Waterfolk's tricks, or maybe the river's own. The river's voracity extended beyond cows: three weeks earlier a pirogue had capsized on the Niger between Mopti and Timbuktu and seventy-two passengers drowned. I tucked the tarp back into the boat. It took in water overboard but the two Bozo polemen said nothing, faces set, stern. To the east, a small fishing craft sailed upstream under a homemade square rig, a solitary Paleolithic silhouette upon it keeping perfect balance against the river's blinding surface, one with his boat like some pelagic centaur.

When the pirogue scraped the mud of the western shore everyone mouthed a prayer. The nomads unloaded into ankle-deep mud. Exhausted by the crossing, the sun, the numbing fear of water, the women huddled on their sacks, scooped out some cold rice for the younger children. Sensing their tension one of the fishermen pretended to steal baby Mayrama. A big man, big face, big hands, big smile. The girl shrieked. He turned to Kajita, lifted her in the air, cooed something in a language she could not understand. Kajita frowned, wiggled free of his grip, slid down into riverside reeds. He made to steal Hashem and Amadou's rice. At last the women began to chuckle, uncrack their tense shoulders, their clenched hearts. Then they were laughing fully, relieved to be laughing. The boys laughed, too. Everyone was laughing to tears.

That night they camped on the bank. After a dinner of rice and tea Oumarou knelt to pray on dry mottles of sedge grass. He faced the river's east bank, where more cows still streamed in from Hayré and the white smoke of cowboy fires seeped down to the water through the brush. Upon the river silhouetted fishers glided soundlessly, cast their diaphanous seines. Handmade sinkers kissed the surface, puckered it lightly, pulled the nets under. Tossed oars dripped water into water. From inland sounded the surprised lowing of cattle. Hmmm? Hmmm? To the west, where the sky faded from orange to blue, Venus rose, and right above, the waxing halfmoon shone like a brimming calabash of milk. In the clearing to the north darkened the compact mud walls of Ballé, where Allaye, his lungs now recovered, was spending his days and nights, flirting with plump rimaibe girls in the smoky crepuscule of empty mudbrick rooms. He was gregarious, handsome, and the girls liked him a lot. They told jokes and took photographs with cellphones they charged with motorcycle batteries, and stripped off their tops, allowed his mind to stray on faraway journeys to the Atlantic shores, allowed his hands to wander.

"It all starts when boys go to the village and drink tea all day," said Oumarou. "That's where corruption begins. We used to just herd cattle, that's it. If we went to town, we'd just go to buy or sell animals. Now they want cellphones, motorbikes. Radios."

He squinted into the night toward the village walls. The walls of settled lifestyle: so impenetrable to him, so open to Allaye. Generation barriers. The walls of disconnect.

"Sons! They are very hard. And we love them best of all."

Ousman walked to Hassan's new camp and returned to make tea and report the latest. His brothers had staked the calf rope next to the spiny twisted hump of an atil bush. The long swale near the camp was full of dry grass on which the cows grazed to fullness, and the cows' udders hung heavy and low. The piebald dogie whose mother had died during the crossing was doing well and Hassan was feeding it rice-flour pap from a teapot spout four times a day. Two Sankaris and a Diakayaté set their cows loose in Ballé rice fields and the farmers were demanding a cow's worth from each owner even though the harvest in this year of late and meager rain would have been not worth three goats. Two officials from the Department of Forestry confiscated the broadsword of a fourteen-year-old goat-herd, accused him of cutting down trees, and ordered his father to report the following market day to court in Djenné.

The Diakayatés would move to their new camp in the morning. Half a mile to the north of that campground rose the hummock of Ballé, with its cool pump well and its sultry girls. A mile or so to the east, inaudible, ran the Bani. To the south and west, reaching almost all the way to Djenné, stretched the red Sahelian expanse. Sunbaked to brick under limpid skies. Breathtaking, austere, un-welcoming with barely any shade and so many thorns. Sparse aca-cias, some shrubs. Creepers blooming fuchsia trumpets. From here the women would resume their long walks to barter buttermilk in Djenné, where mango trees already flowered once more. There was no permission yet from the *dioro* of Senossa for the Fulani to enter the bougou, and the women would return carrying grain and salt and tea and tales of fens full of hippo grass that waved taller than the horns of the tallest bull and tales of other Fulani families wait-ing for the clearance to pasture their herds in that grass. Here Ou-marou would spend days and weeks perched on his goatskin. He would look west. Toward the invisible green swales, the next camp, the next reunion. Fixing himself once more in the savannah, in the world, in the Stone Age ritual of wandering cowboys who always reached the next campsite but never quite arrived.

How long would they have to wait? Days, weeks, a month? No one could tell. There existed no calendar for the nomads, no dates. There was barely time at all: only cycles. The sunrise like a huge white celebration in the east, the molten fisher's float of sunset. The children dying in the night, the women circling back to sit with one another in mourning. The droughts and the deluges. The slow spasmodic migration to and from seasonal grazing lands, and the shorter rhythmic patterns of ferry rides back and forth across the river and its anabranches and seasonal affluents, the roundtrip slogs to pasture, water, market. And the waiting, always the waiting: for rain, for thicker grass, for the next move.

For now, they prepared to spend the night by the river. Boucary's wife, Abba, stretched a mosquito net between six lopsided poles in silver moonlight, like a lunatic fisherwoman cast ashore. Salimata and Fanta quietly gossiped. Hairatou, who was afraid to sleep by herself, spooned her body against Bobo, who lay listless, fatigued. Hashem cuddled against my right leg and covered himself with the frayed hem of my skirt and Kajita fell asleep against my left, holding my hand. Oumarou tucked us in. Much later it became very cold and someone's newborn goat joined us on the mat. I dreamed that a little colorful bird, like a sunbird, red and blue and yellow, lived on my breast.

Evening outside Ballé. The animals sang the sun down, sang the Sahel to sleep. Women talked quietly over their cooking, clattered their pots. Hairatou hummed a song of syncopes and half-steps, and young Amadou, naked as usual, danced in the dust. When the blood moon rose in the east the men and women prayed toward it like sectaries of some eldritch nocturnal cult. Then they went to bed. Several hours later Hassan drove the cows to nightherd.

The night swale was all the breath of cows against the stubby soil, the rhythmic cropping of hay, the moist chewing, the large nostrils exhaling into the earth. Pale clouds smeared the hemispheric sky. On the grass lay blue and green cocoons, bundles of resting cowboys. They napped, rose, checked to see that their cows were still nearby, lay down to nap again. After a time the cows, too, lay in the grass. The sun had sponged up all the rainy season's water, and the night wind, harmattan's precursor, blew cold and dry from the north. There was no longer any dew. The moon paled as it rose and in its blue light shadows fell hard and angled and it was easy to imagine that the world comprised nothing else—just the open palms of the cyanotype valley and the cattle in it, the sleepy herders speaking and not speaking, the few bright stars competing against electric moonlight.

By dawn the bush was fully awake, rock pigeons and dogs and chickens, and the many herds that had slept in the valley had risen and shuddered and mooed together and deeply, and slowly gathered into one enormous milling herd. Egrets lifted off their island shelters and winged across the pinking east in dark lacy outlines, finding room among the cattle. The savannah lowed in the cold wind. When the sun was a palm above the horizon it was time to head back to camp for milking. Hassan stood up from the bare impress his body had made in the grass and wove through the animals, separating out his father's cows one by one. He worked quickly, surely, almost without looking.

"How can you tell which cows are your father's?"

"I can tell."

"But how?"

"These cows were born into my hands. I know."

ACKNOWLEDGMENTS

The Fulani say: "A person who asks questions is never lost." My Fulfulde teacher, Monsieur Koulibaly, taught me this. I asked many questions of him, and of my big-hearted hosts, and also of the *diawando* Afo Bocoum, Abdoul Aziz Diallo of Tabital Pulaaku, Dr. Lisbet Holtedahl at the University of Tromsø, and Dr. Doulaye Konaté, president of the Association of African Historians. Thank you for your generous mentorship.

The Fulani also say: "One man's footsteps don't make a path, and one tree doesn't make a forest." My families in Africa, Europe, Asia, and the Americas accompanied me on this journey—some on foot, others with long-distance encouragement, a steady supply of poetry and succor, and indispensable help for my son, Fyodor. Your caring buoyed me. Charles Digges: you were my first reader and compelled me to write better. Becky Saletan, Katie Freeman, Maureen Klier, Anna Jardine, and Michelle Koufopoulos at Riverhead Books: your attention and your love of word continue to honor my work.

Paul: you believed in this book first. Mi yiɗiima.

Monsieur Koulibaly died after a long illness in the final weeks of 2013. I treasure all the lessons and all the bearings he gave me, and I sorrow over his death.